RAINBOWS *in the* STORM

Journey Through
My Daughter's Heart Transplant

ANGELA FLEMMING CAIRNS

Copyright © 2018 Angela Flemming Cairns.

Drawings by Angela Flemming Cairns; 'Heart In His Hands' by Fred
Photography by Abby Muendel; Lucas Cairns & Angela Cairns

All rights reserved. No part of this book may be used or reproduced by
any means, graphic, electronic, or mechanical, including photocopying,
recording, taping or by any information storage retrieval system
without the written permission of the author except in the case of
brief quotations embodied in critical articles and reviews.

This book is a work of non-fiction. Unless otherwise noted, the author
and the publisher make no explicit guarantees as to the accuracy of
the information contained in this book and in some cases, names of
people and places have been altered to protect their privacy.

WestBow Press books may be ordered through booksellers or by contacting:

WestBow Press
A Division of Thomas Nelson & Zondervan
1663 Liberty Drive
Bloomington, IN 47403
www.westbowpress.com
1 (866) 928-1240

Because of the dynamic nature of the Internet, any web addresses or
links contained in this book may have changed since publication and
may no longer be valid. The views expressed in this work are solely those
of the author and do not necessarily reflect the views of the publisher,
and the publisher hereby disclaims any responsibility for them.

Any people depicted in stock imagery provided by Getty Images are
models, and such images are being used for illustrative purposes only.
Certain stock imagery © Getty Images.

ISBN: 978-1-9736-2246-8 (sc)
ISBN: 978-1-9736-2245-1 (hc)
ISBN: 978-1-9736-2247-5 (e)

Library of Congress Control Number: 2018902959

Print information available on the last page.

WestBow Press rev. date: 05/02/2018

Scripture quotations marked (CEV) are from the Contemporary English Version Copyright © 1991, 1992, 1995 by American Bible Society. Used by Permission.

THE HOLY BIBLE, NEW INTERNATIONAL VERSION®, NIV® Copyright © 1973, 1978, 1984, 2011 by Biblica, Inc.® Used by permission. All rights reserved worldwide.

Scripture quotations marked (NLT) are taken from the Holy Bible, New Living Translation, copyright © 1996, 2004, 2007 by Tyndale House Foundation. Used by permission of Tyndale House Publishers, Inc., Carol Stream, Illinois 60188. All rights reserved.

Scripture quotations are from the ESV® Bible (The Holy Bible, English Standard Version®), copyright © 2001 by Crossway, a publishing ministry of Good News Publishers. Used by permission. All rights reserved.

Scripture quotations marked (GNT) are from the Good News Translation in Today's English Version- Second Edition Copyright © 1992 by American Bible Society. Used by Permission.

Scripture taken from The Message. Copyright © 1993, 1994, 1995, 1996, 2000, 2001, 2002. Used by permission of NavPress Publishing Group.

Scripture taken from the Amplified Bible, Copyright © 1954, 1958, 1962, 1964, 1965, 1987 by The Lockman Foundation. Used with permission.

Scripture taken from the New Century Version®. Copyright © 2005 by Thomas Nelson. Used by permission. All rights reserved.

Scripture taken from the NEW AMERICAN STANDARD BIBLE®, Copyright © 1960, 1962, 1963, 1968, 1971, 1972, 1973, 1975, 1977, 1995 by The Lockman Foundation. Used by permission.

Scripture quotations marked HCSB are taken from the Holman Christian Standard Bible®, Copyright © 1999, 2000, 2002, 2003, 2009 by Holman Bible Publishers. Used by permission. Holman Christian Standard Bible®, Holman CSB®, and HCSB® are federally registered trademarks of Holman Bible Publishers.

Scriptures taken from the Common English Bible® (CEB). Copyright © 2012 by Common English Bible and/or its suppliers. All rights reserved.

Dedicated to my highly treasured and courageous daughter Luka-Angel Lillian Cairns

Acknowledgements

First and foremost I want to thank my Heavenly Father and Creator God. I want to say that Jesus is my example, my strength giver and his Holy Spirit – my peace provider. I am eternally grateful for the grace and undeserved mercy God has shown me, and the fact that he never gives up on loving me.

Thank you to my husband, Lucas, who is a man of great integrity, gentleness and strength. He has always encouraged me, as we vowed at our wedding, to fulfill my dreams. I feel so blessed to have him by my side in the ups and downs of life. Lucas, I love you!

I must acknowledge my beautiful daughter whose amazing peace, positive spirit, outward-looking, kind heart and strength inspire me daily. Thank you Luka, for allowing me to share our story. I love you with all my heart, even though you love me with both of yours!

To my three sons, Elijah, Jazziah and Jayjay, I adore and love you each beyond words and greatly admire your adventurous spirits, bravery, generous natures, your caring souls, and your perseverance and resilience through the toughest of times!

I would like to acknowledge our wider family (the Flemmings and the Cairns), their over and above support through Luka-Angel's heart transplant was truly invaluable. We absolutely love each family with all their quirks and strengths. Both families have faced many challenges, and both have shown incredible strength, greater faith and care and concern for others through it.

Special thanks to my mums, Jan Cairns and Francina Flemming, for the long hours you spent editing, I am so grateful!

Our heartfelt and sincerest thanks to the amazing medical staff at The Royal Children's Hospital (the transplant team, nurses and doctors, surgeons, physiotherapists, cardiologists and pathologists). This team work harder than anyone I have seen. They are passionate and compassionate, professional and highly capable; they are absolutely the best team in the world! It is because of their study, their hard work, and care that our son and daughter have a chance at life. An extra special thanks to Rob, Jacob and Anne.

With deep reflection and thoughtfulness, from our whole family, we say thank you to the beautiful family we may never know who had the courage, strength and generosity to give our girl an invaluable gift in the midst of their deepest sadness. We will forever remember the tragic loss of your loved one and although we could never understand your pain, we grieve with you, and will never forget what you have done for us!

Finally I want to thank our closest friends, family, Christian brothers and sisters and strangers who prayed for our Luka-Angel from all over the world. When we needed you, you stood in the gap for us! We fully believe this unified voice saw God move and miracles take place!

Contents

Acknowledgements ix
Introduction xiii

Chapter 1	The Beginning 1
Chapter 2	The First Still Waters – The Still Waters of Grafton 17
Chapter 3	The Second Still Waters – Another Surprise 30
Chapter 4	Building Her Bravery 33
Chapter 5	The Fire & the Water 38
Chapter 6	The Amazing Things that God has Done 43
Chapter 7	A Mother's Letter 52
Chapter 8	Learning Through the Hardships & Curve Balls – Part One 55
Chapter 9	Learning Through the Hardships & Curve Balls - Part Two – 'A Tsunami' 66
Chapter 10	Athletics Carnivals, Hats and Sunglasses 74
Chapter 11	Timor Leste & Some Lessons in Perseverance 84
Chapter 12	Joy Amidst the Sorrow 92
Chapter 13	More Lessons in Perseverance 97
Chapter 14	Our Journey to Transplant 108
Chapter 15	A Glimpse into my Journal – Early 2016 124
Chapter 16	The Rainbow & Listing Luka 128
Chapter 17	The End & the Beginning 139
Chapter 18	Luka-Angel's Heart Transplant – Day One 164

Chapter 19	Waiting	178
Chapter 20	Full of Hope, Full of Faith	182
Chapter 21	Moments of Joy in the Storm	187
Chapter 22	The First Big Miracle	193
Chapter 23	You Make Me Brave	201
Chapter 24	Mighty To Save	206
Chapter 25	Break Every Chain	219
Chapter 26	Somewhere Over the Rainbow	226
Chapter 27	Getting Better Every Day	232
Chapter 28	The Cup of Tea	240
Chapter 29	Out of the Blue – Another Miracle!	244
Chapter 30	A Well Deserved Trophy	246
Chapter 31	A View From Above	248
Chapter 32	The Lady & the Blue Bracelet	252
Chapter 33	'Little Dude' & Finding our New Normal	256
Chapter 34	A New Day	263
Chapter 35	Sheltered From the Storm	270
Chapter 36	The Burden & the Cartwheel	278
Chapter 37	Finally Able to Dance	283
Chapter 38	The Choppy Seas	288
Chapter 39	Home is Where the Heart Is	291
Chapter 40	Snakes & Adders	296
Chapter 41	King of our Hearts	303
Chapter 42	Not Alone	307
Chapter 43	Trust	310
Chapter 44	Living Life to the Best	314
Chapter 45	Luka-Angel's First Run	320
Chapter 46	God's Little Gifts	325
Chapter 47	Indescribable	328
Chapter 48	Beautiful Things Out of the Darkness	333
Chapter 49	Cartwheels of Joy	341

Epilogue: Gaining a Greater Perspective 345
Luka-Angel's First Blog: "Look on the Colourful Side' 355

INTRODUCTION

In 2011 I felt the first call upon my heart to share our story. God knew I needed time to process, as it wasn't until five years later that we launched our YouTube video ('Share your love, save a life') to raise awareness for organ donation. This was followed by sharing our family's heart journey at The Salvation Army women's conference for the first time in public. I didn't know that just half a year later my precious daughter would be undergoing a heart transplant! God knew the best timing for me to share our journey with others though. So when The Salvation Army leader, Commissioner Jan Condon, rang me at home and said she knew it was short notice (just four days before conference started), but she felt God had put on her heart to ask me to share my testimony about our family's health journey I knew instantly that I was meant to do it. She told me I could think about it and I could say "no". Little did she know that just that afternoon I had stopped on my run at a local duck park to pray, "God, I know you've been calling me to share our story, if you really want me to share our story, you need to give me opportunities. I am willing, and I open my heart to your leading." Any wonder my answer was an immediate yes when The Salvation Army leader rang just a couple of hours later.

I shared our story publicly twice more before Luka-Angel's heart transplant. One of those times was a Salvation Army youth event in Sydney, just six months before transplant, where I preached on 'Life' looking specifically at the story where Jesus raised a dead young man back to life. The other time was at our church the Sunday before we went to Melbourne for Luka's listing appointments where I preached on the account recorded in the Bible of Jairus' twelve-year-old daughter being raised to life by Jesus. This story had become my rock just the year before when we were initially invited to list Luka-Angel for heart transplant.

God knew that in the sharing of our story many people would devote themselves to praying for our family. This great chorus of prayer would join with many others to lift us up to our Heavenly Father in dark days to come. Through sharing our story, God would do miracles in a time when we were desperate for them. I couldn't have possibly comprehended that he would bring tens of thousands of people from all over the world to their knees on our behalf! I had thought initially (as it took great surrender to share my story) that I was presenting an offering of obedience to God that perhaps could help someone else in their own pain. In turn, I was the one who was truly blessed by it. He did something wonderful with it. Out of something so devastating, he brought love, care, community, healing and even a new friendship with a Salvation Army Officer who lived within half an hour's drive of the hospital where we would need to go for Luka's eventual heart transplant.

It was on 7th June 2010 (just six months after diagnosis), when I wrote in my journal, *'Felt very, very sad last night and today. I am so scared and sad for what Luka-Angel and Jazz have to go through. The kids have cardiac catheters in Brisbane on Thursday. I'm scared. Not as scared as the first time, but scared. I watched such a beautiful sunset on the beach after my jog tonight – I was praying and giving all of this to God. I know his arms are around us. I told Him I felt alone. He said to me, as I watched the sunset sky and the beautiful beach in its glow, "If only you could see… you are so not alone!" I instantly had the sense of many angels around me, and then a vision: people all over the place, lifting us up in prayer.*

Kind of like the feeling when you stand in the middle of a group of people and they all lay hands upon you to pray. I could feel many hands on us as they prayed, then I heard God's voice remind me again, 'I will uphold you with my righteous right hand. When you walk through the waters, I will be with you, and through the fire. You will not drown, and you will not be burned.' I find it both miraculous and beautiful, that he showed me, long before we were in the midst of transplant, that he would send his presence, a force of angels and people, to uphold us.

Although this book is intended to share our story, the reality is, sometimes sharing our family's story feels too hard. Sometimes it feels too precious to give away. I wouldn't go and throw my favourite jewellery to the fish in the river in front of me right now, or as the Bible says, 'throw my pearls to swine'. Sometimes when I have shared some of our story, people have accidentally said the wrong thing. Sometimes they have said too much. Sometimes they haven't said enough. Sometimes I have walked away and had a big cry after I have managed to talk about such sad things. It's precious. It's ours. It's my baby girl and my second baby boy and my husband, three of my most valuable people. Perhaps that's why it's hard or perhaps because some days it hurts too much, and words seem futile in conveying the tiniest part of what we go through. Everybody has a story though. Everybody has pain and sadness in their life. I'm sure sometimes I have inadvertently said the wrong thing to others too.

There are times now when strangely I miss the hope, the rawness of joy in the little things, the community, the very real presence of God and the peace I knew over those hard days of Luka's transplant. However, this is not a place I want to go back to again. Seeing my little girl lying so still, and not being able to talk with her, laugh with her, have her hold my hand back was so devastating. I am so thankful now, that she is with me. It is like watching her learn her milestones all over again. Nothing is taken for granted. I stand in awe and appreciation each and every day. Though words just seem impossible to give a picture of our journey, I plan to attempt it. I also have thrown in some excerpts of my journal entries, hoping they can give a very 'real' glimpse into some of the journey I went on.

This is my pain, my sadness, my overwhelming joy, a glimpse into my heart, our family's hearts and a part of our story from my perspective.

I believe I am meant to share this with you, and somehow writing it out has helped me process some of our cloudiest days, as well as to smile as I recall some sunny ones. I hope that in some way, this book can help you through your cloudy days too and that as you read, you may see some rainbows of hope in your own journey. If you are one who prayed for our Luka, may you grow in your faith as you read about the answer to your prayers!

> 'That is why we never give up. Though our bodies are dying, our spirits are being renewed every day. For our present troubles are small and won't last very long. Yet they produce for us a glory that vastly outweighs them and will last forever! So we don't look at the troubles we can see now; rather, we fix our gaze on things that cannot be seen. For the things we see now will soon be gone, but the things we cannot see will last forever.'
> 2 Corinthians 4:16-18 (NLT)

Chapter 1

The Beginning

'I look behind me and you're there, then up ahead and you're there too.' Psalm 139:5 (The Message)

It was dark and the roads were empty. My neighborhood looked quieter than usual as we walked outside. The morning air made me shiver, so I pulled my scarf closer to my face. There wasn't much to say as we put our bags into the car. I longed to pick up my little girl and carry her in my arms, oh how I missed those days (she was nearly my size now). I desperately wanted to keep her safe. My heart beat so hard and felt physically sore like it hurt from the inside out. Glancing back, I wondered how long it would be until I saw my house again. I wondered how long it would be until I saw my two other sons. I wondered if they would be able to get back to sleep. It was only 4:20 in the morning. I wanted to hug them and tell them again that I loved them. Our rush out the door didn't seem to give us enough time to say "goodbye" properly. My husband, Lucas, sat in the front of the car and my dad drove. My thirteen-year-old Luka-Angel sat between Mum and me. My son Jazz (who had only just turned ten) was in the back. I suddenly noticed how serious we all looked and mustered the strength to lighten my face for the sake of my precious girl.

At the airport, I sat unusually still, and stared out at the slightly brightening sky and wondered why it was no longer dark. My heart felt the pure darkness of night. What seemed like only a few seconds later, we were on the plane and I wondered if anyone around us knew our circumstances. I wondered if the air hostesses knew the truth about our situation as they treated us so kindly that day. When they came and offered us muffins and cups of tea, I declined. I had made my decision that I would not eat until Luka could. I resigned myself to thinking that perhaps the plane might crash, and we could get this thing over with, before it even began. Then I thought about my sons whom we had left behind, and decided maybe a crash wasn't the best idea.

As the plane started to take off, everything within me wanted to stop it and say we were getting off. It was now in motion and I knew that there was no turning back. I knew we had to go through this at some point. I never dreamed that it would be now or that I would be witnessing my little girl go through this before her dad. It all felt so horrible, and on the inside I was in an absolute panic. I knew I would never be okay with it at any time. My heart was so heavy, and I tried the best I could to engage with Luka-Angel and just treasure being in her presence. We watched the sun begin to shine from outside of the window. The clouds looked so pretty. "Looks like heaven," Luka said. Luka's face lit up as we flew south over some snow-kissed mountains, and I wondered if she would ever get to the snow. We had always planned to take our kids one day. I pulled out the plain white cards I had packed, supposedly for the ward when she was recovering, and said to her, "Would you like to write notes to anyone now? Before your surgery?" Luka jumped at the chance. She sat with her faithful security toy 'Cowcow' in her arms and wrote and wrote until her hand hurt. I took a moment to swap seats with Lucas to allow him a turn beside her. The tears were threatening to spill over again, and I didn't want her to see me cry. *'She needs to see you be brave and be strong,'* I told myself biting the inside of my cheek so hard it hurt. I closed my eyes quietly beside my mum as if sleeping, and started praying Psalm 58 fervently, 'Have mercy on me Oh God, Have mercy on me for I come to you for safety, in the shadow of your wings I find protection until the raging storms are over.' I had prayed this Psalm over and over again these last few months. Then the quiet tears took over. I quickly brushed them away while my mum tried to console me. "I can't cry Mum, I can't do that to her. I have to be strong," I said. I was interrupted by Luka calling me from across the aisle to come and braid her hair. 'Make me brave, make me brave. Give her peace, give her peace...' I whispered in desperation to God.

As I conspicuously knelt up on the seat beside Luka doing my best to braid her hair, I didn't care who behind me could see. I was conscious I was sticking up above everyone else's seats and we were at the very front in the plane, but I decided it didn't matter. I wanted these two braids to be the best I had ever done for her. I couldn't allow myself to think that they could be the last braids, yet the thought hung wordless in the shape of a feeling at the back of my mind. The day that I had dreaded for so long now, had arrived and a part of me wondered how we got here.

A Different Beginning from Long Ago...

When I was nineteen years old, my parents who were Salvation Army Officers, were moved to Rockdale. Back then Rockdale seemed the other side of the world, although in reality it was only just over an hour's drive from Blacktown where we lived. For some reason though I packed up my stuff and in a sense packed up my relationships and moved on. I didn't say goodbye to that life with coldness, but somehow I just moved on. Perhaps at nineteen years old, and having to share the little blue VW beetle my sister and I had done up with our dad made me feel as though it was too far away to visit. Perhaps it was because I had felt quite lost for some time now.

I had a hard year the year after school finished. I somehow landed in nursing at university. I didn't want to be there, I didn't make many good choices in my life that year and I somehow spiraled to the lowest point I had ever been. One day, death even knocked on my door. I felt pretty worthless on the whole and perhaps that God didn't have a purpose for me. These thoughts and feelings played out in pretty unhealthy ways, but I won't take the time to delve into that part of my life. I am so thankful to God for his protection, amazing forgiveness, mercy and his pursuing love!

I was so excited when I realised that we knew some people from our annual Salvation Army music camp who were members of this new church, where my parents would serve as ministers. I was nervous, but I thought this would be a good new chapter in my life. I had just applied to study music at the TAFE in Goulburn, so Rockdale would become my second residence. I would only come home for the weekends while I studied for my two-year diploma of music. I remember the first day we went to church at Rockdale. The six of us got ready in our tiny house, which still was larger than any house we had lived in up to that point. Mum rushed around getting my younger siblings ready. Half-dressed, in her petticoat and stockings, she reminded Karen and me that we were going to someone's house for lunch after church.

"I don't want to go!" I remember saying. "I don't even know them! Do we have to go?!" I had only just turned nineteen and craved more independence. The thought of having to go to someone's house for lunch where there would be no one my age, felt like an intrusion into my world. Besides, I was over eighteen now, I could do whatever I wanted. Couldn't I?!

I remember Mum explaining they were old friends, and good people and I had to go. Mum told me that Mrs Cairns' father had dedicated (christened) me as a baby. In those days, it was Mum and Dad's roof, Mum and Dad's rules! Although I was nearly out on my own, I was technically still living with them.

My recollection of walking through the front door of the Cairns family home was the smell of a cooked lunch and the oddity that there was no folding on the lounge. In fact the house looked spotless. I remember sitting very awkwardly in the neat, little, lounge room with my big sister Karen, having been introduced to their two teenage sons. Matthew (sixteen years old) was skinny, with big round glasses protruding from his face, and curly, fuzzy, almost black hair. He had a coloured checked shirt on and shorts, and did very well in holding polite conversation with two older girls who weren't overly excited to be there. My sister, Karen, and I remembered meeting Matt last year at music camp and it gave us something to talk about. At the time he had a broken hand and he was put in charge of helping people in the beginner guitar group. I had commented to my sister that Matt had reminded me of Beeka (the mad scientist puppet) off The Muppets. I had been so excited to finally join the guitar group. We were some of the very first girls to do so. For so many years girls only joined the 'Timbrel Brigade' – unless they had been taught a brass instrument (which was rare). This particular year I could not wait to finally give up the wooden round thing with ribbons that at camp, gave me blisters, and move onto something a little more interesting. On reflection I feel sorry for the timbrel leaders I had over the years. I never really wanted to be there and I made sure they knew it. Many timbrel practices I was sent out of the room to stop distracting the other girls, or for being disrespectful. I knew guitar would be a whole lot more fun than being in trouble for not standing straight enough, holding my arm and fingers out far enough with my thumb tucked in, or wearing peppercorn-coloured stockings! Oh how I hated stockings! Even as a teenager they made my legs itch. I could not wait to lose the stockings and learn to play the guitar, but the truth was I had heard the guitar group pretty much had a party every session and was a real bludge. Matt had seemed a sweet guy, was a good musician and I noticed his kind eyes, even though his glasses were a little too big for his face.

Lucas was much quieter than his older brother but looked nothing like him. He had tanned skin, and a trendy, long hairstyle, but I couldn't really get a picture of who he was. He didn't seem to talk. I remember thinking Mrs Cairns seemed very nice and friendly with a smile that hardly left her face. Major Cairns was quiet, but quite a handsome, well-spoken and refined man. *'He reminds me somewhat of Sean Connery,'* I had mused, early at the lunch that Sunday.

Lucas seemed like he thought he was 'a bit too cool' for us and took an opportunity as soon as his mother left the room, to go hide in his bedroom.

I could hear my extroverted dad loudly talking and laughing and became aware that my younger siblings, Michael and Christelle, had disappeared to play 'Mouse Trap' with the little girl who was nine. Her dad called her Tammy, and when he said her name, it was said with such admiring affection it sounded like honey being poured carefully over a crumpet. Her mum called her Tamara (pronounced like 'camera') which I thought was pretty strange having two cousins called Tamara (Tam-arr-a). I hadn't really heard the name pronounced that way. I had noticed Mrs Cairns' accent, and wondered if it was a 'Kiwi' thing.

Karen, her usual extroverted self, held the conversation with Matt while I quietly pretended to engage. Soon Matt disappeared too and I wondered how long we had to go through the torture of being at someone's house we didn't know, uncomfortably sitting in their lounge room.

I found a chance to slink away from the spotless lounge room and peek into Tammy's room at my younger siblings. They seemed to be having a blast playing a board game and my eleven-year-old baby sister Christelle was laughing and playing happily. I didn't realise at that point my little sister had noticed Lucas, and thought he was a 'spunk'! I didn't think twice about him. At nineteen years old and about to move out of home, fifteen seemed a whole lot younger!

Tammy was a cute and quiet little girl. She had pretty dark brown eyes and a sweet smile. Her room looked very neat, girlie and well thought out. There was a floral look to this house. Not something I was used to seeing at my place. Our lounge was overflowing with washing and ironing, there was never a quiet moment, we only ever seemed to be rushing and there was always work to be done! However, in amongst 'work to be done', there was also fun, a lot of laughter and mischief to be had. Most meals at our house now sat far away from the meals of childhood where we couldn't leave the table without eating every single thing on our plate (I spent hours there). Most meals now consisted of crazy behavior, sticking carrots to our forehead, throwing a pea or two at Dad encouraged by our father's chuckling reprimands, and poor Mum frustratingly departing the room, annoyed at our immature behavior.

I could never have known that day at the Cairns' house, all that they lived with and were going to go through, or the fact that one day, that family, along with the health challenges ahead they had to face, would become mine too.

Some three-and-a-half years and many varying experiences later, fifteen-year-old Lucas was now eighteen. Even though we went to the same church, I hadn't noticed him or spoken to him as far as I recall, since that first day at his house. This particular day though, Lucas was taking up the offering at church. I remember turning to my older sister as he passed the offering bag down our row, and us discussing his nice smile. Well, that was it for me.

He had gotten into my head.

Youth camp was coming up, my sister, Karen, was about to leave on a twelve month trip to England (which she had pleaded with me to save for and go with her and her friend Linda). I gave up before I even tried. I had incredible commitment issues and couldn't be bothered holding down a job long enough to earn enough money to go. There was too much fun to be had here and I couldn't imagine being able to save enough money to get myself to England. I was fairly reckless. I didn't have a cent to my name and my dad's little black book told him I owed him lots of money. Especially since the little blue VW and I had been in a big accident that wrote the car off just a year before, for which I still had some scars to remember it by. I was car-less, money-less and travelling sounded like something I could never save for, besides there were too many parties and social events to attend. Karen on the other hand was a hard worker, a good saver and responsible in many ways. She also had dreams, ideas and wanted to get a larger world view. I just wanted to do music, hang out with my friends and party.

I was at a point in my life where I had just come out of a community of musos that I loved at our TAFE course in Goulburn. They had become my people. Many of them though, lived far away and our lives had gone fairly separate ways at that point. I didn't quite fit in with the girls at church and although I really liked them, I was living two lives. It was hard to find my place in either. In my church life, I sincerely wanted to follow God's ways but I was very, very weak. Although I spent many church events with my heart being drawn to God, outside of that I felt pretty mixed up. I felt quite lost and that no one really loved me. My self-value was low. I was still able to smile, seem confident, loud, and was able to have a lot of fun, but inside I felt incredibly insecure. There were times when the loneliness overtook and I felt like no one really knew me, I couldn't even work me out. Often I would play the guitar in a candlelit room, write songs and poetry. Most were sad and revealed the darkness within. There were many times when I felt like life was not really worth living anymore. I often made choices that only reinforced my feeling of worthlessness. To those around me, I appeared 'happy go lucky', but most of the time, deep within I felt completely empty!

I went off to youth camp initially excited. When I got there though, I remember feeling lost. I had friends at church, but no really close friends. As people walked over to the first night of activities in their friendship groups, I hung back in the room for what I thought would be a minute. I needed a moment to get myself together, as I felt lost and didn't want to be there. I sat down on the cold floor leaning up against the bottom bunk, and pulled out my trusty poetry book. Karen had tried so hard to convince me to walk over with her, I could tell she felt sad for me, and didn't quite understand why I wouldn't come. As I started to write in my poetry/song book that I carried everywhere, about feeling like an autumn leaf drifting in the wind, tears streamed down my face and I attempted to stifle my brewing cry. I was so keenly aware of my isolation. I felt so lost. In my mind, I was gearing up to find a way to leave camp and go back home. If only I had my own car. *'Stupid accident! Stupid telegraph pole,'* I thought.

A quiet knock on the girl's dormitory door suddenly disturbed my poetic thought. It was so soft and tentative, I wondered if I had imagined it.

I quickly brushed my tears away, knowing that by now my eyes would be red, and wondered how I was going to hide that. I quickly grabbed my pressed powder and tried to cover the red in just a few seconds. As I opened the door, to my surprise, eighteen-year-old Lucas Cairns and my friend Ben were standing there sheepishly. Lucas kind of hid back behind Ben a little. I knew Ben well. We had recently caught the bus together to a Sound Tech course for 'Dole Bludgers'. Our parents had convinced us both that we should do this course together. Ben was a few years younger than me. We had many conversations and in some ways felt in a similar space in life. We both felt like we didn't fit anywhere and didn't know if there was any purpose for us in this world. Funny how if someone had told me that he would one day marry my little sister, I wouldn't have believed them. Sometimes when I was younger I would long to see into the future. Perhaps if that had have been possible it would have been too confusing, all these people that I knew then, and many would one day become my family. Besides, looking into the future may have proved too shocking and painful.

"We happened to notice you brought a guitar..." Ben said in his almost-monotone, deep voice. "Lucas and I were wondering if we could borrow it?" It was obvious to me that Lucas made Ben do the talking.

I wondered why they weren't attending the Friday night games in the hall either. The program was usually compulsory at youth camp.

I went and got my old, well-loved guitar off my bed. The drawing and painting all over it showed some creative license, and perhaps revealed that it had been rescued off a tip pile by my dad. Oh how I *loved* that guitar. It had seen me through so much, and it knew so many of my secrets and feelings that no one else in the world had heard.

As I handed it over to the two guys, Ben muttered, "You can join us if you want."

I didn't take the time to think through whether the offer was genuine, but for some reason, even though I felt so low and ready to leave camp to retreat home, I followed them.

"Let's go in there, good acoustics in the bathroom." Lucas said. I followed them into the stench of the boy's toilets and we pulled up a seat against the wall on the dirty floor.

Lucas pulled out an old notebook and started to play a song he had written. As he sang, "I feel for you, I feel for you..." and asked me to harmonise, something began to unfold that none of us could have imagined. As I sang those words over and over in harmony to his, I realised they held truth, and it took me by great surprise. His voice was low and his tone mellow, but it drew me in. He was a great song writer!

All night long we sat up and talked, and laughed and talked. I really liked Lucas' way of thinking and humour and felt something unfolding in my heart.

"When did you two become such great chums?!" Ben had asked annoyed as we all snuck into the kitchen attempting to steal our midnight feast! Ben had been friends with my sisters and me for some time, and Lucas and he had known each other all their teenage years. It had only been a few hours of talking, but Lucas and I had connected on such a level that Ben had become the third wheel. My feelings of deep loneliness started to fade into the background...

That night as we talked, Lucas shared with me a little about the night his dad had a heart transplant, a couple of years before and what a difficult time it was. He also explained he had recently been diagnosed with the same genetic condition, hypertrophic cardiomyopathy. I didn't understand at the time all of what that really meant, but it sounded hard.

Around 3am, after a long night of jamming, talking, and laughing at Lucas' silly antics, I sheepishly snuck back into my room, and left Lucas and Ben to sleep.

Gradually my life changed, friendship groups changed and evolved, and I became committed to something for the first time in my life. His name was Lucas. My life became less about partying and more about him. Music remained a point in which we connected and we just loved playing together. We went to gigs, played in some bands, got more involved in church and more committed to God. The foundation of my life became a little stronger all the time, and I became more able to follow through on the tugs and desires of my heart which was calling me to live a pure life.

Three years and two months later, I stood on the platform at my wedding and as I said, "I will look after you when you are sick..." I choked up, tears welling in my eyes, paused a moment, then managed to continue, "And also when you are well". Followed shortly after by a fun conga line by the bridal party with us in the lead, around and then out of the church to the upbeat song 'You and Me Always'.

I had begun praying two years earlier, as I saw where our relationship was headed, that our children would never get what Lucas and his dad had. I prayed with all my heart. I believed in faith. Completely believed, that this gene that we hardly knew a thing about, would never be passed on.

A Little Surprise

As I sit by the river on this February day in 2017, the sun glistening on the water, the blue sky and the feeling of the breeze on my face doesn't seem so different to the setting in Sydney in the year 2000. I had been married just a few months before, I was working full time for The Salvation Army Olympic Team 'More Than Gold'. I often went and sat on a certain bench seat along the city river and prayed in my lunch break. Often I fasted from lunch and spent time praying and being in God's presence. I was always drawn to my creator and keenly aware of his presence when looking at the water and the sky. This particular lunch break, the clouds above me opened, and I felt a beam of sunshine wash over my body. I felt warm and tingly from head to toe and I heard the voice of God whisper, "You will have a son and he will bring you great joy!" I was shocked. I was overwhelmed. I was overjoyed! I hadn't even thought of having any children yet. It certainly wasn't on my radar. I wondered if Lucas and I would eventually have trouble having children. I wondered if this was a message I needed to write down and remember one day. I wrote it in my diary, there on the seat that day, just in case I would forget. There was no doubt in my mind that this was a message from the Creator God. The feeling of his presence was so real. The feeling of his warmth was so tangible. I knew that he had spoken. I was somewhat excited and relieved by this assurance that one day I would have kids. Little did I know that I was pregnant at the time, with that very son who would bring me great joy. Approximately four weeks later, I found out I was eight weeks pregnant!

I reflect now that God not only brought forth his promise in Elijah being a boy, but this fifteen-year-old has always brought me great joy! He still has the ability to make his mum smile every day. From the little toddler that delighted me with his intelligence and funny behavior, to the teenager who has so many similar interests to me, I have only ever known great joy from Elijah! It was right that God would give him to us first. Even though he didn't know what sleep was, he knew how to bring joy to his mum and dad even as a smiley little baby. His overwhelming and protective love for his younger siblings has always been so evident. There was never a moment when I had to ask him not to fight with his younger sister. They have always been the best of friends, from making chilli soup together, to finding worms in the garden, making cubby houses out of boxes under our old mango tree in Tweed Heads. They always made poisons and mud soups and got up to the beautiful mischief that little kids should, but he would always do his best to do the right thing. He always has and at fifteen, still does, bring me great joy!

I remember the doctor's initial response when we went to him to confirm our pregnancy. Looking back at photos now, I see we both looked so young. We only looked like we were in our mid-teens. Needless to say we were absolutely shocked when his first response to the test results to this married young couple was a quiet, muttered, "Do you want to keep it? I know someone who can help."

"Pardon?!" I had interrupted incredulously! I couldn't believe what I had just heard! Lucas and I had looked at each other to see if we had heard correctly. "Yes. Of course we do," we said, knowing that never in our wildest dreams would that have been an option we would take. That was the last time we went back to that particular doctor. The next GP we saw through pregnancy was an old GP for my family. I remember feeling surprised when she referred us to Westmead Hospital for an in-utero scan to see if the baby's heart was healthy. She had explained to us that given the Cairns' family medical history, we should get the baby's heart checked. We were young and naïve, but I was convinced that my faith (in the gene not being passed on) would come to fruition. I wasn't at all worried.

When the ultra sound results were all clear, I barely flinched. I had only gone to the appointment because the doctor said we should.

Elijah wasn't checked again after that. Life went on, and I occasionally reflected on the fact that God had honoured my faith, and the gene would be finished with Lucas – never would it be in the Cairns family again (or so I believed)! Life was a whirlwind of joy, fun, adventure, sleepless nights, socialising, part-time work at The Salvation Army Sports Centre, then three months travelling around the other side of the world, including a great adventure of climbing Mount Fuji with my dad, then visiting friends in the UK. We camped around Europe on next to no budget including a stint of staying in our car, due to having no money left. Eventually we moved back home to Rockdale for a few months. Somewhere in that mix, God had provided an opportunity for us to move to Grafton. My initial response was, "No way!" But I felt God tugging on my heart, and I heard him say, *"I will lead you beside still waters, I will restore your soul"* (Psalm 23). I didn't even know at the time my soul needed restoring. I loved my job at The Salvation Army Sports Centre. I loved being a mum, loved being married to Lucas and had a lot of fun hanging out with our friends. I hadn't yet allowed God to have every single area of my life, and was still reluctant to follow his will and path for me wholeheartedly. I was certainly involved in the church, my faith was growing, I read the Bible a bit and prayed, but Jesus wasn't necessarily the centre of my life. Reflecting now I can see there was much restoring of my soul required. After three weeks of arguing with God about moving to Grafton, I decided that he knew better. So Lucas took up the full time position managing the music shop, a job he had kindly been offered by an old family friend. It made no sense to me at all to leave our life in Sydney. I knew deeply and firmly though, that for a season, Grafton was where we needed to be.

Chapter 2

The First Still Waters – The Still Waters of Grafton

'He leads me beside still waters, He restores my soul.'
Psalm 23:2b-3a (ESV)

As we drove to Grafton the week before we were to move there – I wondered what this place was like. I had never heard of Grafton. I knew nothing about it. I understood it was a country town somewhere up north – but that's as far as it went. All I knew was that God had not just knocked, but repetitively thumped on the door of my heart about going there, after the initial job offer came. We were both active musicians at the time. Managing a music shop seemed a far cry from playing music.

When we had looked on the real estate websites from Mum and Dad Cairns' lounge room in Sydney, it seemed there were many places available for rent in Grafton, and at a much lower cost than Sydney. So the day we arrived to look at which house we might rent, it came as a shock as we went from real estate to real estate to discover there were only three houses for rent in all of Grafton. They had not updated their websites. The first house we were taken to had broken walls, a broken floor and looked like it needed a decent renovation before it was even livable. The carpet was ripped in many places and the whole place stunk. As we followed the well-dressed real estate lady with bright, red lipstick on, I wondered how she could even pretend this was a viable rental.

The next place we went to was on the town side of the bridge, according to locals, this was the 'nicer' side. As we drove over the bridge I pondered the fact that Grafton had a river, perhaps these were the 'still waters' God was talking about. Up until that point, I didn't know whether it snowed in Grafton, let alone had a river.

The third house we went to was next to the famous Grafton bendy bridge. We followed the lady up a driveway which turned out to be a small street with one house, McClymont Place. As we walked around the side of this big, old, run-down house with shabby paint, I could hardly believe my eyes. There in the backyard was the river. As I stood quite shocked and surprised at the view, the voice said again, "I will lead you beside still waters, I will restore your soul."

"This is it." I whispered to Lucas.

"We haven't even been told how much a week it is yet Ange. Just wait," he responded quietly.

"No, this is it! These are my still waters, I know it," I said smiling at God and how he just knows stuff. He never ceases to amaze me. Having looked at the biggest house I had ever contemplated living in, I felt so blessed. I had only ever lived in tiny houses with my whole family, and then when I left home it was just a unit or a small share house with friends. I could hardly believe just the two of us, our eighteen-month-old Elijah and the baby now five months in-utero would be living in a four bedroom house with the hugest living room I had ever seen, a large back verandah with the view of the water, and a huge backyard with an avocado tree. Although old and run down, this house was a far cry from the shabby, smelly, tiny fibro shack we had just seen. This was an old house with character.

"How much is it a week?" Lucas asked tentatively at the end of our tour.

"$210 a week," the lady said. We had been paying more than that for our little unit in Sydney. We looked at each other smiling but trying not to look too eager and said, "When can we pay our bond and sign our rental agreement?"

Less than a week later, Lucas drove the truck out of Sydney while Elijah and I followed in our little car. I was so tired as we drove out I had to pull over before we had even driven an hour, to have a sleep on the side of the road.

"This will be a looong trip," poor Lucas said frustrated. I was pregnant, I had been packing, I had a toddler who still hardly slept, and in a sense I was probably tired from my busy Sydney life. This life was about to change so dramatically. It was such a big decision to leave our home church, our friends, our family and walk into a whole other life we couldn't even imagine.

As we pulled into the driveway of our new home for the first time, we were met by the local Salvation Army Officers Pam and Colin Robinson. Pam left a poster in my kitchen that read, *'I will lead you beside still waters, I will restore your soul.'* (I didn't know if a 'little birdie' had told her my Bible verse, but I could hardly believe it!) They helped us unpack the truck, and then came over a day or so later to build a make-shift fence in our backyard to protect our toddler from the river. It was pouring rain, but Colin stood there diligently, soaked through, building us a fence.

Living in Grafton was a lonely season for the first while. We were so used to having lots of people around us who knew us so well. There was never a dull moment in Sydney – always something to do and our social life was buzzing. Grafton was much slower. Not something we had been looking for, but something most 'Graftonites' thought was a major bonus. "Bet ya glad ya got outta the big smoke," a man with a big, red beard had said on our first Sunday at church. Trying to convey to him the incredible sacrifice it was to leave Sydney and the sadness I felt, seemed futile. Instead, an awkward smile and a stammered, "Oh… I like Sydney… umm… yeah but it's nice here," seemed to take him aback. He was a friendly guy and I hoped I hadn't caused him any offence. Grafton was a beautiful country town, but it was over seven hours away from the home we had known in Sydney.

Many days Elijah and I would wander down our backyard, through the long grass hoping we didn't encounter a snake and swim in the big river to cool off. Grafton was *hot*! Sometimes the shampoo felt like I had microwaved it when I went to wash my hair at night. Although the change of living in the country felt hard on many days, our view of the river was refreshing and renewing. With this new slow pace of life, I began painting and writing songs again, took up kayaking and I even learned to crochet! I also began to pray, meditate and read the Bible a whole lot more.

As we got to know Pam and Colin's daughter Leah, she became the babysitter for our Elijah. She was only seventeen years old, but she had maturity I had never seen before in someone her age. At times I felt there was a lot I could learn from her, and her strong faith. I knew she encountered some health issues, but wasn't fully aware of what they were. She also had a big dream to move to Africa and one day it would become her home. (Leah is now living in Uganda with her husband, who grew up in a Salvation Army orphanage, and their two miracle babies, working on setting up an orphanage and medical camps for women through their charity 'The Mbuyu Foundation').

I loved my days with little Elijah, but often I felt sad and lonely. Even at two-and-a-half, he felt it too. I'll never forget the day he had packed his little suitcase, walked out to the lounge room where I sat, and stated he was moving to Sydney. "Nana and Papa in Thydney, Aunty Karen in Thydney, Aunty Chrithtelle in Thydney, Aunty Tam in Thydney, Caitlin in Thydney. I'm going to Thydney and I need thome chocolate!" After I reasoned with him that running away to Sydney when you are only two years old, might prove quite difficult, he relented. Despite missing our friends and family, he and I had our fun, and made some great memories together. He certainly continued to bring me joy and make me laugh with his bright sense of humour and intelligence beyond his years. We went for lots of walks together, and he would pick a flower for me every day from our yard or beside our house and say lovingly, "A fower for you mummy, I wuv you mummy. You're boo-ful mummy." Nearly everywhere we walked he would pick up rocks and carry them in his hands or pockets and they would stay there all day long. Rocks were his security blanket, and he would even take them to bed with him.

A Little Light Enters the World:

On 17th May, the day I was due to have my baby – also my mum's birthday, I woke up in the morning with a sign the baby would be born very soon. This was such a surprise to me, as Elijah had come eleven days late after induction. Lucas' mum and dad happened to be visiting at the time and were out for dinner with some old friends when we called Leah to come and mind Elijah. My waters had broken and my contractions were less than five minutes apart. Two-year-old Elijah insisted to Leah that the baby was a girl. He told her he was getting a 'dista'. He wasn't wrong.

I was so excited with the contractions seemingly full on and so close together that this precious baby would be born on my mum's birthday! However, by 11:59pm a tear rolled down my face as I said to Lucas, "It's not going to be born on Mum's birthday is it?"

2:55am the next morning, to my absolute shock, my baby girl entered the world! I had been so convinced she was a boy. "A girl?!" I asked, "Are you sure?" This birth experience was different to my first. Elijah had been born in a candle-lit room with music playing and placed straight into my arms. He hadn't cried, just looked at me peacefully, wide eyed, gazing straight into his mum's eyes and hearing me excitedly ramble, "I have a boy, he is so gorgeous! He recognises my voice. Lucas look at him, he's so chubby! He's so big!"

My baby girl however, had been taken straight from me. She was placed on a bench in the corner of the room while I said, "Is she okay? What are they doing? What's wrong? Is she okay?" The nurses explained, "She is okay, she just needs some suctioning." I didn't really even know what that was.

Eventually, she was placed in my arms. I held her close, feeling the shock that I had a girl. Soon they whisked her away again, taking Lucas with her and saying she would have a bath. I thought this was so strange considering I had to ask the nurses several days before baby Elijah was allowed a bath. "It's better for his skin to wait." They had told me. Feeling baffled why in Grafton they bath the newborn immediately, and away from her mother, I felt disappointed and as though I didn't have much say in things here. The nurses offered to keep her in the nursery so I could get a good sleep but I declined firmly. I wanted my baby girl beside me the same as Elijah had been in Sydney.

The next day my still nameless baby started choking very badly. I ran down the hallway of the maternity ward with her in my arms, calling out, "She's choking. She's choking." They grabbed her quickly, and took her for further suctioning. She had swallowed a lot of amniotic fluid on her way out, and the scratches over her face revealed the fact that she had decided to come out unusually with her arm raised up and her hand on her head. No wonder the birth had been so much more painful than Elijah's, even though he was more than a whole pound heavier!

In contrast to Elijah's entry to the world, we had very few visitors. We hardly knew anyone in Grafton. It was strange, but a good chance to rest. Sixteen hours after she was born we named her Luka after her father (meaning 'bringer of light) Angel, after me (meaning 'messenger of God'). The last few days when the nurses did Luka-Angel's 'obs', they commented on her slightly raised temperature but nothing further happened. I recall the night one nurse came into the room and said, "I love coming in here. There is something about this room while you have been here, it seems filled with peace and warmth. I feel something every time I come in here with you guys."

I said confidently, "I believe that's God's presence. There are angels in this room."

No one at any point in time suggested due to the Cairns family heart history we should get Luka-Angel checked. I believed that just like Elijah, Luka would be a healthy little girl and the heart gene had stopped forever! I believed it wholeheartedly!

On our fifth day in the maternity ward, a couple of the lovely nurses begged me not to go. "What are we going to do without you here?" They asked. "Who are we going to look after? We'll be so bored!" I laughed at them, tempted to stay a little longer, but said it was time for me to go home to my Elijah. I had missed him so much whilst in hospital!

I remember the morning vividly, when Luka was ten days old. My mum-in-law, who was visiting us, and I sat at the little table on our front verandah in the sun whilst Luka slept in her little navy blue, vintage basket at our feet. The view from the back verandah was so much nicer, but we decided we needed the sun's warmth on us that cool May morning. While drinking my cup of tea, I noted that Luka seemed very quiet, sleepy and she felt hot. I took her temperature. When the thermometer read 41 degrees Celsius, we could hardly believe it. Jan and I quickly jumped in the car and raced over to our GP on the other side of the bridge. As he examined Luka I noted again how much he looked like Hugh Grant. I wondered how many times he had been told that. He took her temperature again and seemed quite shocked it was 41.5 degrees. He told me he would ring the hospital and that I shouldn't wait for an ambulance, but drive over there myself as it would be much quicker. He told me he was on call for rounds at the hospital and he would see me up there shortly.

When I got to the Grafton Base Hospital, I remember feeling in a bit of a daze. Lucas and I had not long left with our brand new baby in pink and our chirpy toddler Elijah, on our way home from this hospital. This time in the ward felt different. I remember feeling isolated, alone and somewhat frightened. We hadn't lived in Grafton for very long and our family and close friends lived so far away. The doctors explained to me they would need to take Luka off me to do a spinal tap on her, and that I wouldn't be allowed to come. I recall sitting in a four bed ward by myself, hearing my baby scream. This was a scream I hadn't heard before. Her voice began to go hoarse and there were large gaps of silence between cries as she gasped for breath. If I wasn't allowed to console her, I wished they had have taken her further away from where I sat. They told me they had to pin her down on the bed for fear of damaging her spine. I had already noticed in labour (my second one) that they seemed to be doing things the old fashioned way at this hospital.

Rainbows in the Storm

I was a city girl. The high, decorated roof, large rooms and old fashioned windows felt so cold. Luka Angel was so little, and only fresh out of the safety and comfort of my womb. I remember in that room by myself, it seemed dark for this time of the day, it felt sterile and cold and I had nothing there to keep me comfortable or distracted. I hadn't had time to pack a bag. I remember feeling unable to bear the uncomforted screaming of my baby any longer and so my tears joined in with hers. Hunched over and trying to smother my broken sobbing into the tissue in my hand I wondered if I was going to lose my baby girl.

When the nurses came back they explained the fluid they took from her spine would be tested for meningitis. If she had bacterial meningitis there could potentially be long term affects and her life could be at great risk; they resolved to hope for viral meningitis which although not good, was not quite as bad.

I remember feeling alone for a very long time up in the empty hospital ward. On that first night, my baby was taken to another room to be monitored and brought in at times for feeding. My first shower in the shared parent's bathroom gave me a welcome moment of hot water comfort and an opportunity to allow myself to cry again. Once again, the loneliness felt almost as painful as the fear I had for my Luka-Angel.

The next day Lucas and two-year-old Elijah popped up to see us. We contacted our friends and family from a distance (my parents lived in Japan and were working as Salvation Army Officers in Tokyo – so we tried to get a message to them).

Sometime over the next few days the doctors confirmed Luka-Angel had viral meningitis and although it wasn't bacterial they decided to continue to treat her with intravenous antibiotics. Due to her veins being so tiny, they had to put the cannula in a vein in her head. Her head was bandaged up, and she looked so vulnerable and sick. There was a moment where she had a fit. She had gone completely still and the colour grey and the doctors told us there may be some long term effects on her and we would have to watch her milestones.

On the third day, Lucas' parents (who had travelled north for work), came to the hospital but explained that Phil couldn't come into the room due to his immunity. He stood at the door looking compassionate and somewhat helpless. I didn't really stop to think about it at the time, but I thought it was strange. Now that I have a thirteen-year-old with a suppressed immune system, I comprehend completely why he would do that.

Something miraculous happened over those days. I am not sure now exactly which day it happened, but I think it was about day four. Lucas and I have a slightly different take on the timing of when we saw, what we saw, but I can only tell what I recall and have held fast in my heart for so long now.

I remember feeling the physical pain in my heart every time my baby needed another needle (nothing has changed – and now she has had hundreds & hundreds of them). Every time she needed another needle the process would go like this: my baby Luka would cry and I couldn't hold her, she would scream and I could only witness. One nurse told me to stand back and not touch her so she didn't think it was me inflicting the pain. I took that on board at the time being a young mum. Since then though, for any immunisation my children needed I held them wrapped up in my arms of love and comfort.

So it was about day four when the doctors reassured me that Luka would need no more needles or tests now. I felt so relieved. The doctor had told us he still didn't know how this would turn out, and informed us that anything could happen. It was a case of wait and see if she gets better. He had explained that the antibiotics going in through the cannula probably wouldn't do much as she had viral meningitis which can't really be treated. He felt it was worth continuing with the antibiotics in case. So when the pathologists turned up to take another blood test from Luka's foot – I turned to the two of them adamantly and said, "No! The doctor said no more needles! He said she didn't need anymore tests!!" It was about 4pm.

"I am sorry," the lady said gently but firmly, "The doctor has ordered these," showing me a piece of paper. I took a resigned step back as they lay my baby girl, who was not quite two weeks old on the bed in front of me. One pathologist held her still and one held the needle.

I grabbed Lucas' hand and started to wince as they stuck the needle in my baby's foot. All of a sudden a very bright light (brighter to this day than I have ever seen) lit up the room – a fast, flash of light. It was daylight and the lights in the room were all on. I hadn't seen a light like that before. One pathologist turned to the other with baby Luka still lying on the bed and said, "*What* was that?!"

"I don't know," the other pathologist had replied. Lucas and I looked at each other confused and asked, "Did you see that?!" It was ever so brief, but ever so certain and we had all seen it. One pathologist went and looked out of the window as if trying to find the source, then shrugged her shoulders. Peace filled the room.

About an hour later, our sick baby began to pick up, her temperature had dropped, she suddenly wanted her milk and started looking around quite alert and less lethargic. A little later in the evening, the doctor checked her over and said, "Well, looks like she has turned a corner! Doesn't make sense to me, but she looks good."

As I reflect a moment on these stories and consider the goodness of God, I am also aware of the value of Luka-Angel's life. I can't help but recall the maternity ward when a few nurses said to me, "There's something different about walking into this room. There's warmth in here, a peace, an aura."

Something I already knew so well as the presence of God. It was holy ground we were standing on, from that first ward room to every hospital room since. He had sent an angel that night to heal her. There is not a doubt in my mind. Wherever Luka lay, God was evidently present, right through to the ICU room at the children's hospital in 2016, when she lay so still on life support. She was not the only one fighting for her life. The Kingdom of Heaven was fighting harder – fighting for her life as prayer warriors all over the world fell to their knees for our Luka-Angel. God was present, he heard, held her heart, upheld us all and healed her. Yet again her life hung in the balance and yet again it was restored to her. I know she will accomplish great things for God. Our little, 'Bringer of Light, Messenger of God,' fulfills her name's meaning each new day.

Pausing a moment just now as I write (2017), I see the glistening still waters in front of me. I reflect on this day that God has always led me, always been with me, always held my hand, always guided, and always adorned me with his love, his grace, his peace that passes understanding. Always helped me grow through all the challenging things my parenthood has brought me. I reflect how he has always provided me with still waters, everywhere I have lived and always provided me with opportunities for my soul to be restored. There's something about the water. Something about the way I feel God heals me and fills me when I look at his beautiful creation of water. The way the sun glistens and sparkles on its surface, the way it gently moves and caresses, and the refreshing it brings. He continues to lead me beside still waters. The shade of my big tree here by the river in Newcastle is fast running out and I feel the sun begin to burn my skin. The view of these waters will have to be put on hold for another day. Besides, the magpies currently sneaking up on me tell me maybe it's time to go eat some breakfast.

Chapter 3

The Second Still Waters – Another Surprise

'I will give him to the Lord for all the days of his life...'
1 Samuel 1:11 (NIV)

When I found out I was pregnant with our third child we had been living in our next lot of 'still waters' (in Tweed Heads) for about a year. We had reached a crossroad in Grafton, and looked into moving to East Timor with some new close friends who were going there indefinitely to see where they could help the Timorese people living in the aftermath of the unrest of the 90's. Believing that our season in Grafton was over, we were deciding between moving back to Sydney or moving to Timor Leste. A doctor had cautioned us it wouldn't be wise to move to East Timor with Lucas' health. Not long after that we received a phone call to see if Lucas wanted to apply for the Ministry Assistant position at The Salvation Army in Tweed Heads.

Very soon after we were told he had the job, the youth and children's pastor position became available. The day I was told about it my heart beat so fast and I knew without a doubt that was exactly what

God wanted me to do. As I walked along the Grafton bendy bridge praying about it, I saw a boat down on the river, and I felt God tell me, "It's time to step out of the boat." Although we made some close friends and good memories in Grafton, the move to Tweed Heads was a great one! We both absolutely loved our new jobs in the church at Tweed Heads and found it a real privilege to be in these roles.

One night, I was lying in bed in the early hours of the morning and it dawned on me all of a sudden that I might be pregnant.

It seemed the sun couldn't rise fast enough that night, so around 2am I got out of bed and undertook a pregnancy test. As those two, little, red lines appeared, I sat down in shock and opened the Bible asking God to speak to me. I closed my eyes and let the Bible fall open and stuck my finger on a verse (not always my method of choice, but that night it was what I did when seeking direction). Opening my eyes and reading where my finger had landed, I read the first chapter of Samuel. Specifically I read 1 Samuel 1:11, *'And she vowed a vow and said, "Oh Lord of hosts, if you will indeed look on the affliction of your servant and remember me and not forget your servant, but will give to your servant a son, then I will give him to the Lord all the days of his life..."* (vs. 20) *'And in due time Hannah conceived and bore a son and she called his name Samuel, for she said "the Lord heard".'* Now I wasn't looking to fall pregnant, in fact this was quite a shock. I loved my job as youth and children's pastor and it was very busy along with having two kids under four years old. I didn't know how a baby could possibly fit this scenario, but I couldn't contain my excitement or the knowledge that this was meant to be, and this little one inside me was a gift from the hand of God.

It was when I was thirty-seven weeks pregnant, that I had a night where fear swept in. I heard it rustling in the trees outside my window just before it came and invaded my sleep. I had grown up with a brother who is quite severely developmentally delayed. I have always loved being big sister to Michael and he has always been very special to me. I have always felt a fierce protection of him, but the reality is that life for Michael has always been very challenging. This particular night as fear crept in, the thought came into my head that something could be wrong with my baby, or that it may be a troublesome birth as was Michael's (resulting in his brain injury) and I was afraid for my baby. After some time, I began to pray and I felt God's peace flood me and his words whispered into my mind, *'Don't worry about your baby. He will be a great man.'*

The next morning when I woke up I told Lucas about the whisper, and told him we are definitely having a son, so we began to prepare for a boy. There wasn't a doubt in my mind that God had spoken. I went shopping the next day and bought a blue blanket.

The day he was born my heart felt so full, and as tears filled my eyes, I turned to the nurse and said, "God told me I would have a boy – he also told me that he will be a great man." They were the first words out of my mouth. So Jazziah Samuel Michael Cairns entered our world on the afternoon of my little sister's birthday. He was everyone's little joy and blessing and both Elijah and Luka-Angel just loved him so much. In fact, three-year-old Luka-Angel loved him so much I had to keep reminding her gently that he was not just her baby, he was everyone's baby. She wanted him all to herself and he became her dolly. It was around this time that my perfect little angelic Luka became rather strong willed. She was really quite perfect in behavior most of the time, but she certainly knew what she wanted and would express it strongly at home. This strength in her has blossomed into something so beautiful, and I am sure is a part of her character that has held her strong throughout her battle with her health.

Chapter 4

Building Her Bravery

'Two are better off than one, for they can help each other succeed. If one person falls, the other can reach out and help.' Ecclesiastes 4:9-10 (NLT)

There is a bond between all of my children that is both admirable and special. When they were little they cared for each other in the most delightful way. Elijah, even when he was very little, was a respectful, loving son and big brother who revealed his love with the kindest of words and little presents. Elijah and Luka were the closest of siblings and identified so much as a unit that they would refer to each other at that time as 'our chuther' (each other). Every time they talked about what they did together, or the other one, they would say 'our chuther'. I remember not so long after Jazz was born, the day that my five-year-old Elijah and three-year-old Luka started screaming in the yard. Their tears were flowing, their faces and hands were red and swollen, and I was sure their screams could be heard throughout the whole neighbourhood. It was the first time I had heard them crying loudly in unison and I was confused. They were trying to tell me what had happened through their tears, "We gave 'our chuther' the potion (screaming tears). We made poison soup." Their tongues were swelling up and they kept scraping them briskly with their hands. Their eyes were red, Elijah's eyelids had swollen up, and both of their hands had patches of bright red on them. On showing me their 'poison' in the bowl I realised quickly what the problem was. They had made a soup of water, grass and chillies off our little chilli tree and then drank it together. Then their fingers had touched their eyes. I grabbed the milk and as much as I was concerned for them I did see the amusement in it as I could hardly make out their words from their swollen tongues. I knew this memory wouldn't fade fast. I had never seen Elijah cry like that before. I reckon it took a few hours for the swelling and pain to subside. Jazz being younger, was lucky enough to dodge this particular event.

It wasn't so long before this moment when little Luka would not go to sleep one night. We were living in a tiny little house in Banora Point and her bed was a cot mattress that we would pull out from underneath Elijah's bed. She refused to lie down on her mattress that night saying, "A wok up my nose." I kept checking up her nose, and seeing nothing, became quite frustrated she wouldn't go to sleep. I even rang Lucas who was working at the church sports centre to talk it out. She kept repeating, "Ay gotta wok up my nose." I would check her nose and see nothing and so it would go on. Finally I gave her a tissue and told her to blow. Still nothing. She had become quite distressed. I was still feeling frustrated thinking perhaps she was being silly. Finally around 10pm she gave up and went to bed. A few minutes later she came out of the room with little tears rolling down her face but a relieved smile and a tissue in her hand. She pointed on the tissue and said, "Ay got the wok outta my nose." There on the tissue was a pebble larger than her little nostril. I couldn't even work out how she had got it so far up her nose I couldn't see it, but I was relieved it had come out, and resolved to believe her next time.

Another time I took Luka-Angel (four years old) on a special mummy-daughter walk to the Tweed River. She would usually wear gumboots or go bare feet. This particular day, the bare feet won and no matter how hard I tried to encourage her, shoes didn't seem to go on right (sometimes her socks and shoes apparently felt "too funny on her toes"). We were having a lovely afternoon looking at the water and combing our feet through the little sand bank near the boat ramp. Then we took our bread up on top of the bridge at the Kennedy Drive Park where we liked to throw small pieces into the water to see all the fish come up for a feed. We were in the middle of the large foot bridge when my little budding dancer twirled around and then yelped, screamed and began to whimper in pain. When I picked her up to see her 'splinter', I was absolutely shocked! I had never seen anything like this before. Luka had managed to get at least forty or so splinters deeply embedded into her foot. Some were very large, more like spikes than splinters. After my initial shock, I quietly turned to her and said, "Okay, I think we need to go home now. Don't look at your foot, Mummy will sort it out. We might need to go to the hospital for this". I put her on my back and took her home and Lucas too was shocked by what he saw. Luka had the bravest face on and with wet dirty streaks from her previous tears down her face she simply said, "Mum, don't take me to the doctor or hospital. You can get them out." I tried to explain to her how deep and big some of the splinters were (she desperately needed to look of course). Even after looking, she was so adamant that she didn't want to go to the doctors and promised me she would hold still and be brave, and I should get them out.

I could not comprehend her bravery!! After one and a half hours of sitting on a bathroom bench in our little old bathroom at Panorama drive, lots of digging with a needle and tweezers, we finally had them all out. Her foot looked as though someone had taken a knife to it. Her bravery and courage and quiet strength amazed me!

Personally, I felt sick to the stomach, it had been such a feat to have to dig out all those splinters. We rewarded her bravery with her favourite movie 'The Little Mermaid'.

The little scar on her forehead keeps us reminded of the time she tripped on her thongs and fell head first into the gutter on Elijah's birthday. This was yet another moment of seeing her bravery. She had split her head open and needed stitches on her forehead. At Emergency, she sat still, only pulling faces and not even crying as the doctor talked to her, pulled at her wound and stitched it up. He seemed very surprised by how brave she was. Luka was the most intriguing and mature girl whenever she encountered doctors from such a young age. She would stick her hand out to be shaken and with a big smile say "Hi, I'm Luka-Angel". She would then answer questions as asked and sit so still when she needed to. She never seemed afraid, but only at peace whenever we were at the hospital or doctors. Medical staff would often refer to her as a little angel or talk about how brave she was. I believe God was preparing her for what would be a life time of hospital visits and interactions with doctors and nurses.

When Luka was three, we started to notice she didn't really run. She would always get sore legs whenever we walked anywhere. Running was something that she rarely did, but when she tried, she would often trip over and we noticed her legs would swing in a little bit. Any time we would go on our beautiful Coolangatta to Rainbow Bay family walks she would cry from sore legs and sit down until we picked her up (we soon realised she needed to be in the stroller for a long time yet).

After some investigation, she was diagnosed by a local pediatrician with 'Diplegia,' a mild form of Cerebral Palsy. (The doctor explained this may have resulted due to her viral meningitis or one of the three febrile convulsions she had had in the first three years of her life. The convulsion she had at eleven months old had been so significant, I ran outside with her while waiting for the ambulance, looked up to the night sky and called out, "Please God save her, help us!" I thought we would lose her). This diagnosis of 'Diplegia' felt so devastating at the time. I recall him saying, "Your child is no different to who she was before she walked into my office, she is still the same Luka. She now just has a diagnosis for what was already there." This felt comforting to me, to remember she was the same little Luka. I remember though, as I walked to the car from his office with my gorgeous three-year-old on my back, fighting back the tears as his words rung in my head, "She may never be a netballer or sportswoman, but I am sure she will be great at other things." I look back at that now, and see how minimal that diagnosis was in light of what was to come. Perhaps it was good preparation for me as I came to terms with my daughter having a medical condition. We were instructed to do leg exercises with Luka daily in order to keep her legs from being too stiff. In hindsight, this diagnosis protected her heart, as we were suddenly far more compassionate in allowing her to remain in the stroller on long walks. Just three years later, we would receive a much greater diagnosis for our Luka-Angel, and the diagnosis of Diplegia would consequently fade into the background to the point where we would never really mention it again (until now).

Chapter 5

The Fire & the Water

> '*When you go through deep waters, I will be with you; and when you go through rivers of difficulty, you will not drown. When you walk through the fire of oppression, you will not be burned up; the flames will not consume you.*' Isaiah 43:2 (NLT)

Jazziah was a beautiful baby, so calm and at peace and he hardly ever cried. He seemed quietly happy. He was not as smiley as his big brother, or as animated as his big sister, but he seemed content. However, Jazz was often sick, and amongst the times he was hospitalised, three of those were with pneumonia. It was the third hospital stay with pneumonia when Jazz was about two-and-a-half years old and Easter (2009) was approaching. We were due to drive ten hours south from Tweed Heads to Sydney for a family holiday. This particular visit to hospital felt hard and lonely and no one came to visit. Doing life away from family and close friends was always a challenge. On the fourth day when Dr. Cherry (a local pediatrician) did his rounds, he listened to Jazziah's heart. This was the very beginning of what would be a permanent change in our lives. I was no longer certain that God had answered my many prayers that the Cairns' (Woodland) cardiomyopathy gene would not be carried on to the next generation.

After taking a look at Jazz on his hospital rounds, Dr Cherry asked me if my husband was around. He then took us to the parent's room and sat us down while Jazz stayed in his bed in the ward. He told us he had heard a third and faint fourth heart sound in Jazziah and this usually was a sign of something quite significant. He mentioned that due to the family heart history, he or a colleague would be in touch with a pediatric cardiologist in Brisbane, and Jazziah would go on a waiting list to see him for further investigation. There were no pediatric cardiologists on the Gold Coast or within the North New South Wales area. Jazz was dismissed from hospital a little while later and Lucas met us there with our bags all packed for our Sydney trip. It was Thursday before Good Friday and we wanted to arrive in Sydney for Easter. I remember the silent tears that kept resurfacing as I sat in the front seat on that long trip. What Dr Cherry said deeply alarmed and concerned me and it felt like I cried on and off all the way to Sydney. I couldn't believe it. Every now and then Lucas and I would look at each other on what felt like the longest trip to Sydney ever and I only saw fear and concern in Lucas' eyes.

However, it only took a few weeks for our busy and distracting life to set back in and perhaps a little denial. The wait for the cardiologist was going to be long. I remember receiving a letter just after our initial hospital visit for us to see him in the August (six months later). I then managed to put the whole thing out of my mind, and in a sense forgot about it until the day I had an encounter with God on the beach.

It seemed like an ordinary day. Sunset was on the way and as I did several times every week, I left home for my run. The minute my feet hit the sand down on Coolangatta beach the whispered voice began, "I will uphold you with my righteous right hand." I thought it was interesting and sounded like a Bible verse but I couldn't recall which part of the Bible it was from. It went on repeat. Then I began to hear something different, "When you go through the fire and the waters I will be with you, you will not be burned and you will not drown." Again, on repeat. The verses began to alternate to the rhythm of my thumping feet on the sand, "When you go through the fire and the waters, you will not be burned and you will not drown. I will uphold you with my righteous right hand." After about half an hour of this I stopped dead in my tracks as it hit me! That sounded like something hard and troublesome. I looked out across the ocean and up at the sky and I said, "What fire, what waters?" Again I heard, "I will uphold you with my righteous right hand." Well, I thought, I don't know what the fire and waters are, but at least I have the assurance of being held.

As I reached the car I suddenly remembered the waiting list we had been on to see the cardiologist from Brisbane. I contemplated that we were now in August, and that appointment must be soon. My stomach suddenly dropped, as I realised that perhaps that would be the fire and the waters.

As I got home and checked with Lucas and went through some letters, sure enough to our shock, we discovered the appointment was to be the very next day in Coolangatta. It seems without the voice that day, we would have completely missed the appointment.

After breakfast the next morning, I felt a very strong urge to take Elijah and Luka-Angel to Jazziah's appointment. It made no sense to me. They even had to skip school to be there, but I just knew God was urging us to take them along. So we did.

I remember leaving them in the waiting room when Lucas, Jazz and I went in to see Dr Ward and telling them to just sit and read quietly. They were always very good at things like this when we were out.

As the doctor listened to Jazziah's heart, he commented on what an amazing two-year-old he was. He just sat very quietly, and did exactly what he was asked to do. He was only just about to turn three, but he had always been very good at sitting still and doing the right thing. Dr Ward confirmed straight away that he agreed with Dr Cherry and could hear a third and fourth heart sound and this pointed to something potentially serious. After doing a run-down of our family history, he then asked us if we had other children.

We told him that we did and they were both sitting out in the waiting room.

"Do you mind if I see them?" He told us that he would like to take a listen to their hearts as well.

Sure enough, just after Luka-Angel, always charming the doctors, did exactly what he said, and introduced herself in her usual sparkling way, he told us he could hear a third heart sound and she would need to go for further testing in Brisbane. We were stunned! Worried! I decided he must be wrong, considering all of the times she had seen doctors and no one had picked up a third heart sound. The doctor informed us that Elijah's heart sounded normal, so there would be no need for further testing at this stage.

Instantly I knew without a doubt, this definitely was the beginning of the fire and the water! But as soon as it hit me, I grabbed onto the fact that God had already told me he would uphold me with his righteous right hand, and he told me I would not be burned and I would not drown. I believed this was for my children and Lucas too.

Little did I know at that point in time that the fire wouldn't be a little campfire, but more like a bushfire! The waters would come in a variety of ways. Some would be floods that built up and slowly overflowed the banks, some would be like a flashflood that would come out of nowhere, and others like a terrifying Tsunami!

Chapter 6

The Amazing Things that God has Done

'The Lord is close to the brokenhearted and saves those who are crushed in spirit. The righteous person faces many troubles, but the Lord comes to the rescue each time.' Psalm 34:18 (NLT)

Journal Entry - 30th May 2010

'The Amazing Things that God has done'

For about the last two-and-a-half months after our children's diagnosis, I have cried every day that Jazz and Luka-Angel have cardiomyopathy. It seems that I had suppressed my grief. See, leading up to that dreaded day on 16th December 2009 (which was supposed to happen in November but couldn't go ahead because Jazz had pneumonia again), I had sunk into two weeks of utter despair. I felt as though I was drowning and a massive cloud enveloped me. I kept imagining myself flailing in the middle of the ocean with waves coming hard at me, and I was only just able to keep my head above the water.

Then we had the phone call to take in a two-year-old boy with the potential for it to become permanent care (we had applied to become foster carers and been approved approximately eleven months before that phone call). The timing seemed so wrong because of the grief I was going through, but it also felt right and so we said, "Yes". Just nine months before, I had a moment whilst driving when I felt God told me I was having another child. I thought at the time it meant naturally, but just nine months later, along came our two-year-old Jayjay.

The couple of days in the lead up for Jayjay to enter our family, I felt a whole lot better within myself and my focus shifted off my impending fears and onto caring for another child.

The appointment day at The Mater Hospital in Brisbane arrived. Our good friend from church, Leanne, who had become like a surrogate Grandma to our kids, came to support us. I remember the kids' excitement as they had climbed in the car in their pyjamas. Getting up really early was nothing unusual to them, but Mummy and Daddy both getting up early was exciting. Even more exciting to be driving to Brisbane with Leanne in the car with us, and knowing they would receive some little surprises off us. Lucas went with Jazz to take him down to pre-op for his cardiac catheter. Luka and I waited for her Echo (Echocardiogram - heart ultrasound), *with Leanne by our side. The person conducting the test turned to me half way through and said something about her restrictive cardiomyopathy which came as a shock! Luka hadn't yet been formally diagnosed, so I felt confused. I remember feeling very sick, and wondering as my stomach churned if I might vomit. I couldn't decide if I was going to vomit or cry. Leanne turned to me knowingly and shuffling through her handbag said, "Chewing gum can be helpful in stressful situations. It can help relieve stress, I learned that in my counselling course". With that, she handed me a piece of gum apologising that it was all she had and that it looked a little old and tattered in its wrapper. As the gum turned to tissue pieces in my mouth, I recognised that it was indeed very old and weathered, and I turned to Leanne to tell her that it hadn't quite turned to gum but tissue.*

Although terrified of what was unfolding beside me, it did make me laugh. Looking back, I now think it was really quite amusing as I tried at first not to tell her but as the tissue-textured pieces of old chewing gum stuck to the insides of my cheeks and got caught in my teeth. I couldn't deny this piece of 'gum' would not be turning to gum. Its particles gradually slipped down my throat leaving a bad taste and texture in my mouth. Pieces of the gum stuck there for quite some time as I didn't have a bottle of water to wash them away.

Lucas came back up to where we were, having seen Jazz off into theatre. I whispered to him, feeling absolutely terrified, that something had been said during the echocardiogram about Luka having 'Restrictive Cardiomyopathy'. He told me to wait, as that person wasn't the specialist and we would be told formally later if that was the case. His calmness and certainty reassured me.

It felt like the next thing we knew, we were seated in recovery as our little three-year-old Jazz gradually came around. He looked very, very pale and fragile. Luka was her usual funny and engaging self, and seemed very interested in what was happening around her. She sat on Leanne's lap chirping away and reading a story we had given her, whilst Lucas and I sat quietly beside Jazz's bed, waiting for him to look a little better.

A few hours later, a large team of medical staff surrounded us and pulled the curtains partially shut. Doctor Ward told us that both of our children had Restrictive Cardiomyopathy which would mean a pediatric heart transplant. He said something about the fact that if we were in the USA they would immediately be put on the heart transplant list. I couldn't really follow what he was saying. I had never heard of Restrictive Cardiomyopathy. This made no sense to me. Lucas had Hypertrophic Cardiomyopathy. They must be mistaken. He told us they would fly us to Melbourne to see the heart transplant team.

I bit my cheeks and put on my brave face as I didn't want to upset Luka. Leanne looked at us quietly, also in shock. I looked at Lucas and he was just nodding. This couldn't be real. I looked at my cheeky two, and wondered how this was even possible. How could they both have this strange thing I had never heard of? I convinced myself they must have what Lucas has. The doctor went on to say Jazziah's pressures had risen too high in the cardiac catheter and they would need to keep him in at least overnight to make sure he was safe. I thought of my baby boy's heart being pushed to its limits. I pictured him lying there in theatre and his heart being pushed, and then it all became too much. We were told Luka-Angel would also be booked in for a cardiac catheter soon to measure her pressures and they would need them regularly. As the team of doctors walked away, my brave face accidentally fell off, and I started loudly sobbing. I was aware that people started to stare at me, but I just couldn't stop it. Lucas quickly ushered Luka-Angel out of the room, and I collapsed into Leanne's arms sobbing into her chest like I was a toddler. "This can't be true" I cried, "I don't understand. What do they mean they need a pediatric transplant?" I howled. I was too traumatized and devastated to care what people around me thought. As far as I was concerned, no one in this recovery room understood what I was going through. How could they possibly?!

Lucas and I were shell shocked. I remember the quiet trip home the following afternoon and then pulling into the driveway. Our neighbours (and good friends) came out to say, "Hello" and see how we went, but I couldn't speak, so I disappeared inside and tried to stay there as much as possible over the next few days.

It was just a week later we were on our way to Christmas holidays. Christmas didn't feel the same that year. Our new child suffering from his own terrible trauma was like a little two-year-old tornado in our life. I had never parented behaviours like his before, and was unsure how to deal with what I was facing from him. Along with that stress, was the constant realisation that two of my children had just been diagnosed with a terminal heart condition. One of my favourite distractions that camping trip was sneakily and illegally setting off fireworks on the beach with my sisters, my brother, the older kids, my dad and my brother-in-law. As the noise of our fireworks got louder, we ran to hide behind some rocks so we didn't get caught. Often with my siblings, I laughed until I cried! As often happened in our family, Mum turned a blind eye and sat that one out, minding the younger children.

The days went by, my grief was somehow pushed to the side and a certain numbness set in.

It was late February 2010 when the grief monster reared its unpredictable head again. I remember that most of the time I was very happy and distracted. I had lots of things in my life from parenting four children to working part time as the Youth and Children's Pastor at church. I absolutely loved my ministry, loved the teenagers and kids in my sphere of influence. It added so much joy and fun to my life, and I loved seeing their young lives changed for the better! I worked hard and gave everything I had to my ministry! It gave me a greater purpose and I knew I was doing exactly what I was meant to do with my life. With four kids, a husband and many teens and kids to invest in, being alone was rare. Being alone was also very hard. I tried to avoid being alone wherever possible. Whenever I found myself alone, the grief monster would come and visit me and I would be overwhelmed with sorrow because of my children's diagnosis. If I was alone during that season, I would cry. I didn't like to cry.

Running had always been like my best friend and so most of my runs were now filled with silent, flowing tears (besides the runs I would invite my good friend and neighbor Jodie to, in which case we would laugh nearly the whole way, even to the point at times of having to stop and cross our legs). When I was on my alone jogs, I would put my hat and my sunnies on and run bare foot down on the sand where the water lapped the beach. This was my favourite pastime. I felt so free when I ran. It was the perfect outlet for my sadness, my stresses and concerns. Most runs I would talk to God the whole way, and have a moment where I would stop and listen to him. Running at sunset was my usual practice as I would look at the sky and remember how amazing our Creator is. It was as though he would paint the sunsets in the sky just for me.

One particular run, the tears weren't soft and quiet and intermittent. I felt deep sorrow and isolation in this journey I was on. I felt as though I had no one in my entire world I could talk to about this face to face. Perhaps no one I could openly talk to full stop. Mum and Dad were working for The Salvation Army in Papua New Guinea, my sisters lived far away. It was often too hard for Lucas to talk about it. I started begging God to send me a like-minded woman I could talk with face to face specifically about this health stuff with my kids. That evening I was deeply overwhelmed with sorrow that every step I took along the beach, more sorrow and grief emerged. I was just so sad for my Luka-Angel and Jazziah that this would be their life. Doctors' visits, hospitals, heart transplant in childhood, no sport, no exercise, no jumping castles, no trampolines, no chasings or tips, no 'duck, duck, goose'... I was frightened and very, very sad. Normally my stamina was big and I never stopped during my run from Kirra beach to Point Danger and back. This day, I got just past Rainbow Bay and around the corner up the hill. Then I felt the heavy weight of my invisible backpack that was filled with grief and I thought, *'I can't possibly go one more step!'* I plonked onto a bench seat with a beautiful elevated view of the ocean and I began to cry out to God, "Send me someone that I can talk to. Send me a like-minded woman. I need someone to talk to – help it to be the right person!" My head fell into my hands on my lap and I started sobbing quietly. All inhibitions were out the window, and I could sense people passing me by, but I just could not stop. The grief monster had finally won! I was done. I couldn't even complete my jog because my sadness was far too heavy to carry any further.

As I cried out to God to send me someone, I heard him clearly whisper to me, "She is right in front of your eyes". I quickly looked up. I looked at the beach in front of me, gazed at the empty footpath and then said to God incredulously, "Where? I don't see her. Where is she?" Then I started to think he must have meant it figuratively, not literally. In my mind, I started looking through the faces of the women I knew, *'Not that one, no she is not the one God is providing'*...I felt I needed someone outside of my 'work place' which also happened to be my church. There were other women in my life that I loved, but no one seemed right. Then I heard God say to me a second time, "Look up! She is right in front of your eyes". This time I knew in my heart that he meant literally. Once again I looked up from the place where I had buried my teary face. A face appeared very suddenly from around the corner of the footpath directly in front of me. "Angela?!" Tammy exclaimed with a beautiful smile and the warmest brown eyes. Tammy lived just five doors away from me, and I had met her through my other neighbor, Jodie.

Instantly knowing she was God's provision for me I said through my tears, "I need to talk, have you got some time?"

As she sat beside me, I poured my heart out, and she listened perfectly. She put her arm around me and spoke at the right times, asked the right questions and said some encouraging Bible verses and prayed with me. At the end of our conversation she went on to tell me about her day.

Tammy never jogged. That evening she had said to her husband when he got home from work, "I really need to get out. I need to go for a walk." This was unusual. She began her walk from Rainbow Bay towards Kirra Beach (the completely opposite way to me). As she walked, she prayed. Just after she started walking, she felt God suddenly urge her to turn around now. Unsure as to why, she obeyed the urge and as she did, she walked closer and closer to where I sat crying. When she came across me, she knew instantly why God had told her to turn around. Tammy explained how blessed she felt that God would use her in this way. She felt so privileged to be the listening ear outside of 'my world' that I really needed.

There was not a doubt in my mind, that for that moment in time and a couple of months to follow, Tammy was God's gift given to bring me strength. Living just five houses away from each other meant I was able to visit her easily. I went over there a few times for a cuppa and a chat. She was a great listener, a beautiful follower of Jesus and so perfectly outside of my world. Through her at that time, God was able to bring me the comfort and strength and listening ear I needed. There was no judgment or expectation, just Godly love and concern. She even shared a similar taste in music and shouted the kids and me to a concert at her church one night when Lucas was away. She bought me a CD and it was filled with songs that helped bring healing to my hurting soul.

Music is a God-given gift, and can bring miraculous soothing and healing to one's soul. Many times through my seasons of grief, I have written a song, or heard a song that has been exactly what I needed at the time. It is no wonder that music is the common language of the world. Music can speak to every human being. I also believe God can send someone just at the right time, to come alongside us on his behalf. They may even be right in front of our eyes.

Chapter 7

A Mother's Letter

'The Lord is my rock, my fortress and my deliverer; my God is my rock in whom I take refuge, my shield and the horn of my salvation, my strong tower.' Psalm 18:2 (NIV)

23rd February 2010

Dear Luka-Angel and Jazziah,

Tonight I was leading worship in 'The Upper Room' gathering at church and singing 'Made Me Glad' (by Hillsong). This song is so special to me as it reminds me Luka, of when you had meningitis as a baby... and the PEACE and the ASSURANCE and STRENGTH I felt from my God. I sang and played this song at your dedication Luka a few days after you got out of hospital with meningitis. So singing this song tonight reminded me of that and then my mind travelled to now.

We only found out two and a half months ago that you both have Restrictive Cardiomyopathy. Tonight, I started to cry while leading worship and I could barely get it together to continue. I left early and haven't stopped crying for the last hour or so. My heart hurts SO much knowing all that you will go through – it tears me to pieces because I love you both so, so dearly!

You both (& Elijah of course) mean the WORLD to me.

But, in all of this pain and all this grief, all this uncertainty, I KNOW our God cares! I know he has a plan to work all things together for our good. I know he will hold our hands, hold your hand and carry you through the water, through the fire so you will not drown and you will not be burned. You are both SO, SO strong and SO brave and God can make you even stronger! He is after all, the strongest in the whole universe! Every night Luka-Angel, we quote together at bed time Psalm 42:5 'Put Your Hope in God.'

Every night Jazz we quote together Isaiah 40:29-31 'They that wait upon the Lord shall renew their strength. They shall run and not grow weary, they shall walk and not be faint, they shall rise up on the wings of eagles.' You are only three years old and every night you say it from memory with me.

Your big brother Elijah every night says Proverbs 3:5-6 'Trust the Lord your God with all your heart, and lean not on your own understanding. In all your ways acknowledge Him and He will direct your path.'

These are verses we can rely on.

Chorus of 'Made Me Glad' (in case when you are older you don't know it):

> 'You are my shield,
>
> My strength, my portion,
>
> Deliverer, my shelter, strong tower,

My very present help in time of need' (Hillsong Music).

I love you with everything within me.

Eternally,

Mummy Xo xo xo

Chapter 8

Learning Through the Hardships & Curve Balls – Part One

> *'...suffering produces perseverance, perseverance character; and character, hope.'* Romans 5:3-4 (NIV)

Sometimes it feels as though we have had seasons where hard times came in thick and fast, and there were only short breaks in between. We have always had so much joy and so much to be thankful for, but it seems that life has often presented our family with many hard times among the good.

When I reflect on these times, I see that we grew, and I found God in a new and profound way. I also see how he sent help when we were desperate and on our knees.

A year or so after we bought our little blue duplex on stilts, down the end of the worst driveway you have ever seen, some people moved in next door who were soon to become some of our best friends.

The day I met Richard, I was playing in the front yard with Elijah who would have been about seven years old. As we introduced ourselves, my bright eyed and confident Elijah stretched out his hand to Richard and said, "I am Elijah. Do you believe in God Richard?" Richard has never forgotten it. I watched apologetically as Richard stumbled over his words saying, "Umm.. oh? Umm.. kind of. I went to a Christian school…" or something to that effect. I wondered if Richard thought, *'Oh great, moved in to share a wall with some Bible-bashing Christian crazies.'* It was very amusing and I thought Elijah's faith and innocent courage was something I should learn to follow. Dee was expecting a baby and we soon found out his name would be Henry.

One night not so long after they moved next door a violent storm blew up. Our duplex was surrounded by very large trees and the noise of the branches falling on our tin roof made us wonder if the house would actually fall down. It took some courage for me to run out into the wild weather and check on our new neighbors. Arriving on their doorstep I discovered they had set up camp for the night next to the only brick wall in the house. Considering they had a background in construction and had decided to do so, we decided to do the same on our side. We gathered the kids into our loungeroom to sleep on mattresses next to the brick wall. This was the wall we shared with our neighbors, so in amongst the storm we took joy in tapping 'hello' backwards and forwards until we fell asleep. As the storm blew wildly around our little duplex, it felt like safety in numbers as we took refuge on either side of the shared brick wall. This wasn't the only storm we would face in our little blue house.

Months later, I was delighted the day Henry was born to go visit this precious little baby boy. Little did I know at that point, that Dee and Richard would become close friends, and friends who also knew what it was to have a child with significant health issues - Henry was later diagnosed with a lung condition - bronchiectasis. Dee's father moved in with them for a time as he was very unwell with mesothelioma cancer (from asbestos). They like us, lived life with a storm brewing constantly on the horizon and there was no doubt God had placed us in each other's lives for numbers of reasons.

After the landlord put up the price of their rent, Dee & Richard moved out, but our friendship remained.

The day that our new neighbours moved in with their six kids, I knew instantly this would be different.

From even the first night, we heard the violence and the first week was a real shock. Things would be completely quiet, we wouldn't see any of the kids, then the man would get home and the harrowing sounds would begin. We would hear yelling, banging and profanities, then after an hour or so there would be complete silence. It was terrifying. Elijah and Luka-Angel became very aware of the sound and it used to petrify Luka. She would lay there awake and worry. Then together we would pray for the family next door.

We called the police numbers of times. By the time they would arrive the screaming would have already stopped. I often wondered what had happened and why they couldn't just take the man 'in', or at least rescue the kids. I wasn't sure if he actually lived there, or just came to visit regularly.

I tried to befriend and reach out to the lady, and we managed many conversations in the front yard, but most of them ended up with her asking me for money. Then she became braver and she would come up to my front door all through every day, asking to use my phone and very often asking for money. I decided early on not to give her money but to offer her food. I would ask how her children were, wondering who was watching them, knowing they were all so young.

One day she walked up our stairs for the phone with a black eye the size of an egg. I told her I know she gets beaten by her partner. I told her I wanted to help her. She shut down very quickly and left.

The one time their eldest child was allowed to play with our Elijah, he told Elijah he didn't go to school. He also told Elijah that his mum had never had friends. This made me more determined than ever to help and I would look for opportunities to try and have a conversation, and would often give them food and clothes for the children.

One day as I lay in my bed in the afternoon with my three-year-old beside me, the banging next door and the shouting became louder and louder. It sounded like someone had been thrown down the front stairs. I peeked out the window to see the man next door with a shovel. He was banging it as hard as he could, shouting and swearing. He looked as though he was on drugs. I looked at my clock and knew that any moment now, my husband and my three other kids would be driving down that driveway straight into the path of someone who looked like he was ready to kill someone. My heart beat so hard and I rang Lucas saying, "Don't come home! I am petrified but you can NOT come home! Don't come down the driveway. I am worried he will hurt you or the kids." I called '000' and waited next to my little boy on the bed, covering his ears as the yelling and the banging of the shovel continued.

This time it only took about fifteen minutes for the police to arrive and to my surprise they came in full force. There was a combination of uniformed police, some in no uniform, and some in a uniform I didn't recognise. They were decked out with batons and weapons. A team of fifteen or so ransacked our shared yard and the house next door. I gathered there was a reason for this. After about twenty minutes one of them knocked on my door and explained the man had run, was missing and they hadn't found him. They told me he was 'wanted' in three other states, and that he should be in prison. We stayed with some close friends from our church that night, worried for our safety.

A number of days after that, the lady clambered up my front stairs so bruised and beaten she could barely walk. She came over to ask for $20. My dad was visiting and I quickly asked him what we should do. I told her there were people who could help her. I began to plead with her to get some help and to step up and protect her children from him. She 'threatened' me that she was afraid he, or worse still that his brother, who had just gotten out of prison and was far worse than him, would come after our family.

I invited her to come in and sit down and have a cup of tea. To my shock she came in. It was the first time she had been willing to sit down in my house and not just bang on my door because she wanted something. She finally said she would like help, as I had explained to her about a refuge I knew for women and children. I said we would need to act quickly. I told her I would borrow our church bus, get some children's car seats and we would leave in the next hour. I rang the refuge to check they had space for her and there was just a little more organising to do when something shifted. She suddenly stood up and said she had changed her mind. Walking briskly towards my door with $20 in her hand she explained to me that it just wouldn't work and she could never escape 'him'. She felt it was just too dangerous for her and the kids. I was extremely disappointed and my heart sank. I had truly believed she was so close to allowing help.

We were fostering already at that time, so we had regular visits from a government department. One day they accidentally knocked on my neighbour's door instead of mine. We never told our neighbours that one of our children was fostered, so from that moment on they believed we had reported them to the authorities and we started to face many insults and threats.

Living with fear for our children's safety was very difficult. Deciding it was no longer safe to live in our little duplex, we made a plan to leave quickly. Over a couple of days we quietly packed boxes as much as we could with the plan to come in with a truck the next day and get out of there. Mum and Dad had just bought a retirement house in Banora Point and they were going to rent it out while they travelled Australia. Instead they kindly offered for us to stay there rent-free. We took a car load over to Mum and Dad's place, and decided it was more important to move us out safely, before the rest of our things. Although we had planned to go back the next day for the boxes we had left behind, nervousness set in. It was about 8pm when Lucas said, "I am suddenly not comfortable with all the expensive gear we have left at our house. I think we need to at least go back and get the instruments, the camera and the computer." So Dad and Lucas left.

When they arrived back at Mum and Dad's place, they were shaken. They had encountered our violent yelling neighbor, who threatened to break in and take everything we owned.

The next day, when Lucas and I went over to get some more boxes from the house, we felt nervous as we drove in. As we got to the front door, it was apparent immediately that the door was open! "I feel scared," I said to Lucas, "let's just go".

Ignoring our fears, Lucas walked in, and I followed. Becoming aware of the mess in front of us, I felt so shocked and started to instantly cry and shout! "How dare he do this!! All we have ever done is help them!! We have given them so much food, and so many times I have offered to help..." I just couldn't believe what I saw. I felt so foolish and so betrayed. It made no sense to me. We had shown them such kindness and genuine concern, and this is what we had been given in return. All of our packed boxes had been ripped open and poured out. Our music room was knee deep in paper, sheet music, letters and equipment. I was surprised to see my digital piano had not been taken, but clearly had been thrown across the other side of the room. There was garbage mixed through all of our stuff and it stunk. Our bedroom and the kid's bedrooms were the same. Packing is so hard, especially with four kids (three who have high needs) and so the fact that they had broken in and trashed our house was an absolute shock and absolutely traumatising!

The most devastating moment for me, was when I walked into the kitchen and I saw Luka-Angel and Jazziah's specialist letters from Melbourne and Brisbane sitting on the floor in amongst the poured out rubbish. They were soggy. These letters represented the greatest and deepest pain in my life. They represented my beautiful children who take their sickness in their stride and go to doctor's visits and have needles with such courage. All over the page was a dirty, brown coloured fluid, which the police said later they believed to be urine. I dropped to the floor in sobs that rocked my body and I felt sick to my stomach.

Lucas' next words, after we had looked through the house were, "We should get out of here, we're not safe! We'll have to leave before we call the police."

At the top of the driveway we sat in the car on the phone to the police when wracked with anger and the injustice of it all, I jumped out of the car and started screaming out, "How could you do this to us?!!! You are going to go to jail! We are calling the police! How could you do this to us when we have only ever been kind to you?!!" I was angry and broken! As I picked up some rocks to throw onto their roof in my enraged state, Lucas grabbed my hand and hugged me, telling me it wasn't worth it. He reminded me how dangerous this man was, and that perhaps throwing rocks at their house was not the best idea.

Just an hour or so later when we went back into the house with a police escort to begin the process of assessing what had been stolen I was stunned by an image in our office. We had just noticed that our camera bag and contents had been taken (we were very broke, and so this was very upsetting), Elijah's DS gaming device he had gotten for his birthday and numbers of games had been taken. A jar of a few hundred dollars I had been saving was missing along with a few other things. It was all very devastating!

Right in the middle of the floor, among the piles of ripped boxes and paper, was a painting I had done a few years earlier on one of my toughest days. The day I did the painting, I was in the thick of a busy ministry role at Tweed Salvos, I had a four-year-old and two-year-old and was about three months pregnant. Lucas was away for the first time in our parenthood. I was left alone all weekend and I was petrified at that time of staying alone at night, especially with a big empty property next door. My four and two-year-old had come running inside the house from playing in the backyard screaming, "Snake! Snake!" I came outside and saw the tail of a snake in our garden. I had already felt a great darkness descend and still suffered from post natal depression, which I had been diagnosed with soon after Luka-Angel had a very frightening febrile convulsion, at eleven months old. We had called our local 'Wires' reptile agency to come and remove the snake. When he found it, he told me it was a 'yellow face whip snake'. He explained that if it bit me, it would only make me sick, but if it had bitten one of the kids it could kill them. It shook me to the core. I also felt strongly that we were under some serious oppression!

I couldn't sleep that night, so I put some worship music on, and set up my easel and began to paint for the first time since I had moved from Grafton to Tweed Heads.

I saw an image of a girl (me) sitting curled up, sad, low, but a light shining out from within her. She was completely surrounded by the presence of angels, and she was safe, secure and held. I painted what I saw and although it wasn't anything amazing, it was a moment in time when I felt the thickness of God's presence in my house. I felt his peace descend almost tangibly as my children slept. The Bible verse I painted underneath it read, "And lo, I am with you always" (Jesus' words in the book of Matthew). Even as I looked at it as the morning light arose with the voices of my children, I knew it was real. I had painted what had happened. The girl was safely in a womb of God's protection like the baby within her.

As I gazed at the painting yet again, here I stood surrounded by an act of evil. Surrounded by the biggest attack I had ever experienced. I stood my legs deep in rubbish, ripped boxes and paper work, and right there on the top of the pile was my painting with a rip in the middle of it and the words, '...and lo I am with you always'. I knew I was not alone. I knew I would be helped through this too. I knew there was a 'snake' in the front garden here, and I knew it was time to move on. I had given everything I could, and I was devastated I couldn't rescue this woman who seemingly didn't want to be rescued and I couldn't rescue her six children (or the seventh growing inside of her). I had done everything I could to show love, grace and kindness to this family. It was time to move on, and God would help me through this devastating time, like many more to come. I only hoped that the lady next door would also find some help.

Two of my old neighbours and close friends (Dee and Jodie) came and gave up a whole day helping me pick up our trashed things and cleaning our house. Dee and Richard even went as far as buying Elijah a new DS gaming device. I was so touched and moved by their kindness and it reminded me again we were not alone.

Just a few days later it was the school fete. Our son was entering the school's Talent Quest singing and playing guitar to Michael Jackson's, 'Heal the World, Make it a Better Place'. I had been so low for days I could hardly eat.

I felt that day that perhaps I had re-entered depression, thick and fast. I was also facing a significantly shocking and difficult time as some people within my youth group were going through some extremely challenging circumstances. I now believe I was suffering post-traumatic stress.

My dad who was still visiting us (at his new house) said, "Come on Angie, you're best to come to the school fete. Don't stay at home. It will be good for you to get out."

I put my sunglasses on to cover my tomato-red eyes that had been crying all morning, and I went with the family to the school fete. We entered the holiday guessing competition and I watched as my son sang, "Heal the World, make it a better place, for you and for me and the entire human race…" The words were so timely and the hard wall around my heart that went up so quickly in the last week of trauma, crumbled down. I had been reading over and over in the Bible the last few days about the importance of having mercy on others, and it was up to God to avenge, not me. I got back up on my feet, left my pit behind and decided it was still worth loving others well, loving them big and forgiving their wrongs against me, even if I got nothing in return. This was the love I had been called to follow, the love that Jesus had towards others, regardless of their behavior, race or attitude towards him, even to the point of surrendering himself to die. Elijah won the school Talent Quest and I was overjoyed!

We decided to hang around while they announced the holiday competition winner.

I knew in my heart of hearts that God was giving us that holiday (he had whispered it into my ear earlier that day). Sure enough, our names were drawn out! We won a weekend family holiday to stay in a cabin south on the Coast. This was an absolute gift from God. We could not have afforded anything like this, and it was exactly what we needed.

God was with us through yet another troubled time, he was helping us, and we were being prepared and given skills in perseverance, courage and trust that we could never have known without circumstances like this. We were being taught resilience and coming to understand peace that passes all human understanding. God knew there were darker days ahead. Even amid the immediate pain of our circumstances, I knew he was helping us to trust and to grow through this hard time. God was also rewarding us with little joys and reminders along the way of his love and his care for us, like this free holiday.

Chapter 9

Learning Through the Hardships & Curve Balls - Part Two – 'A Tsunami'

'Do not be anxious about anything but in everything by prayer and petition, with thanksgiving, present your requests to God and the peace of God, which transcends all understanding will guard your hearts and minds in Christ Jesus.' Philippians 4:6-7 (NIV)

A Little Sunshine

It was January 2011 when we were still living in my mum and dad's house while they travelled. It was a two-story house with a pool in the backyard. This house had become our haven. We were now safe from our dangerous neighbours and living in a quiet street in the biggest house we have ever lived in. The pool became a great space for bonding with the kids and lots of special family memories. It also became an outlet for our youngest to expend his seemingly endless energy, and we could enjoy each other again. We had so many happy times in that house and it was an absolute blessing to us! I still really enjoyed my job at our church but we entered a new phase as Lucas' role was made redundant. Lucas still invested in the youth though, and we ran our weekly youth church together. It was during this time too that we were gifted by some close friends with a beautiful puppy. (I had decided years before we would never get a dog. Lucas had decided differently).

One day Jazz came home with a picture and a story he had done at pre-school. The story read of our imaginary pet dog and how happy Jazz would be to play with it. Lucas had secretly asked me just the night before if we wanted a Labrador as our good friends who were breeding, had offered us one. I had said a firm, "No". Then I decided to ask God if it was part of his plan. Earlier that day I had switched on the TV. This was something I never did during the day for myself. There was a documentary on dogs that were aiding sick kids and those with serious illness. The entire show was about dogs helping people with serious health conditions. So when Jazz, who had never previously asked for a dog, had brought his drawing home that same afternoon, I nearly laughed out loud! It was blaringly obvious that we were supposed to have this dog so I changed my mind.

Choosing her name was something! As a family, we all put our best two suggestions in a hat and then drew out her first name, second name and third name. Lucky for her she just dodged four-year-old Jazz's two choices: 'Treetop Grassy' and 'Bubblecuppa'.

'Zibby Sunshine Blaze' became everyone's play mate and was incredibly gentle with the kids and protective of them. She loved to swim, and spent many days in the pool with us.

Angela Flemming Cairns

A Tsunami

It was on an average sunny day in January when our world was once again turned on its head! Lucas had loaded the trailer full of some stuff that needed to be taken to the tip. Elijah's best friend had come to visit for a 'sleepover,' and the five kids were in my care. They all wanted to go for a swim, so we made our way down to the pool at the back of the house. Lucas said goodbye and I went in the pool with the kids for a few minutes, then got out to sit by the pool. After a few minutes, I decided it was probably a good time to mow the lawn. I found it hard to sit still, and there was always work to be done. I was a multi-tasker and decided that I could see the kids well from the whole backyard, so I could still supervise them and get the mowing done at the same time. Elijah, Luka-Angel and Daniel were strong swimmers and could touch the bottom of the pool in most places. Jayjay had a good flotation vest on and could swim well enough with it. Jazz was in a flotation ring. I realise even as I write, the lack of wisdom I showed that day, and it haunted me for weeks. I ducked outside of the pool gate and went under the house for not more than a minute to get the lawn mower.

As I pulled the chord to start the mower, which this particular day started immediately, I glanced at the pool and I could make out four of the five kids. I couldn't see Jazz. All of a sudden with my heart leaping into my mouth, I could see Jazz's hands and the tip of his hair as he splashed around in a panic. His face was completely under water. He had slipped out of the flotation device and I could see his flailing arms begin to slow down. As I ran to the gate, I started yelling and screaming but my words weren't coming out right. Daniel was the closest to Jazz, but they were all having such noisy fun that they couldn't hear me well, and they hadn't noticed Jazz. "Grab Jazz!! Daniel – Jazz!!!" I was in such a state that I couldn't get the gate open on my first attempt! As I got to Jazz and Daniel had lifted him up as much as he could, I dragged him in one swift move out of the water, and his little body flopped into my arms. His eyes were rolling and white! His face was a colour I hadn't seen before and his lips were completely blue. I could hear my voice screaming and screaming for Lucas but I hardly recognised its sound. I was calling for Lucas, even though I knew it had been at least twenty minutes since we had said goodbye to him in the driveway, as he had finished loading the trailer. Elijah ran to get the phone to call the ambulance, and see if Lucas was still around. It wasn't until later that I recalled my precious daughter's voice calling out, sounding very wobbly, "Is he dead? Mummy, is Jazz dead?" She held onto the side of the pool in a corner and began to cry, but I couldn't even bring myself to answer her. I put Jazz into the recovery position and looked at the CPR chart. Although I had my First Aid Certificate, I couldn't even think straight or work out what to do next, so I started thumping his back and shaking his body. 'There is NO WAY I can do this! I *cannot* do this!' I thought over and over looking at the CPR chart. I started sobbing, "I love you Jazz. You're going to be okay Jazz! You're going to be okay." I was picking him up, thumping his back and then laying him back down into the recovery position again, screaming in between at the top of my lungs for Lucas. Jazz remained floppy.

To my absolute surprise and relief, Lucas appeared with the boys running ahead of him. He was on the phone to the ambulance. I was bawling, Jazz was pale and still, with blue lips, and then he began to cough. His colour went slowly from blue to white. He came around quite quickly, his heart thumping so fast. We carried him outside of the pool gate and lay him on a towel on the grass. After about ten minutes, Elijah said, "Jazz, do you want to play my DS?" Jazz whispered, "Yes". I felt so relieved that Jazz was okay enough to accept the offer (the DS was Elijah's new toy, and it was a rare day when I would allow the little ones to play it). I knew by Jazz's response he was okay, he was with us. The paramedics arrived and Jazz was much more alert. He was still pale and very tachycardic and they needed to take him to hospital for further assessment. I was still in my wet swimmers, and had no time to consider getting changed.

As we sat in Emergency, I felt so relieved that my little boy was looking pretty good, all things considered. I kept swallowing and refusing to cry the tears that lay beneath the surface. I felt completely sick about what had happened. Our minister (who was also my boss and our friend) came to visit Jazz and I in Emergency and brought us a McDonalds Happy Meal for dinner. Although the chest x-ray showed no water on Jazziah's lungs, his heart rate was extremely erratic.

After being admitted, I lay in the ward in my slowly drying swimmers until about 11pm before I called Lucas (who was still looking after four kids at home). I asked if he could get someone to bring some clothes to the hospital for me. Up until that point I was so caught up in the trauma of what had happened that day that I hadn't realised how uncomfortable I was.

That night I barely slept. The heart monitor, connected to Jazz, woke me all through the night. Sometimes I would see on the screen that his heart rate was over 220 beats per minute. Other times it fell as low as 20 beats per minute. I climbed into his hospital bed and clung to him. I felt so guilty over my terribly unwise decision that day, and the cost it had nearly come at. I stifled my sobs into my pillow and wondered how on earth we were going to get through this. His heart rate was so unstable and all I could think about was that this was only going to get worse! I knew there would be times in the future when this heart would be failing and I could hardly conceive it! I opened the drawer beside the hospital bed around 2am and found a Gideon's Bible. I begged God to show me something or give me some peace. I stabbed my finger in the little Bible and it landed directly on a passage that up until that point I had never really taken in, *'Do not be anxious about anything, but in everything by prayer and supplication with thanksgiving let your requests be made known to God. And the peace of God which surpasses all human understanding, will guard your hearts and minds in Christ Jesus.' Philippians 4:6-7* (ESV). Instantly, I felt God's peace and calm miraculously wash over me. The feeling was tangible.

The next morning the pediatrician came around first thing and did an ECG (Electrocardiography – records the electrical activity of the heart). He looked at the monitoring from overnight and said he needed to ring Jazz's cardiac team in Brisbane. As my little boy was now propped up in bed, pale, but enjoying the special treat of playing PlayStation, I was told he was at great risk of cardiac arrest. We needed to be transferred by ambulance immediately to Brisbane, which was an hour and a half away. Rather than focusing on the stress of it all, I just took in my son's sweet face and thanked God that he was unaware of what was happening.

All Jazz knew, was that he was getting a 'long ride' in an ambulance. To a four-year-old boy, that sounded exciting. It was a Sunday morning and Lucas was leading the worship music at church. I tried his phone over and over to explain to him what was happening. I then tried to call my contacts at church, although most of the numbers I had, were my youth group members. Finally after about fifteen phone calls, one of the sixteen-year-old girls answered. I spoke to Lucas, and holding in my tears, I told him I was very much at peace. After I got off the phone, I brushed the fresh tears away before I went back in to Jazz. Even though I felt sad and very concerned, I noticed that I felt significantly different to the night before. I was no longer terrified. I knew peace.

Amazingly the same paramedics who had transported Jazz to hospital the afternoon before were the ones to drive him to Brisbane. They had given him a little knitted teddy bear the afternoon before that Jazz had not yet let go of. All through the night he had used the bear to communicate with me, "Teddy wants to go home. Teddy misses Daddy."

Lots of our friends and family began to let us know they were praying for us and we really started to feel as though everything would be okay. By the next day, Jazziah's heart rate had settled down and was back into some sort of 'normal' rhythm for him, erratic, but without extreme jumps. I remember the sick feeling I had when the doctor met with me in that hospital in Brisbane and said he had asked one of the nurses to do children's CPR lessons with me. They explained that Jazziah's heart had gotten into a funny rhythm probably brought on by the trauma and panic of nearly drowning. They told me there was definitely a good chance this could happen again. The nurses encouraged me to get him some swimming lessons and to keep him supervised, especially in the water. He was so vulnerable. I wondered how I was ever going to let him out of my sight again. After my CPR lessons with a child mannequin, I couldn't stop visualising me doing CPR on Jazz and it terrified me.

When we got home from hospital a few days later, Jazz was greeted with a parcel sent by The Salvation Army children's department. He appeared to feel more 'spoilt' by the presents and cards, than traumatised by the event and I was so grateful. I gave him longer hugs, and spent more time with him when I put him to bed. I could hardly believe what had happened. It was devastating to think that we could have lost him.

During this time, I learned a great lesson about God's peace and his intervention. Lucas should not have been in the driveway still that day. He was supposed to have left ages before with the trailer, but he was delayed an extra half an hour or so. God showed me that even on the darkest of nights, he is aware of what is going on in my life. He had seen me. He had seen my depth of sadness, guilt and terror as I lay in the hospital bed in the children's ward beside my precious son that night. When I called out, he stepped in and he flooded me with his peace that passes understanding, and led me to read Philippians 4:6-7, a passage of scripture that would become embedded in my memory, and speak to me in many hard times ahead.

Chapter 10

Athletics Carnivals, Hats and Sunglasses

'Show me the right path, O Lord; point out the road for me to follow. Lead me by your truth and teach me, for you are the God who saves me.' Psalm 25:4-5 (NLT)

Lucas and I have always endeavoured not to label our kids. We did not want them with the label 'disabled', 'heart kid' or 'sick' (or for our youngest 'foster kid'). Ever since diagnosis it became a mandate for me, to make sure our kids knew that their life was so much more than their heart condition or any label. Their heart condition was not who they were, it was just something they had. It may change their outlook on life, the courage they had, but it would not define them. It was also so important to both Lucas and I that they still had adventure, to know they were good at things, even though they couldn't do sport, and to make sure life didn't become all about doctor's visits and hospitals when everything leant towards doing that.

One of the hardest things as a parent of a child, who is unable to do some things is seeing them miss out on activities or knowing that they will.

The first school athletics carnival for Elijah (pre-diagnosis for Luka and Jazz) was so exciting for me. I recall the excitement I felt about my own school athletics carnivals. When I had been at school, this was my favourite day of the year! I just loved athletics carnivals. They also made me incredibly nervous and I remember the unbelievable butterflies in my stomach - a mix of nerves and anticipated excitement. I would do my very best at these carnivals. I was hungry to win, my aim was always high and I was after 'Age Champion', although I only got it a couple of times in high school and never in primary school.

So Elijah's first athletics carnival had me with those same butterflies. Would he be a natural? Would he do really well? I was both intrigued and hopeful. At that point in time we had nicknamed him 'Dash' as when I played Wednesday night basketball at The Salvation Army sports Centre in Banora Point, little Elijah would sprint up and down the lines of the court alongside me whenever the ball came into my hands. He looked so fast and reminded me of little 'Dash' off the movie 'The Incredibles'. Elijah was also very social, and he also laughed a lot. He had a gorgeous inability to contain excitement, and it would often unfold with him jumping everywhere, or trying not to smile and ending up in laughter.

As he lined up for the 100 metre race at his very first Athletics Carnival, Lucas and I stood with a camera, proudly waiting. We had sprayed his hair the colour blue to match his shirt, so even from where we stood, he was unmistakable. BANG! Everyone took off. Elijah was still talking, always the chatterbox, and got left a few steps behind. Then he started a run that took him zig zagging all over the lane. The ground was grass and looked fairly even to us, but he seemed to swerve in and out of his lane, with one of his typical, 'I'm-trying-not-to-smile' expressions, and excitement that sent him into lots of chuckles all the way to the finish line. Needless to say, he came last.

As disappointed as we were that he didn't do his best, it was just too funny and too cute to remain disappointed about. Sadness didn't even enter the picture. Not even a glimpse of it. We knew he could always do better next year, and really it was hardly a big deal at all. I can't help but take a moment of mother's pride, that he went on to win age champion many times later in primary school and high school.

Luka-Angel and Jazziah's school carnivals were a whole different story.

To come to understand the kids could never do sport for me, a mad sportswoman who loved to run, was heart wrenching! To know they would never know what it was to be part of a team, to achieve on the court, the field or at the pool was so difficult. Yet harder still, was the realisation that family walks would change. Even a simple thing like playing tag or jumping on a trampoline would be out of the question. Nothing was worth risking cardiac arrest for.

There was always going to have to be a fine balance between allowing them to 'go for it' and have fun, and keeping them safe. Many of our favourite days as a family encompassed walking from Coolangatta to Rainbow Bay. In order to do this though, Luka and Jazz needed the stroller or scooters. Luka and Jazz stayed in the stroller for a long time, but when Luka was about seven years old and her feet could touch the ground in the stroller, we decided something needed to change. That's when the scooter became a saving grace for us! She could stand on the scooter and we could push her along, one hand on her back. It was amazing! With it we could walk up the incline from Coolangatta beach to our favourite beach at Rainbow Bay. Jazz became so accomplished on the scooter by the age of four! He could speed along and it gave him legs! It was such a blessing.

Going without his scooter for the week after Luka-Angel's transplant was hard on Jazz's body. Then one day he was given one as a gift. As he flew past me on the footpath outside the hospital he yelled at the top of his lungs, "Mum, when I am on this – I feel free! I feel like I don't even have a heart condition!"

Our time of living in Tweed Heads and doing youth and kids ministry at The Salvation Army was a time of great joy and we just loved living there. It felt like we had finally found our 'home'. Besides the fact that we fell in love with the Coolangatta Coast, being around kids and youth kept me laughing, being daring and enjoying life! As much as my role was very tiring, I also received great energy from it. I have many great memories of hilarious games, sleepless nights at camps and conferences, watching young lives changed for the better, serving the community with our youth through car washes, feeding the homeless and helping people with their lawns, visiting the local nursing home, girl's sleepovers, playing music and recording a CD with our youth band, playing basketball, experiencing adventure and hanging out with the youth & kids connected to The Salvation Army.

When the phone call came from someone at head office of The Salvation Army asking us to consider taking on a new role resourcing youth, kids, young adults and youth leaders in the Newcastle & Central Coast area my first answer was, "No way!" I was happy. I was not remotely interested in moving. Lucas, however felt that we were supposed to go and asked me to think and pray about it.

A few months of wrestling with God and desiring to do what I wanted, concluded the day I sat on the rock wall at Kirra Beach. I looked out at the view I was so familiar with and loved so well. I told God I knew he was asking me to go, but sulking I told him I didn't want to. I finally gave in and I felt his peace descend. As I watched the sunset sky over the expanse of a still blue ocean, I heard his whispered words of comfort, "From every sunrise to every sunset I will be with you, and in between. I will never leave you or forsake you. I am with you always." I felt very strongly we were being urged to move to Newcastle for a season and it was God's best plan for us (I felt within my heart that part of the reason was something to do with being closer to Lucas' Dad). It was such a sacrifice to leave. My parents had just decided to move there and had bought their retirement home. We hadn't lived near each other for sixteen years. I had journeyed so closely with some of the young people and couldn't bear to leave them. I felt like I was walking out on their lives and the grief I felt was great. But, how could I say, "No," when I knew God knows everything and I only can see what's around me. God's peace about going was absolute confirmation that I had heard right. We were moving away from the still waters of Tweed Heads, and onto the still waters of Newcastle.

We didn't know where we would be living but I prayed about choosing the right school and I googled some schools within Newcastle. I wrote down the name of the first school that came up. Something within me said if we moved, that was the school our kids were supposed to go to. I didn't tell Lucas about it, and I didn't even look into any details about the school. I just knew it was for us, and truthfully, I was still somewhat sulking about going. I was absolutely shocked the day Lucas came home and threw an envelope to me. I opened the envelope as Lucas said, "I have been looking at schools for the kids in Newcastle, I emailed this school and they have sent us an information pack to look at." It was the very same school I had written down and already believed our kids were supposed to go to. I still didn't look into its distance from the house we would be moving to. When The Salvation Army residence we were to be living at, changed just two days before we arrived at the new address, I just had to trust. After we moved to Newcastle, we went to visit the school to hand in our enrollment forms. I couldn't believe it was less than a five minute drive from our house. If we had been living at the residence we had originally been given, it would have been a twenty-five minute drive. Another confirmation this was the right choice.

On our way to school on the very first day of term, I prayed for the kids in the car. Elijah was in Year Five, Luka-Angel in Year Three, Jazz in Kindergarten and Jayjay at preschool. I invited the kids to pray. Luka-Angel's prayer went something like this (keep in mind she had been watching the movie 'Matilda' over and over at that time), "Dear God, please help me to have a teacher exactly like 'Miss Honey'". She then said, "Mum, he said yes! God told me I am getting a teacher exactly like Miss Honey!" I felt very concerned she was going to be sorely disappointed, and wondered how I was going to work through that one with her.

As we walked into the school the first day to my surprise I saw in the distance my cousin's husband. We hadn't kept in touch over the years, and last I heard their kids were home schooled, so it came as a shock to learn they lived within minutes of us and Luka would be in the same class as their daughter. As I met Luka that afternoon she came to me exclaiming with absolute excitement, "I got Miss Honey Mum!! She is EXACTLY like Miss Honey!" Bewildered, I asked Luka to introduce me to her teacher. As I walked to this petite pretty young teacher with hair so much like Miss Honey she introduced herself. She was softly spoken with the sweetest voice and said, "Hello, my name is Jessica Forbes". I almost burst out laughing! Indeed, God had answered Luka-Angel's prayer – she had a teacher exactly like Miss Honey!

The first school swimming carnival I went to, took me by surprise. Luka had stayed home as she couldn't participate anyway. I had left my disappointed little girl who had wondered why she couldn't participate. I knew it would be too hard for her to sit on the sidelines and watch and not be part of it. It was the second week at their new school. We felt so far from our home in Tweed Heads and I was grateful I had a cap and sunnies on. The tears took me by surprise. When they called Luka's age group up, it was too much for me. I had sobs in the back of my throat. I talked to a few mums around me, but considering they knew nothing about me or our family at that point in time, it felt too awkward to let any tears spill over publicly, so I retreated to the car for a while. When I had recovered sufficiently, I went back into the pool grounds and forced myself to sit there and support my son Elijah through his races.

Jazziah's first athletics carnival was even harder. The athletics carnival for Luka hadn't been so bad as she had a great group of friends by then, and enjoyed dressing up in her colours, cheering and celebrating her friend's races. She also got to participate in some field events. Jazz however was still at that age where they only had the 100 metre race and then some great novelty events but most involved too much 'cardio' for him. I had a big conversation with him in the car on the way, reminding him that he couldn't go in the running race. He had heard it all before. He was very disappointed but seemed happy enough to go in the slower paced novelty races.

When we got there and sat together and watched race after race, I guess it gave him time to contemplate. When they called his age group, he got up and said, "Mum, this is my race!" With that Mr Five took off to line up with his friends. I was initially shocked. He knew that he couldn't participate! I couldn't tell him it could unfold in cardiac arrest, so he just knew he couldn't, but didn't really understand the 'why's'. I quickly made my way to the gate saying to the teacher with urgency, "Please grab Jazz, he can't do this, it's too dangerous!" As he was walked back to me with tears welling in his eyes and a very angry look on his face, I bent down to console him saying, "I am so sorry Jazz. I know you want to do this, but it's just not safe for you." He turned to me and said adamantly, "But Mum, I am fast and I *know* I can beat those guys!!" Then he folded his arms and pulled his hat over his face and slunk down in his seat as my overwhelming sadness for him beat me. So I pulled my hat down too, put my sunnies on and prayed no one would come near me. The minute the race was over and his friends were back I took an opportunity to go to the car to recover. Everything in me wanted to drive home and curl up in a sad corner, but I knew I needed to stay to support all of my children (and to keep Jazz safe from himself). This was the first time I had noticed that this journey of missing out on sport was going to be very tough on Jazz.

Out on the novelty field, a surprising thing happened. Jazz's beautiful teacher Mrs Lowthe, had gently taken my arm and whispered intuitively, "How are you going today?" To which I responded with, "Not very good," and tears instantly took their place again filling my eyes. I briefly pulled my sunnies down to look her in the eye and then quickly put them back in place to disguise my feelings. "You *need* to meet someone!" she said to me, much to my initial alarm! The last thing I felt like doing was meeting someone today (inside I was a *mess*). "This is Lindy," she said, "and those are her boys and she doesn't like athletics carnivals either!" (I looked at the gorgeous twins in front of me). Mrs Lowthe went on to tell Lindy that Jazz has a heart condition and like her boys (who had a different condition), he can't participate in most things either, so it's a tough day for me too.

Lindy had soft, warm eyes and a lovely smile. "I hate athletics carnivals", she said her eyes filling with tears. "Me too," I responded, "They used to be my favourite school day of the year when I was growing up." She kindly offered me a hug and we stuck together for the next hour of torture. Watching our boys do what they could and sit out what they couldn't.

I grew up in a family where you go in everything and give everything a go. I had to come to a new resolve in my own circumstances of parenthood. On days like swimming carnivals and athletics carnivals and cross country, it was okay to allow my child to stay home if they wanted. If they chose to do that, they would be spoilt with movies, cafes and yummy food. I also came to understand that hats and sunnies were vital for carnivals and not because of the sun. I also came to understand that the sadness grief monster could hit me at any time, often out of the blue and so having my car keys in my pocket or within easy reach was so important. The last thing my kids needed to see was their mum unfolding in tears, especially in front of their peers.

We were so blessed to be at the most caring and understanding school in the world! God had gifted us with this school. God's provision is simply amazing!

When we first moved to Newcastle, one of the first things I did was find my new favourite jogging place. As I explored with my feet, I soon learned that running on the beach bare foot was no longer an option. In Newcastle this meant shell splinters, which was quite unlike running bare foot along the pure, white sands of the Coolangatta Coast. I found my way to jogging in shoes again, on a picturesque path near my work from Bar Beach over the beautifully, rugged headlands to Nobby's Lighthouse. It entailed a stack of stairs and hills, but I loved this new challenge and was always one for a beautiful view. On my very first run as I stopped for a moment of meditation at the top of a cliff, my eyes fell on a Bible passage graffitied on an old white fence. It was the very passage I needed and I continued to stop there every run until I could commit it to memory. Psalm 25. After I had it to memory, I would stop there and recite it, even after it had long faded. Although Newcastle felt a far distance from our home in Tweed Heads, we felt so blessed to have water surroundings again. Many of our family days entailed a family walk near the water somewhere. Luka and Jazz would bring their faithful scooters and we would push them along.

Fast-forward some years, our school recently allowed Jazz (year five now) to ride his big off-road electric scooter in the school Cross Country! It was the first one he had ever participated in! He was so excited all week knowing he was able to finally go to his first Cross Country! This off road electric scooter we had bought made it possible for Luka-Angel to attend school camps the last couple of years and could get up to 30 kilometres an hour. Needless to say Jazz 'unofficially' won his Cross Country race.

Chapter 11

Timor Leste & Some Lessons in Perseverance

'I lift up my eyes to the mountains – where does my help come from? My help comes from the Lord, Maker of heaven and earth.' Psalm 121:1-2 (NIV)

When Elijah was about eleven years old with his teenage years not too far around the corner, I decided it was worth asking some parents around me what they believe they did well with their children, and what they felt they would do differently if they could go back.

Three times within the same week, having asked three different women this question, it became clear to me that I needed to take Elijah on a holiday to a developing country, or on a short term mission trip, before high school. Lucas and I decided together that this would become tradition, to take our child in year six on a special one on one mission/holiday.

I encouraged Lucas to take him to East Timor, although it played on my mind that Lucas had already been there once on a mission trip and had been rushed to hospital unwell on his arrival home. Lucas turned the question back to me, "Do you want to go?" I admitted to him that part of me would like to go, but that I was also too scared to be that far away from the kids in case they got sick. For years it had been terribly hard to leave to go anywhere. Even a two day conference in Sydney felt too much. The 'what if something happened to them while I was away?' question, always played on my mind. Lucas said, "You will be okay. They will be okay. I will be here even if something did happen, why don't you go? You've never been to a developing country and I know you would love it!"

I hesitated, as Lucas started to book in the flights. There was a good sale on flights, so it was all very spontaneous really. "Okay, crunch time", he said. "I need to finish this, what name am I putting in there – mine or yours?"

"Ummm… I just don't know if I can do it," I whined.

"Great. It's done," he said, having pushed me into something he knew I would love to do, but was allowing fear to get in my way.

When Elijah and I arrived at Sydney airport with our big backpacks on, a few tears escaped down my face and he reassured me, "You'll be right Mum. This is going to be fun!"

I could hardly believe what I was about to do. The sound of Luka-Angel, Jazz and Jayjay crying loudly in unison was still ringing in my ears, "I'm going to miss you Mummy…" was being sobbed and yelled out the window as they drove away from the airport.

However, a call to adventure and the fact that it was all too late to pull out now, overrode my feeling of uneasiness as we walked closer to the gate.

Our first night a stop-over in Darwin, wasn't great. We had accidentally booked a backpacker hotel room on the wildest street in the city of Darwin. There were party goers and the sound of people who had drunk too much, keeping us wide awake until about 4am. Plus Elijah thought that there was somebody standing in our room several times. I would flick the light on, and no one would be there, but I felt a thick presence of fear. It was about 4am when I pulled my head under the covers and decided that if anything was going to get me I would rather not see it coming.

Our Darwin adventure the next day was really fun. It felt so free to have just my eldest child beside me and to be able to choose to do whatever we wanted. No little ones to carry, consider or look after. We visited a crocodile centre, caught a bus to a beach where there were 'Beware of the Crocodile' signs, then finished with a swim on the water front (deciding not to worry too much about what was underneath), and a sunset dinner on the wharf. As we ate our dinner we could see the hugest fish leaping up from the water below as people fed their left over chips to them. It was just beautiful and I felt so free.

Flying into Timor was quite a shock. The vastness of the land, and the simplicity of the airport in stark contrast to the Sydney and Darwin ones we flew from, was so noticable. I had thought we were about to land in fields when suddenly there was a tiny patch of tarmac. The heat was like someone had opened an oven door in your face as we exited down the stairs of the plane directly onto the tarmac. We kissed our western food goodbye as we left the plane.

The security looked more like soldiers and I had already been warned by Samuel (our friend in East Timor) about the guns they carried. I couldn't even look them in the eye for fear of the power they held in their hands.

As Samuel, his daughter, Serenity, Elijah and I went out to the car park a little girl speaking in Teton began to beg to carry our suitcases. We only had our backpacks, so it certainly wasn't needed. I looked at Samuel as if asking him what to do. He firmly said not to give her any money as she will be taken advantage of at other times if she thinks we are all 'safe'. There were many other ways to help. To my initial shock, Elijah and Serenity jumped in the back of the Ute. As I hopped in beside Samuel, I decided if Elijah was sitting in the back of the Ute, there was no way I would wear a seatbelt. If we had an accident, I couldn't live with myself if something happened to him and I was completely fine because I wore a seat belt. This was the first time in my life I had consciously not worn a seatbelt and I felt strangely insecure.

As Samuel drove to their little village in Dili, not so far away, my eyes were opened to a whole new world. Groups of boys sat or stood around the sides of the road. Cars did whatever they wanted, and motorbikes or scooters transported entire families. I had of course heard about this and seen photos, but this was the first time I had ever seen anything like this with my own eyes. The houses were very basic. Many were simply a straw roof with mud brick or concrete walls. The roads to the village were like dirt footpaths. There were goats everywhere and some very skinny dogs. A graveyard seemed to be right in the centre of their village, and the local shop looked just like a window to a cubby house.

Samuel and Cynthia's house was right on the most beautiful beach of crystal blue water. The grey sand stretched for miles. A group of cows were herded across the beach, which was lined with coconut trees. Thirteen-year-old Serenity announced with a cheeky smile, "Don't stand under a coconut tree while you are here. More people die here of being hit by a coconut than by car accidents." I didn't know if she was joking or not, but I decided not to stand under a coconut tree. I thought that would be a pretty pathetic way to die, and I would rather go out old or in the midst of adventure. Not simply standing under a coconut tree.

Although their second home here had many 'western luxuries' as it had been set up to house mission teams from Australia, a hot shower was not one of them. I was surprised that a simple hose off outside seemed just as good as a cold shower upstairs.

Although I couldn't quite imagine the personal cost of living here for as many years as our close friends had, I felt if my life was different (and there were no heart conditions to consider), this is something I would love to do!

Our big adventure, a few days later, took us into the mountains to climb the highest peak and deliver some goods to villagers along the way. It was amazing and eye opening. When I saw the number of families traipsing up the mountain road with supplies on their heads and in their arms, donkeys carrying goods, and children as young as two carrying large baskets, it was shocking to realise that this was their only option. They would walk for days to go to the markets then walk for days carrying things home. Some people even carried massive rolls of carpet. I could hardly believe it was possible. Many people attempted to flag down our 'Ute' asking for a ride, and I think the most Samuel squeezed in the 'Ute tray' along with Elijah, Serenity and Israel (his young son), and at times me, was about thirteen other people. It was really very different for me to see and quite amusing. Elijah was a little put off by the fact that all of the people silently stared straight at him, and of course Serenity too but she was quite used to that. We were in the country, and many of the country Timorese had never seen 'Malai' (foreigners) before.

We drove up the mountain-side and reached our destination at the foot of Mount Ramelau. Samuel had decided it would be fun to climb the highest peak in East Timor. I was really up for that as climbing Mt Fuji with my dad ten years before was one of the biggest highlights of my life! We packed very little food (naively expecting the local 'bed and breakfast' we stayed at, to supply a bit more than the two sweet potato chips we each received for breakfast). With no running water, and no shops within miles, we also had hardly any water. Then we underestimated the time it would take. As Samuel, Cynthia, their children, their friend, Elijah and I trekked up and up this rugged mountain, I remember my stomach churning and grumbling with terrible hunger pains. The worst thing though, was feeling so, so thirsty! We had run out of water, and there was nothing to drink. Yet, this was a challenge that I was so grateful for. It was a good learning experience to get the tiniest glimpse into what it is like to be hungry, thirsty, and have to watch your child not have enough to eat. So many people in the world live this way every day. Getting past my hunger and thirst, it was something beautiful to stand at the top of the mountain up in the clouds and know we had achieved walking to the top of the highest peak in East Timor! Watching Elijah's discomfort (of thirst and hunger) was hard though, and I longed to give him more food. He was so hungry and expending so much energy, and I wondered how mothers all over the world, including right here in our neighbouring country, cope with such a terrible thing every day of their lives. This for me was the first time I had no water or food to give my hungry and thirsty child.

The next day we headed back to Dili for the nation's 10 kilometre fun run ('The First Lady Cup'). I had always wanted to go in a run like this, and I jumped at the opportunity when I found out Samuel was participating. The only problem was I didn't take my joggers to East Timor with me. The closest thing I had was an old pair of hand-me-down canvas shoes with holes in them. Cynthia's feet were a lot smaller than mine and I couldn't seem to find any joggers for sale on the outskirts of Dili. After exhausting any hope of another option, I resigned myself to going in it anyway. The heat and humidity was grueling and I wondered how I was going to be able to run in this heat when just standing in it was a challenge for my body. When I made my way to the starting line I looked at the hundreds of feet around me, and to my surprise I saw sandals, bare feet, and the odd pair of good Nikes on the foreigners over there. I wondered how the locals were going to run this dirt and gravel footpath in bare feet or old sandals for 10 kilometres!

It was about the '7 kilometre mark' when the heat was all too much for me. The holes in my shoes had let in so much gravel that was now grinding against my skin. The thin soles of my old shoes, meant that every step I took pounded deeply into my feet and ankles. Never had I been in a race like this, but I also couldn't seem to find a breath of fresh air. Most of the locals cooked with fires and so every breath I took consisted of smoke. We were also running alongside the water, and so every now and then I would get the smell of raw or rotting fish! As we passed the markets and the fishy smell got stronger, I began to dry wretch. The smell of fish had been causing that response in me since I was about five, when Dad would cook smoked cod for breakfast on Good Friday (not a fan!).

The heat on my head felt like I was on fire and I poured the water bottle I had been given all over the top of me. I felt like I couldn't step any further and then I looked above the hundreds of shacks on the hill and a Bible verse came to mind, *'I look to the hills but where does my help come from? My help comes from the Lord who made heaven and earth,'* Psalm 121. I began to chant it over and over. Then I began to remind myself of my favourite jogging singlet that read 'Never, never give up'. This singlet had kept me running so many times before on my favourite beach run in Coolangatta. I had used that motto to keep me going when I was tired in ministry, when I was sad about my kid's diagnosis, when I was tired of parenting. That motto had become embedded in my very soul as if tattooed there. Never, never give up. *'I look to the hills, but where does my help come from? My help comes from the Lord who made heaven and earth.'* (Psalm 121) "Don't you stop and walk!!" I quietly demanded of myself, "not even for a second!"

As I approached the finish line I could see Elijah with a huge smile on his face, waving madly at me and cheering, then he and Samuel (the latter who had finished a long way ahead of me – coming in Seventh overall) ran up beside me and jogged me through to the end. I was grateful to have persevered, and I knew even then that some of the lessons I learned that day would remain with me. Although surprised by how much I struggled in just a 10 kilometre race, I was pleased to at least finish in around an hour.

Timor was an eye opening time for me. It was also a time I will be forever grateful for as I shared in some beautiful adventurous moments with my eldest son, who was soon to become more independent. I was also able to witness Elijah, in varying circumstances, remain persevering, caring and full of joy! I was deeply aware that these were character traits he would require into our future.

Chapter 12

Joy Amidst the Sorrow

> *'To all who mourn in Israel, He will give a crown of beauty for ashes, a joyous blessing instead of mourning, festive praise instead of despair.'* Isaiah 61:3 (NLT)

Although it was quite different to what we had been doing, we really began to enjoy our new job as Youth and Children's Coordinators for The Salvation Army in the Newcastle and Central New South Wales region. Being closer to Sydney had also become an absolute blessing. We were able to see our Sydney family far more often and that meant having the freedom to visit Dad Cairns when two years after we had moved to Newcastle, his health was suddenly declining. He had some fairly long stints in hospital, and being so close meant Lucas could pop down and spend time with him at St Vincent's Hospital. It had been nineteen years since his transplant when his health really began to decline. I don't want to write too much about when Dad Cairns went to heaven. I feel as though it is not my story to tell. So I will just say it was both shocking for us each and heart breaking. Phil was always grateful for his new heart and every year in May his family would celebrate his new life since transplant. His journey was often not easy, particularly towards the last few years, but his strength and devotion to his ministry in

The Salvation Army was amazing! I never heard him utter a word of complaint, although he must have found his sickness very tiring and challenging.

Losing Dad Cairns was a huge loss to the entire family. He was a man who loved his wife and his family the way Jesus taught, he had great integrity, compassion and worked hard. We will always feel the hole and the gap where Dad should be, and I guess we won't recover from that until we see him again in heaven.

I will never forget the day we remembered his life and celebrated him with hundreds of others. Although we have the assurance he is celebrating eternity with his Saviour, this of course, was still a very sad day for us, especially his immediate family. One memory of sheer delight on this hard day – will forever be etched in my mind.

During the afternoon tea following Dad Cairns' Celebration Service, Luka-Angel and Jazz and some of their cousins just seemed to disappear. The food around us looked decadent, so the fact that the kids were missing in action, made no sense (my kids love good food)! As the hundreds of people in attendance gradually became 'tens', I started to worry and determined it was time I stopped talking, and started looking.

Lucas came to me sighing and exhausted, saying, "I have found the kids upstairs, they wanted to put a show on for Nana and everyone else here, and they have been practicing this whole time".

"Oh no," I groaned, looking around at the empty room and considering how inappropriate it would be to pull out a kids show at a funeral. "Will they put it on for just us?" I asked. My husband said he was too tired, as naturally it had been a very emotionally draining day. "I'll go see if they will just put it on for me", I said. I told my sister-in-law, Kristen, that our kids had been practicing a show this whole time, and could she come and sit and watch it with me, to give them a bit more of an audience.

When we got upstairs there were some tears. "Everyone is gone?!! We have been practicing all this time!" The rows of chairs were set up for at least 40 people. The skits had been written and rehearsed to near perfection. The tickets had been drawn up, and I stood before the five children (five of the eight Cairns cousins) wondering what on earth were they thinking to put on a show today?!

"Nana said she would watch!" One of the kids said. Kristen and I tried to reason, "Nana is so tired. It will be too hard for her to watch this tonight. Anyway, Nana has gone home now". They all protested, "But she said!! We don't want just our parents to watch. We will just have to do it when we get home to Nana's place."

I thought of my newly 'widowed' mum-in-law, a patient, joyful and loving Nana, yet I reflected on how strong she had been all day, and how exhausted she must feel. I determined that when we got home, I would have to talk some sense into the kids about saving the show for another day.

One hour later (back at home), I inquired again, "Where are the kids? Why aren't they eating dinner?"

"They're practicing still," came the reply. Sigh…

I went in to tell them empathically but firmly, that enough was enough and the show could not happen tonight, it had been a *huge* day for everyone. But when I saw the effort, including the complete set up, the re-arrangement of seats in the formal lounge room, the bouquet of flowers that had been freshly picked for nana (from *her* front garden), the tickets that had carefully been written out (by two Miss eleven-year-olds, the Miss nine-year-old and the Mr seven

Rainbows in the Storm

year old), I said, "Okay, I don't know that Nana or the Great Aunts and Uncles will come, but I will see if all the parents can come."

Word got around. Their devoted nana said she was happy to come to the show.

I pondered on whether this 'top secret', self-authored by the 'Cairns' cousins', well-rehearsed-all-afternoon-show for Nana was going to be full of 80's style contemporary dance and soppy songs. I wondered how we would react if they said anything 'inappropriate' on such a day as this.

As we walked in, we were handed a fresh flower, and escorted politely to the correct seat number on our ticket. Approximately fifteen compliant adults were in attendance. Some seemed to have travelled all the way from New Zealand just for this show, or so the kids seemed to think. It was getting late (after 8.30pm), we were all tired, but everyone was very kind and happy enough to sit back and watch.

Well, the show opened with great drama. It seemed that seven-year-old Jazz had a portable speaker in his voice box, which was the beginning of the chuckles in the room. He boomed, "LADIES AND GENTLEMEN, BOYS AND GIRLS AND NANA". A special comfy chair had been set up for Nana, and she was presented grandly with her bunch of flowers. She laughed!

What unfolded was the most hilarious variety show I have ever seen in all my days of sitting through shows by my kids (absolutely their best yet!). No soppy songs, no inappropriate words or long, sad speeches about Papa (that may have undone us), only comedy – jokes, surprising magic tricks, toilet paper humour, short comical skits with English accents, all concluded with a big group dance and song, "We are the Cairns Family! We are family! We are the Cairns

Family!" Laughter filled the place. Not just chuckling laughter, hysterical laughter, bursts of it, over and over. The kind of laughter that saw tears coming out of my eyes! The applause went wild. An encore was demanded from the audience and the face of the young cousins shone! Nana smiled, Nana chuckled! I thought how my musically inclined Father-in-Law would have been delighted by the unity of spirit and his performing grandkids. I contemplated the thought, *I wonder if God has allowed Phil to see this*'. It was a comforting thought. Warmth and joy filled the room.

On reflection I have thought about all that we would have missed out on that day, had we not allowed our kids to go ahead with their 'Show for Nana'. This momentary distraction from such terrible grief was ridiculous, yet profoundly appropriate and crafted beautifully out of childlike character!

On a dark and sad day, such delight and joy and even great laughter, was brought about by our little people. Even to their nana, who had lost her soul mate, partner in ministry, one and only love and best friend! Any wonder Jesus said, "Truly I tell you, unless you change and become like little children, you will never enter the Kingdom of heaven." (Matthew 18:3)

> *'I will turn their mourning into Joy.'* Jeremiah 31:13b
> (NLT)

Chapter 13

More Lessons in Perseverance

'And let us run with perseverance the race marked out for us fixing our eyes on Jesus'. Hebrews 12:1-2 (NIV)

In the last few years I have intentionally sought some opportunities to learn more skills in perseverance, knowing I have a tough road ahead of me.

In 2014 I decided to go in my first half marathon. I had been sitting at our dinner table as we hosted our good friends Brad and Kirsty. Brad, whose life had recently been transformed by a new fitness bug, was talking about his upcoming half marathon 'The Bay to Bay'. My first comment was one of wistful envy, "I have always wanted to go in a half marathon". Brad and Lucas encouraged me that I should go in it too, and an inner urge to do this not so much for the run, but as a spiritual journey, grabbed hold of me. There was no turning back after I paid the registration fees. The race was only just a month away, and I knew there would be no time for me to train. So I just set my head to making the decision that during the race, I would not give up no matter what, and nothing would cause me to quit. I decided that with my very hectic schedule of looking after a family of four kids and full time youth and kids' ministry, my usual runs (usually three or four a week of about 5-7 kilometres in distance) would have to be enough training.

The day before the race was one of our biggest events of the year 'All in Kids Church'. I worked so hard packing up after the event and with all my energy spent, I wondered as I went to bed after 11pm how on earth I was going to get up at 4am to leave for the race. I was never a 'morning person'.

The next morning, I got up on time, packed my glucose syrups and got my permanent marker out. I wrote on my wrists and on my hand Bible verses about God being my help and strength and little notes to myself like 'never ever give up', 'Jesus gives me strength', 'Don't stop'. It was June and a very cold morning. As I drove down the highway in the dark, many times I smiled at myself and shook my head. Who would do a half marathon with no training? The furthest I had ever run was 10 kilometres in East Timor and I barely got through that. I knew that I could only do this by God's strength and I decided to pray all the way. I knew this would be a spiritual journey and one in which my faith would grow, and I felt a sense of excitement.

Over 700 people lined up. I could see Brad was quite amazed and amused I had taken up the challenge. He had been training for some time now, along with his running mates. I started to stretch (the way I had learned back in high school jogger's club). Brad burst out laughing and asked me what I was doing. Confused, I told him I was stretching. "No one does that anymore Ange. You don't just stand there and stretch anymore, you need to warm up instead." He went for a little run with his mate, but I decided to keep my reserves, and continued with my stretching.

The gun went. I was somehow at the back of the pack and felt at a disadvantage (until someone told me later there was a timer in my number). I prayed as I took off, thanking God for this incredible opportunity and asked him to help me.

Just before the 5 kilometre checkpoint my knee had the sharpest pain. I had never felt this pain before. It was agony, and the disappointment inside my chest was soon overridden by a strong determination and faith. I started to pray, *'God, you are the healer. God I felt your urge to do this, your permission. I need your healing touch. Touch my knee and heal me like Jesus healed people with just his touch. I believe with all my heart you will carry me through this race. I need you. I can't do this without you. You are my help, you are my strength. You healed King Hezekiah in the Bible, you healed the woman who was sick, and you healed the man who was blind. Heal me. I will keep going. I will keep my eyes on you.'*

The pain in my knee was there for at least ten minutes; I refused to walk and continued what became a slow, limping, jog. Many people started to overtake me. I felt like hundreds had overtaken me. I looked at the race volunteers and I considered telling them about my knee. I pictured how disappointed I would be and how this could play out if I let them know I had a knee injury all of a sudden. I continued to pray and believe. I continued to call out to God and beg him to carry me through this race reminding him we were in this together and I was relying on him because I knew I couldn't do it by myself – especially with no training.

It was around the 13 kilometre mark when I felt God whisper into my heart, "I will pick you up and carry you all the way to the finish line. Keep your eyes on me. You will need to remember this again in the future, I will carry you to the finish line. When your kids are sick, I will pick you up and carry you above the pain. I will carry you through it."

All of a sudden the knee pain disappeared. I felt like a cheat and I almost laughed – God would carry me to the finish line? I celebrated! I believed I would not feel that pain again, and that God had lifted me up in the palm of his hand and he would carry me to the end. I suddenly felt a boost of energy and started overtaking heaps of people. We came to a hill and as others slowed down or began to walk, I only got stronger and faster. I honestly felt as though I was watching myself being carried along. My legs kept moving, nothing in me felt any inclination to stop or to walk, my legs just kept on moving. I kept on praying, kept on worshipping. I thanked God for the beautiful water I could see all along the race. I thanked God that he had promised to lead me beside still waters and to restore my soul and he had done that over and over, including today.

It was Sunday morning and I felt like I was joining Christians everywhere in worship of our great God. I mused how this is the kind of worship I love - outdoors, out in his beautiful cathedral of creation.

I felt that this was sacred ground and knew that God was teaching me that he would always carry me through the hard stuff in my life. I only needed to rely on him and allow him to pick me up. I truly felt carried the rest of the way, it almost felt easy!

I ran down the last hill determined to hear the praise and yelling of my kids and Lucas and to see the signs that I had imagined them writing about how truly amazing I was and how much they loved me and were proud of me…But to my incredible disappointment, they hadn't made it in time.

When they arrived half an hour after my finish time I cried to Lucas saying, "You weren't here. You didn't believe in me."

"You were too quick," he replied. "You said you thought it would take you two and a half hours."

Two hours and two minutes it took my awesome God to carry this first time half marathon runner. Two hours and two minutes of glorious time along the water, relishing every minute alone with my Creator, relishing the lessons I was learning. I felt so happy.

The next day I could hardly walk (and I realise now it was probably because of the $20 Kmart sneakers I wore). But although I could hardly walk, my heart was full and I felt a great sense of achievement and joy.

I love how God leads us.

Interestingly in 2015 I decided I would do this race again.

Every time I thought about it though, I felt God's voice whisper, 'Not this time'. I had a great discomfort about participating, so I didn't register.

Of course the week of the race in 2015 I came down with a bad virus. A real assurance that I had heard correctly, that this year it was not to be.

When 2016 arrived I decided to see if this year I could do it again.

The first time was for a spiritual and faith experience.

The second time I decided was because I wanted to learn some specific lessons in perseverance in light of what was to come. I wondered if God would carry me again, or if this time I would find it a whole lot harder. Once again, still far too busy and not a morning person, I found no time for training (other than my usual runs). I felt all good to go ahead, so I registered again for the 'Bay to Bay Half Marathon'.

This time felt different from the outset. We had just put our daughter on the heart transplant list the week before. I felt very raw and emotionally vulnerable. I was going alone this time, and I didn't know anyone else participating in the race. As I drove the hour and a half there, I cried. I felt in my heart that I was doing this one for Luka and for Jazz and my heart beat with sadness and affliction. I knew what I wanted to write on my shirt when I got there. In my mind, I was running this for them. I was running it to learn some more lessons in perseverance, so that when our time came for heart transplant, I would have some lessons to refer to. That was it. I had prayed God would teach me. I knew this could be tough, and wouldn't be the same experience as my first half marathon.

I sat in the car in the dark just a couple of blocks from where the race would start. Tears flowed down my face as I wrote on my arm in permanent marker 'For Luka & Jazz'. Then I wrote Psalm 121 on my hand. I got my shirt out and wrote on the back in large writing '2 of my children need a heart transplant. Please consider organ donation.' Then I wrote the 'Donate life' website. I wondered how many runners would read the back of my shirt as I ran in front of them. I wondered how many would then sign up for organ donation. This was a message I was desperate to communicate. It could be the difference between getting a heart for my girl or not getting a heart...

I quickly wiped my tears away, set my mind on learning some good lessons in perseverance and began my run. The lump in my throat and the heaviness in my heart would not leave. I made mental notes each time I heard God whisper a lesson in perseverance to me. It was unbelievable how my hope of learning some lessons was becoming real. The lessons were almost audible, visual. I knew that I needed to hold them fast in my mind so I chanted some of them over and over until they stuck. I wondered how soon I would be implementing these lessons. I wondered how soon I would need this perseverance in action as I witnessed my daughter go through something that, quite frankly, terrified me!! Every now and then someone would pass me or run alongside me and say, "I read your shirt. I am so sorry. That must be so hard." Each time I choked back the tears, withholding my energy, understanding I needed every bit to get through this race. Sometimes, I quietly brushed away an escaped tear.

One woman about ten years my senior came alongside me and said, "I am so sorry. I have read your shirt. You have brought me undone (tears in her eyes). I hope your children get the hearts they need. I have often thought about signing up for organ donation. I will do that this afternoon. You have made a difference. My family and I will sign up today." With that, she touched my shoulder as the tears rolled down my cheeks and said, "You've undone me." All I could do was whisper a choked, "Thank you for caring."

The race was hard. My heavy heart matched my legs. I wondered how much slower I was going to be this time. I felt disappointed. I knew the kids and Lucas would probably make it on time today (after the last disappointment), and I wanted to do them proud. I have never been one to measure my distance or my steps. I don't really like machines. I like to be organic. I like to enjoy the race, without tracking it, without worrying what pace I need to set. I just follow my heart. Kind of like I do in life. Unmeasured, spontaneous, flexible and creative (sometimes this works for me, sometimes it doesn't). I wondered how far behind I was from my previous time. I did feel determined still to never give up and not to stop or walk. "NOT EVEN FOR A SECOND!" I would demand of myself.

I worshipped God, I prayed, I thought, I chanted the lessons I was learning to embed them. I saw the faces of Luka-Angel & Jazz. I considered how hard life is for them, I considered what they had to go through. I dwelt on what we had been through last week at the hospital. I thought about the seventeen blood vials that had been sent off in Luka-Angel's listing appointment. I thought about how brave she was and how much her consistent courage amazes me. I thought about the bright spark she is and the questions she had for the surgeon. My mind was spinning as I ran and questions plagued my mind: *'How on earth did we get here? Is this the right decision? Should we have waited longer? How long will this wait be? What if there is no wait and I get a phone call next week – I will want to say no. What if it goes wrong? How am I going to kiss my baby girl goodbye when they wheel her off to the theatre? How am I going to pretend to be brave around her? What if I lose it? What if I lose her? How will I live?'*

I decided I needed bravery like hers. I was *desperate* for more lessons in perseverance. I wondered if anyone jogging around me could hear the agony of my thoughts and my heart. I felt God close. He could hear. That's all I needed to know. He knew the time that we would face all of this. He knew what lessons I needed, he would teach me, he would hold me and he would carry us. He had promised that, not only two years before as I saw these same views and ran this same race, but 8 years before as I ran along a different beach, not knowing the diagnosis that was just around the corner.

The *Lessons on Perseverance* God taught me in my second half marathon:

1. Remember your goal, 'So we press on to that which carries us forward' (Hebrews 12).

2. Some days will be mundane as it will seem like nothing amazing is happening but God is still at work, still with us,

even when we can't see him or feel him. Keep putting one foot in front of the other. Some moments in my running the half marathon I felt as though I was getting nowhere, moments of mundane and seemingly 'one foot in front of the other' running.

3. Keep the Bible, the word of God in your hand. Never let it go. It will energise you, fill you, and spur you on. Some days it may taste bitter, but it is always helpful for your growth. I had my glucose gel sachet in my hand for so long – I had opened it and had some but I wanted to throw it in the bin – it tasted disgusting, but I knew it was re-energising my body. I knew I needed it, even if I didn't feel like it. So I held onto it, and had the discipline to sip it every few minutes.

4. Some days are really, really hard and painful – you'll want to quit. Just keep your eyes up and keep perspective. Never, never give up! Some moments of the race felt so hard and I was tempted to stop.

5. Remember the 'Why…' I needed to remind myself that I was doing this to challenge myself and learn lessons on perseverance. Some days we need to come back to remembering why we do what we do. Some days I'll need to remember that we are going through transplant so my kids can have a whole new life.

6. Jesus gives me strength. I had this line written on my arm and I needed to keep looking at it and calling on his name that is so powerful, "Jesus, Jesus, Jesus". I need to call on his

strength in everything. Doing things in my own strength is not enough.

7. When you have hit a wall, intentionally climb into God's hand and allow him to carry you. Sometimes throughout the race I would hit a wall, and needed to allow myself to just be carried along by my legs. Some days, when the pain is too much, curling up in God's hand is the best thing we can do.

8. Run your own race. Don't look around, comparing or worrying about what others are doing. Don't try to copy or compete.

9. There are many people along the way – spurring you on, encouraging you, praying for you. You are not alone. There were volunteers all the way along the race, applauding, cheering, and handing out water. "Keep going." "You can do it." "Great job, you are nearly there". These are words from strangers that spurred me on along the journey of my half marathon.

10. Sometimes God will intentionally place people in your path to give you that extra motivation and boost. Accept their help. He will send them at just the right time. To my surprise, as I was hitting a physical and an emotional wall and about ready to cry, Gosford Salvos had a drinks stand at around the '14km mark'. Seeing the face of someone I knew, and hearing him exclaim, in surprise, "Angela Flemming!" boosted me and once more I determined to do well.

11. VICTORY is ours through Jesus. Just after the '14km mark', I had to cross the road at a little street called 'Victory Parade'. It made me smile the moment I saw the sign. I

knew this was a message from God, right at that time, for me, and one I will need to remember in days to come.

12. No matter the pain, no matter how hard, no matter how sad, keep the end in sight! Keep the 'Finish' sign in mind and NEVER EVER EVER give up!!!

CHAPTER 14

OUR JOURNEY TO TRANSPLANT

'Even though I walk through the valley of the shadow of death, I will fear no evil, for you are with me;' Psalm 23:4 (ESV)

Since diagnosis, Luka-Angel and Jazz were carefully monitored every quarter, rotating between two major hospitals. They were always so cheerful and excited on the way to appointments. Often we would have to catch a plane. Early on I decided that these trips needed a lot of a distraction. Every flight down to Melbourne there would come a moment when I would hand them a surprise bag for the trip. In the bag were presents, lollies, chocolates, stationery, and a Bible verse on courage or strength. For them the trips meant special time with Mum and Dad's full attention, a stay at their second home – Ronald McDonald house, exploring Melbourne and some medical appointments in between. We always felt so incredibly blessed to have such a capable medical team and a hospital that was more like a kid's play centre.

It was on a routine visit in May 2015 when we were first advised by our Cardiologists that it was time to consider putting Luka-Angel on the heart transplant waiting list.

The first time we were told this, our two children sat in the waiting room of the cardiology clinic. Even though Luka was very symptomatic, this came as quite a shock. I was absolutely terrified of us getting to that point. I remember coming out of the room and explaining to Lucas I needed to get to the bathroom before the kids could see me. I had managed to hold back my tears in the medical team meeting, now I needed a quiet space with a door.

I headed to the bathroom, my face crumpling, and just made it to the cubicle in time for the sobs. Thankfully no one else came into the toilets. It would be impossible to explain myself. I took some deep breaths after a few minutes, quickly powdered my nose and around my eyes in an attempt to protect my kids from my sadness, and made my way back out to the waiting room.

"What's wrong Mum?" Luka asked knowingly. "I have a bit of a cold remember Luka?" I muttered, trying some distraction, I could tell I hadn't fooled her.

When we made it out to the park, my precious eleven-year-old girl said to me with excitement, "Mum, can you push me on the swing?" I found it so strange to hear such strong and implicating words from the doctors just now, and then doing something as normal as pushing my child on a swing. I wondered if anyone else in this park could read the shock and sadness resounding in my heart and mind as she went backwards and forwards.

My little girl called out in a big voice from the height of her swing, "What did he say Mum? Did the doctor say I need to go on the heart transplant list now?"

Stunned, I gradually pulled the swing back to ground level and asked her to repeat her question, even though I had heard it. I needed a moment to think through my response.

Miss eleven looked at me with strong, tenacious eyes, emphasising, "I said, did they say I need to go on the list now?"

Taking a deep breath I quietly said, "Yes, Luka. They did. But this is something Dad and I need to talk through, think about and pray about."

Luka smiled quietly.

"Why are you smiling?" I asked her confused. Luka resounded, "Because I am so excited. The sooner I go on the list, the sooner I can dance!"

Sometime later, after days of processing, talking and deliberating we explained to Luka that we wouldn't be saying yes yet (we felt there was so much more she needed to know and none of us were ready yet). I told Luka if she really wanted to dance, she could start preparing her body now by watching YouTube clips and doing flexibility stretches.

My very determined and persevering girl started to pursue her dream. She believed with her whole heart that she was born to dance! At this point she could only dance for thirty seconds or so, without becoming completely tachycardic. Her dancing would be beautiful and graceful and heartfelt but then she would turn herself upside down on the lounge trying to get her heart rate back down, as she puffed and panted and went pale. It was so sad to watch. She built up to doing flexibility stretches every single day. Her routine after arriving home from school each day was to put on her tights and begin stretches. She would watch YouTube clips and her favourite dance show 'The Next Step' and try and mentally learn how to do the moves. Within six months, Luka could do the splits and had learned how to cartwheel (although could only do one and then would become tachycardic). I watched in awe at her sheer determination and perseverance and my heart would ache for her as my head took pride in her courage.

Luka was one to always protect all creatures, even cockroaches. I remember one day Lucas killing a spider and Luka dissolving instantly in big tears saying through her sobs, "Daddy, how could you do that? Maybe that spider had a husband, and now her husband is left without a wife and he is crying because he has lost her forever..." It was always a big concern of mine that she would one day find out, that for her to live someone else would need to lose their life. It was too much to bear. I began praying God would open her mind and she would be prepared to learn these things. I felt we couldn't put her on the heart transplant list whilst she didn't know more information. I thought of her sensitive heart and I couldn't comprehend the pain it would cause her. To hold her off the list against the medical team's advice was always so conflicting, but we also knew the decision was ours to make. One day Luka and I were driving back from a conference, I had been praying so much she would be prepared and open to learning more about transplant when out of the blue she shocked me with her first question, "Mum, where does the heart come from for a heart transplant?"

I took a deep, prayerful breath and began our conversation.

She was quiet and at peace.

"Okay." She responded. No tears, just peace, and more questions.

I began my prayer for our anonymous family. I could never pray that God would provide a heart for my Luka-Angel, it was too sad. I felt as though I would be praying for someone else to die. It felt too selfish. So I would just pray that God would make Luka better. I would pray that if it was going to happen the heart transplant way that God would be with this precious family. I prayed for this family all the time, for beautiful memories, big forgiveness if there were any issues between them, and special moments together. I remember the last Christmas before Luka's transplant, I prayed sincerely that this family would all make it to their family celebrations, that everyone who needed to be there would be, and that they would have some wonderful times together. It broke my heart to pray for them, and in the meantime I kept praying for a miracle.

During this time of holding back on the doctor's invitation to list Luka, we began to collect a list of her dreams, things she really wanted to do. We then determined to make those things happen. Even to the point of allowing her to audition with a local musical theatre company for a musical, 'Seussical'. The musical was being directed by our good friends, Lell and Guil, and we knew they would be able to look out for her a little, already knowing about her heart condition. Luka got a part in the ensemble and we sacrificed our time at least three times a week for six months of rehearsals. Hours of waiting around whilst she rehearsed was always a challenge when we had three other children at home. However, knowing she was achieving a dream was so worth it! The weeks of the performance were such a joy! Watching our beloved girl shine on the stage, sing her heart out and perform to her best in such a heart-warming musical was so delightful! There were a couple of scenes where she would wait in the wings, because the activity was too risky for her heart. The last thing we wanted was to put her at risk, but there was always the fine balance of living life to the full and being wise. We usually leant on the side of living life to the full. As much as it was always a temptation to tuck them away safely at home, we knew they needed to be able to enjoy life. Almost a year later, one of the many touching moments while she was 'sleeping' in ICU, was when our friend and director of 'Seussical' sent us a message that some of the cast were gathered around a piano singing 'Solace Solu' in honour of Luka-Angel. Even as I received

Rainbows in the Storm

the message, I was taken back to seeing her on the stage months before, singing this song, with tears in her eyes as she swayed side to side.

During this time prior to being listed, she was able to go on a mission trip to Cairns with her dad and help out at a Salvation Army women and children's refuge (we thought this was a good choice for her pre-high schoool mission trip/holiday, considering her big dream to one day set up a centre for the homeless). Unfortunately she was sick whilst there and this affected all she could do. She sat in her bed, wrapping presents for the women and children at the refuge for the days she was too sick to get up. On the flight home she became very tachycardic and dizzy. It was frightening for both Lucas and Luka and the flight became a priority landing as they were met on the tarmac in Sydney by an ambulance. After spending the night in a local hospital, Luka was then taken to Westmead Hospital for some appointments with her second cardiology team that had already been booked ahead of time. Over about two years, we managed to tick off much of Luka-Angel's bucket list of dreams. She got to start a garage band, 'The Angel Rockers' with some of her friends (and record a little CD), go to a butterfly house, snorkel the Great Barrier Reef, share her dream about 'The Lighthouse' on our church platform, go to a couple of big concerts including a Demi Lovato concert with her aunty. Luka also set up a blog in which she wanted to inspire people, especially children with challenges. She got to four wheel drive on Rainbow Beach on the Coolabah Coast and collect sand of all different colours, camped with good friends and jumped off a high cliff into the water, learnt to cartwheel, went to see Matilda, the musical (& meet the cast), had a one on one lesson with a professional ballerina, owned a turtle, undertook singing lessons, and had a large birthday party (a bit more like a 21st), where her life was celebrated and she and her friends were treated to a personal performance from her cousin, Brittany Cairns, who had been on 'The Voice' TV show.

Christmas 2015 was a 'Flemming Christmas' (my side of the family). We headed up to Tweed Heads and were excited to be at Mum and Dad's house. There was always fun, adventure and outdoor activity to be had when we were with my family. Unfortunately, this of course, made things very difficult for Luka. She would try and participate as much as possible, but some things were out of the question. If she swam in the morning, by the afternoon she would be very tachycardic. She would even find it very hard to sit up at the table at night and eat dinner. Often I would carry her to the table and try, but usually she would end up lying back on the recliner in the lounge room or on her bed. Her neck would pulsate so hard that we could see the work her heart had to do, just for her to lay there.

One night not long after we had arrived, Luka-Angel was particularly unwell. She had swum in the morning for a little while, and then just mucked around in the house. By dinner, she didn't appear. I went into her room where she was very 'puffed' and lying on her bed. I convinced her to try and come out and join the family, and I managed to get her to the recliner lounge. We were so used to this being the 'normal', especially after an active day or some swimming, so we lay her on the lounge for observation. We got over calling the ambulance or taking her to hospital a long time before, because they never really knew what to do with her (this was the same for Jazziah). Restrictive Cardiomyopathy is so rare, and we have been told that most pediatric cardiologists would never see it in their entire career. Getting help at an ordinary hospital felt impossible, and besides, there was not much they could do for her other than monitoring her condition.

This particular night, her symptoms got worse. It was about an hour of a very fast heart rate, her pulse in her neck thumping wildly. Her face was very pale, and she couldn't even lift her head to speak as it made her heart race faster. Lucas and I subtly exchanged concerned looks and got Elijah to go beside his sister to hold her hand while we grabbed a moment to whisper and decide what our next step would be. It was the 23rd December and I couldn't bear the thought of her being transferred to Brisbane or the hospital in Melbourne and having her miss the family Christmas. I quietly placed the defibrillator next to her and prepared myself for the worst possible scenario.

I went into the bedroom and called my mum (who was out) for advice. She agreed I should call the ambulance. When I got off the phone I began to pray. I felt God's peace wash over me, and him say 'wait ten minutes.' I looked at the clock and then I told Lucas, we are to wait ten minutes. I believe that's what God has said.

So we watched the clock as her heart thumped away, and had someone by her side every moment. As soon as ten minutes was up, we literally saw her neck pulse drop back to normal. The monitor that had been attached to her finger and reading between 160-180, dropped to around 80 beats per minute. Without even seeing the finger monitor yet, she pulled the lever of the chair to an upright position and said with relief, "Aahh, that's better! I'm okay now and I need to go the toilet," and with that she got up.

God had been faithful. Nearly an hour of these symptoms, then God whispered, *'Just wait ten minutes'*. As soon as those ten minutes were up, Luka was fine. Her heart rate went back to normal. We knew calling the ambulance may have been 'the right thing to do', but it would have meant she would have missed Christmas holidays with all of the family, and emotionally that would have been devastating. It was often a fine balance between being wise and having faith. This balance was often scary.

Throughout Christmas that year, I was aware of her having to miss out. She attempted beach cricket for the first time in ages, but just the short walk on the sand to where we were playing, was enough to throw her. One swing of the bat and she was puffed and short of breath. This particular night she was frustrated. She plonked down on the sand and said, "It's too hard, I can't do this." Then we had to carry her back up to the grass where she lay on a blanket with Grandma while the rest of us had fun. It seemed so unfair. She would determine to swim in the beach a little while, and would have a whole lot of fun doing so, but that would exhaust her for the rest of the day. Walking on sand had become practically impossible, but carrying her was also becoming impossible. She was two thirds my size now, and Lucas would struggle too much with walking himself, let alone being able to carry anyone. So in order for her to get to the water, a few of us would push her along the beach as she put one foot in front of the other.

Over the next part of our holidays, I noticed Luka had pretty much given up. She would sit in the holiday unit while some of the family went for a swim. It was too hard for her. She didn't complain, but it was obviously very difficult. She was always a 'get in there and have a go' kind of girl, so this felt very sad and so hard to watch. During this holiday I had caught a salmonella style stomach bug (diagnosed six weeks later). I had daily writhed in pain for weeks, and the feeling of nausea hardly left me. I would determine to still try and participate with the family as much as I could, but it was so hard. Just trying to put a smile on my face, and trying to swim with them, while feeling so unwell, functioning out of very few reserves, felt near impossible. During this time of physical un-wellness, even though I felt awful, I remember feeling grateful for the sickness, as it gave me a tiny glimpse into what life is like for Luka-Angel, Jazz and Lucas. Out of very little reserves, they try to participate and do life to the full and it is so very difficult for them. I remember re-considering the transplant list at this time, and becoming a little more open to seeing what Luka wanted and needed. She had begun asking every few days if we were ready to put her on the list. It was the top of her Christmas list, the top of her birthday list and something she wanted above anything else, she just wanted to be well. I remember reflecting that no kid should have to respond with 'a new heart' when asked what they wanted for their birthday. She had a great love and affection and appreciation for her current heart, but she knew she needed a heart that could allow her to live fully, freely!

In February 2016 Luka had some days at home where nothing particular seemed to trigger her heart, it was just off on its own fast rate. We kept her home and in bed and sometimes brought her down to the loungeroom. Even lifting a glass of water would set her heart off into a fast rhythm. We would closely monitor her and went to and fro about whether to take her to hospital. Four days into caring for her, we gave in and I took her up to emergency. She was transferred to ICU as nowhere else in the hospital could cater for the monitoring she needed.

I recall laying on the parent's pull out sofa at the end of her bed and hearing the medical staff gathering around Luka-Angel's ECG. Clearly they were fascinated. One of them mentioned to the other her condition and then talked about it being headed to pediatric heart transplant. The nurse caring for Luka stuck her head in the curtain and looked at sleeping Luka then beyond her to me. With great compassion in her eyes she said to me, "Wow, you have a big journey ahead of you."

"Yep," I said with my lip quivering. I cried into my pillow stifling the noise and wishing I could shut off my sadness. I was always strong in front of others, especially my children, but when it was quiet, or night or I was by myself, not crying felt impossible.

One night in late 2015 as I was putting Luka-Angel to bed, she said to me, "Mum, I have decided that if you won't put me on the transplant list yet, I am going to pray for healing. Every night, I will pray that God heals my heart, but I also want to ask, if he chooses not to heal my heart, can he heal a child in another country who doesn't have hospitals or doctors like we have here."

The next morning she said to me, "Mum, I woke up this morning and waited to see if I was healed but when I got really puffed getting dressed, I knew that God didn't choose to heal me. I am so excited though Mum, because I really, really believe God chose to heal another little girl, in a country where she can't get help like I can, in a country where they don't do transplants." Her outlook and faith, was overwhelming! These prayers and sentiments went on every night for Luka. All it took each morning to see if she was healed was to try and sit up and get out of bed. Just getting out of bed in the morning was a big struggle on most days. She would get puffed, short of breath and tachycardic. Many times even brushing her teeth would set her heart off. Mornings and nights were the worst for her.

My running had become a bit of a saving grace for me. As I ran I would pray and sometimes I would cry. For the months leading up to the impending transplant, my running prayer had been, *'Lord, make me brave, make me braver, Lord make me brave. Give me courage, give me strength, I need you.'* I would repeat the name of Jesus, over and over again. I pleaded with God over and over to make me brave.

Even though my heart was sad, I chose to live life to the full. It was imperative to me that I enjoy every moment with my children. My ministry and full time work with youth leaders, youth and children was my joy, my passion and once again my beautiful distraction.

One day Luka-Angel joyfully called me into her room and exclaimed, "Mum, I have just realised, my life will *never* be boring!" Curiously, I asked why. "Well, I only have three options: I will either die and go to heaven, have a heart transplant or be healed miraculously! See? My life will never be boring!"

The day we rang our cardiology team resigning ourselves to the fact that Luka needed to be on the heart transplant list (and the fear that we may have 'missed the boat' which was always a risk with 'restrictive cardiomyopathy'), we also decided that a big memorable family holiday was in order. After the dreaded phone call, we began searching for something suitable.

Realising that visiting another culture was out of the question due to the risk of infections for our kids, we decided on a Cruise.

After booking it, the fear set in. The 'What ifs?' played over and over, in both of our minds. The fact that we would be so far from medical intervention seemed crazy! We had just about come to a point of letting the whole trip go, when I began to beg God for a sign that we would be okay.

I prayed and prayed. One day as I ran, I asked, *'Lord, make it very clear to us if it is okay for us to go, put a stop to it if we shouldn't go.'* I heard God's whisper in my mind, *'You can go on the cruise; I will give you a sign.'*

As I drove home after my run, I pulled up at a set of traffic lights and I heard a quiet inaudible voice in my mind, *'Look to the left.'* I turned my head and in bold writing, on a large poster on a shop window I read, 'Trust us to look after the health and wellbeing of your children.' I couldn't believe my eyes. Just as I saw the sign, the sun came out from behind the dark clouds on this rainy evening, and shone straight through my windscreen. I was bathed with warmth, light and peace. I knew it was my sign.

When I arrived home to Lucas I stated with confidence, "We are going on this cruise. I know we are going to be okay, and we are not going to change our minds now. That's it, God has made it clear we are okay to go." I had never seen that sign in the window before that day. In fact, there were many signs in the street but that was the only one my eyes had fallen on. A few months later, that poster was gone.

The cruise was such a beautiful experience. We got to relax and enjoy each other's company and have many new and amazing experiences together. As we walked around the ship, and I pushed or piggy backed my children up some of the stairs that we couldn't avoid at times, or pushed Luka on the old people's walker we had obtained, I took in each moment realizing that this was our last holiday before Luka-Angel's heart transplant listing that would come in June. I wondered if for some people this was 'just another cruise'. For us, it was a once in a life time experience, it was a BIG risk, and it was possibly the last holiday we could ever have together. Every moment was precious, every moment counted.

Luka has always been an explorer. I remember when she was a little girl, wherever Elijah adventured, Luka-Angel was right there behind him or alongside him, and at times she led the way. She would go up trees, walk through bush or long grass, one time (just at eighteen months old) she even found herself stuck thigh deep in mud. Much to our amusement, she couldn't move an inch! The last few years before transplant, it was sad to see her unable to adventure in the same way. She still had an adventurous spirit. She still gave things a go, but things like bush walks had to completely stop. We used to go on a family bush walk at Glenrock. I would take turns of piggy backing her and Jazz so they had enough reserves to enjoy it. Gradually we had to cut the bushwalk in half because they were getting too big for me to carry. I recall the last time we attempted that walk, was in 2015. My mum and dad were with us, and Luka turned back as we went on, after just a few hundred metres of flat walking. It was just too much for her now. No pushing her along would be enough anymore. Even that short walk she had already done had her stopping along the way, short of breath. She never seemed to complain, she just took things in her stride, and knew her limits.

To see her on the Isle of Pines (on our cruise) snorkel for an hour was amazing! She always found leisure swimming fairly manageable, and it was only after it that she would be completely wrecked and unable to do a thing due to shortness of breath and tachycardia. She had a long enough adventurous snorkel to enjoy the beautiful colours of the tropical reef fish and then for the rest of the day at our island stop, she lay on a towel, completely tachycardic as the boys and I explored the Island. We brought her back shells and a coconut to drink from, but it broke my heart that she couldn't come on the adventure. I know I pushed her a little too hard, and after too much encouraging, Lucas looked at me and said, "She can't come," pointing to her neck, which was showing the back pressure of her fast heart rate visibly. Hours of lying down didn't help. She was still wrecked that night on the cruise and just getting to dinner was tough for her.

For some heart conditions it is black and white when they need to go on the list. For Luka and Jazz's condition, it is a little grey. Every day there is a risk, we also risk missing the boat of transplant, but we know that heart transplant is a major operation, and post-transplant and living with a suppressed immune system also has its own risks. On days like our day on the island, I feared we had 'missed the boat' (no pun intended).

Luka just wouldn't complain, so the fact that she managed to get around school, go to classes and live a fairly normal life, to me was quite phenomenal! Every day was hard work for Luka's little heart and most of the time it was at the end of the day when she got the sickest. Luka was blessed to have absolutely beautiful and supportive friends at school who would carry her bag, link her arm and drag her along, or wait with her while she caught her breath after walking up a few stairs. I always felt thankful for such support. At home her brothers would run up the stairs and grab what Luka-Angel needed, time and time again. As Elijah got bigger, he was able to help me push Luka or Jazz on the scooter if we walked somewhere, or piggy-back them to the park, so they could go on the swings. Elijah and Jayjay have never once complained about helping their sister or brother. The care they always show their sister and brother is simply inspiring! Doing normal things like going to the shops or walking on the beach in the last couple of years had become way too hard for Luka-Angel.

To the world, my bright and cheerful, even energetic, spirited daughter, looked like a normal girl. No one would blink an eye if Luka or Jazz walked down the street. It was (and still is for Jazz) like an invisible sickness. The reality was that they were living with a ticking time bomb, right in the centre of their chest, always at risk of cardiac arrest, always at risk of sudden fast decline and heart failure. Their Dad's time bomb was seemingly on a long timer and I imagined we would get plenty of notice when it needed to be dealt with. Having Lucas with hypertrophic cardiomyopathy was hard enough. Often for me, it felt like we were standing on the edge of a cliff. I could only try to hold them back off the edge, but I was never sure if a wind would blow up, and we might all fall straight over into the abyss. Some days I felt like I had already fallen over the edge, and I was spinning out of control, unsure when I was going to land.

Chapter 15

A Glimpse into my Journal – Early 2016

'O Lord, God of my salvation; I cry out day and night before you. Let my prayer come before you; incline your ear to my cry! For my soul is full of troubles...' Psalm 88:1-3 (Holy Bible)

Some journal entries early 2016

My prayer: (16th March 2016)

O God I need you. So desperately I need you! My heart physically hurts. I feel its deep ache and it runs up to the back of my throat.

The pain of death and sadness daily swirl around me.

Shed your love and the light of our eternal hope into these dark and low places.

Pour yourself into every ache and carry me in your comforting hand. I climb into your hand and I know I am safe.

May the unfairness of life be met with the fairness of you - a mighty powerful force.

God deep within is a place that can only be filled with your fullness.

Bring me into the fullness of life you have planned for me. Encompass my family with your ever-loving, never-changing presence. I sense your promise, "I will never leave you or forsake you…" and "I am with you always."

My prayer (18th March 2016):

Lord, I need you now more than ever before.

So sad.

My world feels as though it is beginning to cave in. So much heartache, so much pain; such deep-set grief, without an obvious end or solution.

Help me to stand up!

Help me to keep my head above water. Help me to reveal you to those around me, even in this mess.

Shelter me and protect me from this.

'Be merciful to me, O God, be merciful, for I come to you for safety. In the shadow of your wings I find protection until the raging storms are over.' Psalm 57:1-2 (GNT)

Journal Entry - 13th March 2016

I imagine most parents would have conversations with their children about what they want for their birthdays. My daughter's daily plea at the moment is for a new heart. It was the top of her Christmas list, now it has become the top of her birthday list.

She doesn't care for money or even things very much. What she wants most in the world is a new heart so she can dance.

Tonight for the first time ever Jazz said he felt sad about his heart condition. We had a beautiful dinner at Thai and then were going for a family walk along the foreshore. Just after Jazz said he felt sad, Jayjay came sprinting past and Jazz tried to join him. Jazz's attempt at running resulted in him collapsing on a rock wall, pale and tachycardic. I have seen this many times, so I just observed to make sure things wouldn't deteriorate further. Tonight I could feel his pulse even in the top of his head.

Jazz recovered and went on to tell us that at school they have been doing training for the athletics carnival. The school our kids go to, are always so accommodating and helpful in regard to my children's needs, allowing Luka-Angel and Jazz to have a choice of what they do whilst the kids participate in sport. For Luka this looked like helping out in the Kindy room. For Jazz, often it meant doing what he could in sport, and then giving out prizes or awards or going to the Library.

No child should have to sit on the sidelines all the time though. No child should be held back from a simple childhood thing like running, chasings, tips, hide 'n seek, races, soccer, sport – these are all childhood gifts. It seems so unfair and it makes my heart so sad.

Journal Entry - April 2016

Something Luka said to me recently:

"Mum, I love you with more than my heart, because my heart is a tiny little one that doesn't even work properly." With that she threw her arms around me and proceeded to say, "AND... one day, I'll even love you with someone else's heart!"

It is such a strange and peculiar reality we live in.

Chapter 16

The Rainbow & Listing Luka

'Wait for the Lord's help. Be strong and brave, and wait for the Lord's help.' Psalm 27:14 (NCV)

It was June 2016 and it was the week I had been dreading since February when I first made that call. Lucas and I had finally given in to the reality that our daughter needed to be listed for heart transplant. It was inevitable, as perhaps anyone would have realised from the medical advice, but we had to live pretending it was never going to happen. One can't live life well, fully comprehending that their daughter will go into heart failure while still just a child.

I watched my grandma as her heart began to fail. She was such a beautiful and amazingly strong woman who was generous in so many ways. Her home was always open, she had the most incredible collections of all things imaginable, and she would welcome people from all walks of life into her home, notably those who were lonely or had complex lives. My grandma was a woman whose actions reflected her words. Whose hands prepared food not only for those she loved, but also for those in need. When she was retired, Grandma would devote regular time to running 'Jumble Sales' in her yard to raise money for mission. She was a woman of initiative and leadership even leading her Salvation Army 'Silver Threads' group for those over fifty, until she was in her late eighties. She was energetic and still hanging out her own washing, doing her gardening and collecting her own mail even at ninety years old. Watching her heart begin to fail was devastating, but somehow seemed appropriate. She was after all, ninety-three years old when she died. She had a good innings and lived it well. Sadly she had tried to resuscitate her beloved husband, my grandpa, when he had a fatal heart attack at home nearly twenty years earlier and outlived him for such a long time. She had watched as her seven siblings died before her, even though she was older than three of them. It seemed appropriate that her heart would begin to fail after all of these years.

My grandma was someone who always said what she thought and sometimes the things that came out of her mouth were a bit of a shock! I guess she had some old fashioned views, but she still had such a loving, giving and caring heart. In her last weeks, Grandma had incredible grace and gratitude. She got less and less able, but was able to stay in her own home, in her own bed as her family took care of her. That last month it was as though she had one foot in the door of heaven. She shone! She would see her family in heaven and talk to them, even though they had been gone a long time. I remember the last time I said goodbye to Grandma. My heart felt broken, but I could accept that she was ninety-three years old, and she was ready to go to heaven, to be with her Lord and Saviour and her family. She would always write on the birthday cards of her twenty-four grandchildren '8 years of love and learning. 9 years of love and learning' (depending of course on the age you were). She had lived it - 93 years of love and learning!

To somehow comprehend that my daughter and my son would be in heart failure as children felt impossible, unnatural, devastating and unfair. *'How could we be at this point?'* I often wondered how a thirteen-year-old could already be in heart failure. Grandma was eighty years older than Luka-Angel, so that made sense. This made no sense, not even a little bit. Thirteen years of loving and learning was just *not* enough!

We decided as usual with our visits to Melbourne, that we needed something to make this a good trip and not all about needles, tests and specialist visits. So we booked a trip to Phillip Island. The man who owned the motel I was booking, had asked me if we were on a big family holiday. I had told him we were there to go to the Royal Children's Hospital but wanted a day at Phillip Island. (He didn't realise I had cried my eyes out before the phone call and had to take a deep breath before I rang. I didn't even want to go to Melbourne. To me at that time, it only meant impending doom). The reality was we couldn't afford more than a night at the little cheap motel anyway. The cost of the hire car, and the visit to the penguins was already draining our finances, so when he decided to throw in breakfast, I saw it as a gift from God. When I later saw he had just one arm, I wondered if breakfast was thrown in from a point of understanding as well, not just generosity.

It was the 3rd June 2016 and we were on a plane to Tullamarine airport. Lucas and I felt somber, although managed to put on a smile for our children. I glanced around the plane and wondered how many people were on their way to Melbourne for a holiday. I thought of the farce it was that our kids were excited. We looked like an ordinary family going on a big holiday. Our bags were packed, our winter garb was on, and our kids were excited about going to Phillip Island. We knew in our heart of hearts that Phillip Island was the calm before the storm. Phillip Island was our way to appease what was about to happen. Phillip Island was a means to an end. A way of once again, bringing some joy into our pain. This would be something to look forward to and relish, in amongst a tough time.

We landed in an overcast Melbourne and headed off to pick up our hire car. The kids sung, laughed and made movies in the back of the car. The front of the car felt like there wasn't much we could talk about. Our hearts weighed so heavy. This date had been looming like dark storm clouds. This week had been hanging over our heads, booked into our diary since February, the week we would be putting Luka-Angel on the list for a heart transplant. This was the week we would find out in Melbourne if Jazz now needed to be listed too, after his results at Westmead Hospital in February, had revealed further deterioration. I had countless nights in the lead up to this moment, when I would wake myself up screaming. I never quite knew if my voice had really been audible, but the sound of it had definitely woken me many nights. Most of the time, I was screaming at doctors, "Get your hands off her!! Leave my baby girl alone!" A deep, dark agony and buried fear had surfaced. I would go downstairs and write a song, or wake up sobbing, my face wet before I was even aware I was crying. It was the primordial in me. It was the very being of my protective mother instinct come to life, and given a voice that I would quickly suppress.

My counsellor told me to allow this voice, acknowledge it, and soothe it. The repression of this voice had felt near impossible, but had been something I had been doing for some years now. I would stifle her, telling her not to disturb my sleep anymore. My heart would be thumping so hard I felt the house would shake and I would tell her to go away. She was a fruitless voice. There was nothing I could do. If I let her take charge, there would be no remedy for my daughter! The doctors would have to go near Luka-Angel; they would have to cut her chest open, they would have to take her beating heart out of her body. Ironically, it was the only way she would live.

The dark clouds loomed. They hung over. They were cold, they were frightening.

As we drove along, heavy hearted but with an attempted smile periodically on our faces and admittedly looking forward to the overnight holiday, dark clouds literally threatened to rain on our sunshine. Threatened to rob us of this little adventure we needed as a family before we drove back to the hospital for a series of tests and meetings with specialists and surgeons. Even though freezing cold, we had a great night witnessing the penguins' parade.

The next day was a Sunday and we drove off to Nobby's Lookout. The clouds, no longer in the distance but overhead, threatened to stop us from our beautiful boardwalk. The power of the surf way below, the waves crashing into the cliff faces, was breath taking. The smell of the penguins and their homes around us was pungent, but somewhat softened by the smell of the fresh, crisp air and the scent of salt water. The scent of impending rain hung heavy. Then a light sprinkle began. "It's definitely going to rain hard." Lucas stated matter of factly, "maybe we should come back another time."

I blatantly refused, saying with positivity to the kids, "Come on, out you get. It's worth us going on this beautiful walk even if we get a bit wet". It was freezing!

Others ran for their cars as the rain started to come and the sky got dark. The wind blew hard.

Something within me knew that we needed to push through this storm in order to enjoy our surroundings. I didn't know if we'd ever make it back here again, everyone intact.

I prayed that the rain would hold off just long enough for us to enjoy the walk along the board walk.

The rain stopped, and the tourists had mostly disappeared.

As we walked and looked for penguins, I felt in awe of God's great creation, amazed at the hugeness of the sky and the power of the ocean against the lush green towering cliff faces. Every small set of stairs that we came to along the way I would automatically do what I had done for years. I would push or drag Luka up the stairs, and then carry Jazz up. It was the only way we could enjoy family walks. There were many stops on the way as we dawdled along and three in our family would need to stop, catch their breath and wait for their hearts to calm down.

The view was also breath taking. If God could create this, how big must he be? How powerful must he be? As I walked, the cold air enticed me to snuggle my face deep into my wooly coat and I prayed, "Lord, give us strength, give us courage as we face this scary week. May things come to pass in your perfect timing, give us and the doctors wisdom. Thank you for Luka's bravery. Help her to continue to know your peace." These were sentences I had whispered many, many times before. My soul chose to worship our great big God regardless of what was coming.

I gathered my family as we stood above a high cliff, looking down to the ocean. I told them to look out at the sea and the sky as I said a Bible passage.

Psalm 46:1-2 'The Lord is our refuge and strength, a very present help in trouble. Therefore we will not fear though the earth gives way, though the mountains fall into the heart of the sea'. Looking at the huge cliff in front of me, I pictured it crumbling into the sea below and it felt strangely familiar.

Then I quoted:

Psalm 121 'I look to the hills but where does my help come from? My help comes from the Lord who made heaven and earth. He will not let your foot slip; He who watches over you does not slumber. Indeed, He who watches over you does not slumber or sleep.'

Even if our world caved in, I believed God would help and strengthen us if we allowed him to.

All of a sudden as I came to the end of the second psalm, "The Lord will watch over your comings and goings both now and forever more," a rainbow began to appear in the sky. Luka-Angel had only just put up her 'rainbow' blog (see end of book). The rainbow had always meant so much to me, and truly was a reminder of the promises of God. There is a story in the Bible about a man named Noah and God's deep sadness that most people on earth were treating each other terribly, hurting each other, killing each other. This was not part of God's original plan for a loving, happy, peace-filled community of people so he started again. God painted the very first rainbow in the sky for Noah as a sign that he would keep his promise to all people, to never destroy the whole earth again.

Many times along my walk of faith when I have needed reminding of God's promises and been praying as I gaze on his creation, a rainbow has appeared in the sky. Here I was, yet again, praying, seeking, with darkness looming, and a rainbow formed in the sky. On looking at this rainbow I instantly remembered the day my one-year-old Luka-Angel had said the word rainbow for the first time. Her big brother (three years old), and I were standing in the sprinkling rain at the top of the hill beside our house in Grafton. We were overlooking the river next to our house when Miss One, who still didn't even have any hair, had exclaimed, "Wainbow". To which I jumped up and down and said, "What did you say?" Pointing to it again she had emphasized, with a big proud smile on her face, "Wainbow!" A few days later, I had painted that moment onto a canvas. A beautiful reminder of the day Luka-Angel first noticed a rainbow. I had no idea at the time what that memory would mean for me, and I am so glad I captured it in a photo and painting.

Here we were at the lookout being threatened with a storm, and out of nowhere, God had painted the largest rainbow in the sky. We could see the end of it, travelling into the water in front of us. Luka-Angel stood in the foreground excited about the rainbow and claiming it as hers. Having just written her blog, 'Look on the Colourful Side' (about her rainbow after the storm), she wholeheartedly believed it was put there just for her. Luka knew this 'holiday' was the calm before the storm. She knew the very next day we would be driving to the hospital where she would be listed for what she referred to as her 'rainbow', a heart transplant. It would be this rainbow that would get her bravely through blood tests, chest x-rays, Echos, ECGs, a halter monitor, and discussions around the surgery. This rainbow would keep her bold and strong, surprising those around her with the most direct questions and a peace-filled spirit.

It was just five days later, when Luka-Angel looked the cardiac surgeon in the eye and stated, "I have some questions". He nodded as she pulled out a slightly scrunched, over-folded piece of paper from her pocket. I had asked her a few months before, to make note of her questions (I knew many I didn't even think I could bear to hear, let alone know how to answer). Her questions seemed to know no inhibitions. They were real, unnerving and some quite shocking!

"Will I die when you take out my heart?" she asked in a matter of fact tone.

The surgeon seemed thrown. It looked as though he hadn't heard this question before out of the mouth of a child.

I looked at Luka and she was completely at peace, quietly waiting for his answer.

"What will you do with my heart after you take it out?" she asked as I felt myself flinch.

Once again, he seemed thrown.

He stumbled, and he stuttered, but he answered as best as he could.

The questions went on and on. With each one I felt both proud and devastated. I was devastated that she had to ask such questions but proud that she had such courage and tenacity.

He talked about the process of heart transplant, and he said with assurance and sudden passion, "Luka, I have done many, many heart operations. Some of them are very tricky. Some children have problems with their heart that no one else has, and I have to come up with a way to solve the problem and fix their hearts. Some heart operations are very complicated. Heart transplant is very straight forward. It is a straight forward operation. I have never forgotten what it felt like the first time I saw a heart transplant. To see the heart spring to life was like a miracle. It was magical. Every time I do a heart transplant, and the heart springs to life, it is magical! It is amazing!"

After she had left the room he turned to us and said, "She is remarkable! What an intelligent, strong and assertive little girl! I have a twelve-year-old daughter. She could never ask questions like that!" I recall feeling so relieved that he had a daughter of similar age. Perhaps he would take more care of our girl being a 'Daddy' and having heard her questions. I quietly prayed that this would be the surgeon she would get, as we knew on the day it would depend who was rostered on.

None of us had a clue at that time that our Luka would indeed get this particular surgeon. And this surgeon would never see the 'magic' of the new heart springing to life. He would not be allowed the privilege of watching this heart receive the miracle it would need to function. This heart would only lie dormant, still. The next time I saw this doctor, he looked crushed, he looked exhausted and he had no words to tell us. He sat reflectively beside our cardiologist who told us things had not gone as expected. That the new heart didn't work. There was no magic in this particular heart transplant. Only long, grueling hours followed by confusion, despair and resignation. In this heart transplant of the little girl who asked, "Do I die when you take my heart out?" a machine would be hooked up to all her vitals, just to keep her blood flowing. A machine would keep her alive. Meanwhile, we would wait. Every minute would seem like a day, every hour like a year, and in every moment of that wait, my heart would feel like it had been ripped right out of my chest along with my baby girl's.

Luka-Angel nearly one year after her diagnosis of Restrictive Cardiomyopathy.
Credit: White Wish Photography

Chapter 17

The End & the Beginning

'You will keep him in perfect peace, whose mind is stayed on you, because he trusts in you.' Isaiah 26:3 (ESV)

It had been the hardest two weeks. It was our busiest time of year with our hugest youth camp having just happened.

I had been busily preparing for our work youth camp for months now. Most of the time at my workplace I didn't stop for lunch, nor did I go home with a completely free mind. I had to intentionally leave all the left over work in the car before I walked into my house, and make a decision to revisit it in the morning when I was back in the office. These were busy weeks in the lead up to the hardest days of my life.

Jazziah's big birthday party was on 20th August (we have always thrown a big party for our kids every second year, it was his year). As usual I had gone over the top along with being frugal and trying to do everything myself, and so every spare moment at home was taken up with creating games, piñatas, dress up outfits and decor. He wanted a Black & White themed party this year. He wanted to wear a tuxedo. For a kid turning ten, I thought this was both quirky and delightful! We had twenty kids at his party and it came off so well.

The next day however, I came down with something.

What followed was days and days in bed of the worst virus or flu I had experienced in ten years. I had only ever felt sick like this twice before. Lucas had banned me from going anywhere near the kids, and I was banned from leaving the room. I understood it. If Luka-Angel or Jazz (or Lucas for that matter) caught the flu, they could die. I felt delirious and my fevers were high. All I could think about was the huge event coming up on the next weekend, and I wondered how on earth I was going to get things done this week. It was going to be one of my busiest weeks of the year. Being sick was just completely inconvenient. On the Sunday after Jazz's party, Lucas realised I really was very unwell. From my 'sick bed', I heard him come home from church, take a look at me still lying in our bed, and then take the kids out again. I wondered if they were going to get some lunch, or perhaps buy me some flowers or some soup or herbal tea. Lucas was often sweet and thoughtful like that. However, when they arrived back home, Lucas marched up the stairs, a man on a mission. He emphasized a clear instruction to the kids, "Don't go near Mummy!" I often made a joke of how 'OCD' he was, although perhaps it wasn't always such a laughing matter. He then proceeded to come into the room, I felt quite delirious, so it took me a minute to realise what was going on. He was so particular about keeping things germ free, so it shouldn't have come as a surprise when he sprayed our entire bedroom with 'Glen 20'. He then started spraying above me from my head, down to my toes, pulling the covers back as he sprayed me just above my body. I was shocked. The smell of lemon and eucalyptus filled the air. I looked at him with glassy eyes and delirium and mumbled incredulously, "Are you spraying me with disinfectant?!!" Tears sprung to my bloodshot eyes as I said, using the only energy I could muster, "I thought you went to the shops to buy me some treats! You only went to buy disinfectant?!"

After Lucas left the room, I rang my sister (even though I hardly had any voice) who I knew would find the whole thing highly amusing. I cried a little and laughed hysterically at the same time, on the phone to her about my germ-a-phobic husband and his strange and funny ways.

The next afternoon there was a little tap, tap on the door. My precious thirteen-year-old walked in with a tray for me. Raisin toast, a cup of tea in a special cup and saucer, a frangipani and a little love note. She whispered, "Sshh, I'm not meant to come in here." And with that, she was gone. I hadn't eaten all day, and I knew I needed to try, so this was a welcome tray. I contemplated how she had spent many times sick in bed, or in a hospital bed with a tray of food. I thought of the beautiful care she had taken, with an opportunity to look after me this time. It blessed me so much!

I tried and tried to get out of bed, but every time I did I nearly fainted, or I heard myself speak gibberish. I knew I was really unwell, but I couldn't get myself up to go to the doctor. Lucas was very busy doing the last minute preparations for our youth camp, and managing the family. It had turned into such a big week for him when we usually prepared for our big work events together.

The next afternoon after school another little tap, tap on the door. In walked Jazz, "Shhh, Mum, I am not allowed near you but I will sit over here and read you a story okay?" I was given two choices (a ten-year-old's choice of course). Neither story particularly interested me, but I was delighted in the sweet gesture and even though feeling so sick, my heart danced to his little voice bringing the words to life. He sat there for half an hour and read to me.

Once again I thought of this precious boy who had endured so many stays in hospital, he knew what it was to be stuck in bed sick. I was moved, and secretly recorded him on my phone. This was something I wanted to always remember.

On Thursday I was well enough to sit up in bed and go over the sermon I was grateful I had written four weeks beforehand. It was titled, 'Living life to the max despite hard circumstances'.

The words hit home as I had written it out of a space of what it meant to face an imminent heart transplant or two. I had written it from my own personal journey of learning to trust God, and some insight into someone with difficulty, living life to the full.

Friday was the first day I managed to get out of bed. I went to the chemist and loaded myself with as much medication as I could manage. Then, off to youth camp, praying that I would be able to stand up and preach that night. I was not willing to allow sickness to come between me, and my favourite event of the year, or the message I felt I needed to bring to the 140 youth who would be there.

With hardly any voice I explained in my team meeting that I wasn't well, so to stay a little clear of me, but I wanted them to know I was so happy to be here, and I knew God would move in the lives of young people and leaders. By the evening, adrenalin had kicked in and I felt pretty reasonable, although wished I had a bit more voice.

Our good friend Elyse arrived at camp around 4pm having picked our kids up from school. One look at Luka-Angel told me things were not really okay. Even with the patchy, left over yellow face paint she had put on for her Book Week dress up (Bananas in Pajamas outfit), she looked really sick and I could see immediately by her eyes that she had a temperature. She had hundreds of high temperatures throughout her thirteen years of life. I tried to give her some empathy, and then still feeling unwell myself and with a lot of setting up to do, I gave her a Panadol and got on with the afternoon. By 6pm, I realised as Luka clung to my side whimpering, that things had gone downhill pretty fast for her. I took her to the house on the property we were at. We knew the Salvo Officers who lived there quite well and I thought perhaps Luka could stay there a while. When I read that Luka-Angel's temperature was 40 degrees Celcius, I quickly asked for nurofen and contemplated leaving. My desire to stay there overruled my mother's instinct. They kindly offered to look after her for me.

I stood up on the stage with great purpose and knew that surge of energy well. I believed God had a word for me to bring that night and I was excited to deliver it. I had just enough voice to preach my sermon of living life to the full in adverse circumstances. I was grateful I had included a couple of video clips including a clip from Nick Vujicic from 'Life without Limbs' (if you haven't heard his story, I encourage you to look it up). Nick was born with no arms or legs, yet lives a life of great purpose and joy as he invests in others, encouraging people to reach their full potential. I spoke to the youth of the importance of relying on God to give them the courage to live life to the max regardless of their circumstances. I shared briefly that living with two children who need a heart transplant meant I had to keep my eyes up and keep getting my strength from God, as did they.

Around 10pm, I cut my night short and took Luka-Angel back to our cabin to care for her properly. I wondered how this would unfold. I was so aware that when Luka goes down, she usually goes down hard.

By the morning, to my surprise, Luka hadn't gotten any worse, although she still wasn't well. As often happened when Luka-Angel went down, Jazz was now sick and his temperature was up. Regularly, the two of them were sick together, having a lower immunity than our other two children. They often shared a journey of being home sick from school together, or both going off to doctors.

"Great," I whined to Lucas, "now it's both of them. How is this going to go? I don't want to leave and go home."

We decided to keep an eye on them, and be prepared for anything. Often if their temperature was up, their heart would play up too. Sickness for Luka and Jazz was never a simple thing.

By the afternoon, Jazz lay curled up in a ball in the front room of the building where our main event was happening, I sat with him wondering what I should do. He had taken both Panadol and nurofen and he only seemed to be getting worse. He couldn't eat, and drinking was now hard too. He had no energy and just lay on a mattress. Elijah was lead singer with his band over the dinner break and I really wanted to support him, besides the fact that I just loved our youth weekends, and didn't want to leave. It was also my last event for a while as I had received permission for 'leave without pay' due to Luka-Angel going on the heart transplant list, and all the preparation that needed to happen at home. I believed God had called me, one night on a run (months earlier) to 'prepare for the marathon' that was ahead. I wanted enough time at home to get things in order, and I wanted to be there for Luka. I had pictured keeping her home from school some days, and taking her to a café or just spending some beautiful quality time with her. I knew the coming time would be a lot of pressure on the whole family, and also wanted to be there for the kids after school.

At 10pm I was still at the venue, and Lucas was now back in our little cabin across the road with our younger boys. Lucas suddenly rang me, "Jazz is not good. He is lying down but his heart is hitting 180bpm. He is really tachycardic and he now has chest pain. I think we need to go to the hospital!"

I responded instantly, "I am coming straight away!" With that I gave our friend Scott a heads up that we may need to take Jazz to hospital, and he offered to drive me. When I reached Lucas at the cabin I had already made my mind up. I took one look at how sick Jazz was. This wasn't worth cardiac arrest. I pulled our defibrillator a little closer, and rang the small local hospital explaining the situation.

We were told quite sincerely that they wouldn't be able to assist a child with a condition like Jazziah's. They told us it would be quicker for us to drive him straight to John Hunter Hospital ourselves, than see them, and wait for an ambulance.

Scott drove Jazz and I the one hour trip to hospital, and I sat in the back of the car with my son curled up on my lap. I was worried for Jazz and feeling a mix of fear, disappointment and deep sadness. That was the end of Youth Councils for me (there was still another day to go) but no event, camp or thing was more important than keeping my son safe. I already knew awful mother's guilt in that I had probably allowed things to get too far already. We sat in emergency and surrounded by coughing people I whispered to the nurse Jazz's condition and as usual we were whisked off to a different room for his protection. His temperature was right up, his heart was playing up and then, all of a sudden the vomiting began. I sheepishly told the pediatrician that we had been running a camp and he had been sick since this morning. I mentioned how I had been in bed sick all this week too.

As Jazz lay in the bed so sick, I draped myself across his little body and quietly shed a few tears, praying and wondering how I was ever going to cope when this story was actually so much worse. I envisaged me sitting by his or Luka-Angel's transplant ICU bedside and once again I felt isolated, alone and the deepest sadness and fear. I was also sad that I hadn't been able to say my "Goodbye" to the youth and leaders we had now been journeying with for five years. I began to pray, and God's peace descended upon me, I had vomit all over my shoes and cardigan but that blended with the smell of peace that surpasses human understanding and hospital. I watched my sleeping son, and realised again that I loved him so much it hurt.

Late Sunday afternoon our friend Elyse brought Luka to the hospital so we could give her some 'Tamiflu' medicine at the hospital's recommendation. Elyse brought me some things including a painting she had done for me that read, 'Eyes Up, Never give up.' I had mentored Elyse for some time now, and I had told her that this was my life's motto and I had based it on Hebrews 12:1-3: *'And let us run with perseverance the race marked out for us, fixing our eyes on Jesus'*.

Luka had been sick most of the day (and her temperature was clearly still up). Elyse took her home to her house to watch a girlie movie and relax while Lucas continued to pack up at youth camp.

The next day my church minister Colin came in to see us, to bring some encouragement and pray for Jazz. I had known Colin and Pam for years, and they had been there for our family on many occasions when we had gone through hard times, even when Luka-Angel had meningitis those years ago in Grafton. I told him how I felt terrible grief at leaving our youth weekend without being able to give my final goodbye and encouragement to the people within our ministry. I felt so disappointed having had no real closure and also how much fear I felt knowing I had to 'get used to this.' Colin and Pam were people of great faith whom I really admired and loved.

Colin had been dying of cancer just three years before and had miraculously beaten it. The visit from him really uplifted my spirit.

My heart felt very low as I had a keen sense that there was much more of this to come in the near future. I didn't have a clue just how soon that would be.

A couple of days later Jazz was dismissed from the isolation room at hospital. We were advised to keep him at home and resting all week.

As I left the hospital to my surprise I heard someone say my name. I looked up and saw another Colin I had known from my church in Tweed Heads. He too was someone I saw as a man of great faith and had also miraculously beaten life threatening cancer that had been diagnosed as terminal years before. He still lived up in northern New South Wales, so I was surprised to see him (eight hours south) in Newcastle. He asked me what I was doing at the hospital and as I told him, some silent tears escaped. There on the main footpath in front of the hospital he placed his hand on my shoulder and prayed for healing and strength for our family. I thought it strange that the only two people I had seen whilst in hospital were two Colins of great faith who had beaten cancer miraculously. As I reflected on my drive home from the hospital that this was no accident, I felt my faith increase as I was reminded that God had done miracles before and perhaps he would do some in our family.

On Wednesday, Lucas had gone to Sydney for his own cardiologist appointment. The children had a concert on at school, and Jayjay was dancing with his class. Although I had the pull of staying home with my two sick kids, I felt I couldn't miss Jayjay's performance. So Elijah stayed home to look after Luka and Jazz.

As we turned up to the concert (just Jayjay and I), my heart felt broken and tears were ready to spill over at any moment. It had been such a hard few weeks and I was tired! I firmly told the tears to stay there, and they weren't welcome tonight (I just didn't trust myself and wondered if I might have a melt down on some random person I hardly knew). I felt such deep sadness that yet again my kids had to miss out. Luka was supposed to sing in a group performance that night. When I bumped into my cousin Triniti, a couple of tears escaped and I told her I was so glad she was here because I needed her tonight. As we sat together and some beautiful songs were performed, I bent down low, pretending to shuffle through my bag and briskly wiping away the tears that had escaped. The music sung to my heart. In the intermission I went and sat on a seat in another part of the school in the darkness, hoping to be well hidden. One of Luka-Angel's teachers came past me and said, "Are you Luka-Angel's mum?" I told him I was. "She is such an ANGEL – she just breaks my heart!!! I just love her and she is amazing!!" He said dramatically pounding his chest - he was a drama teacher so for me having seen his flamboyant personality it came as no surprise to hear his beautiful and dramatically delivered statement.

Thursday came and went and I sent Luka back to school despite the fact that she still had a terrible cough. Her fever had at least gone and I was concerned about all of the school she had missed over this year and in years gone by. Besides, she was in her first year of high school and I didn't want her to get too far behind already.

By Friday Jazz was doing much better, so I went off to work and took him with me. It was to be my last day in the office for an indefinite period. Lucas was in Sydney and was unable to make my farewell morning tea. The staff sat around and I said my goodbyes, explaining to them that I needed to have a season of preparation with Luka-Angel having gone on the transplant list. I told them I also wanted to take some special time to be with her, and just wanted to be available for quality time with my kids with the impending storm ahead. I explained to them that at any time we could get a phone call to say we need to urgently get to Melbourne for her transplant. In my mind, that phone call was probably going to be as far away as next year. At the very soonest, I had decided it would be November (on reflection, I sometimes wonder if this was a self-preservation thing).

After those incredibly hectic weeks, the house was an absolute mess. Having been sick in bed, followed by Jazz's big party, followed by youth camp and then Luka and Jazz needing extra care, and Jayjay's birthday mid-week, there was a major backlog of washing, folding, left over party things, wrapping paper, and you could hardly see the floor in some spaces. Even the fridge seemed to be merging into a new creature never before seen by mankind.

No surprise then that on the Saturday morning as soon as my youngest woke me up, well before my body was ready, I immediately made a mental list of everything that needed doing. I told Lucas, when I already felt half way through my day by 9am, that we needed to have a family meeting and give out the jobs. There was just no way I could do it all myself. I was fairly grumpy and feeling overwhelmed. I wondered why when I stopped, the mounting housework didn't. Surely others could see what I could see all around me. Clearly though, it didn't seem to trouble anyone else.

All day we worked. We turned the music up, and everyone diligently did their allocated jobs. Their reward was my appreciation. It got to around 4pm, and I said to the kids, "We don't have anything for Dad for Father's Day tomorrow. Unfortunately I'll need to go to the shops. Who wants to come and buy Dad some presents? We're not going for long, we'll need to go as quick as we can!" I was conscious of the fact that the very next day we would be flying to Melbourne for Luka-Angel and Jazz's quarterly routine appointments, and I hadn't yet packed any bags. Elijah and Jayjay were to be going to Triniti's house while we were away a few days, so there were six bags needing to be packed.

After we had rushed around Kmart buying some presents for Father's Day, we went to Coles to buy bacon and eggs and apple cider for breakfast. As we walked through the baking aisle in Coles, Luka did something she never really did. She begged me to buy something, "Please Mum, can I buy this brownie mix to make brownies for afternoon tea?" My first response was, "No Luka, it's already 4:30pm! It will be too late for afternoon tea by the time we get home and you cook them." Uncharacteristically she didn't accept my answer, "Please mum? I'll clean up all my mess!"

Instantly I decided to live life to the full and stop being such a grump!

"You know what? I have changed my mind. Who cares?! It's been a hard day, yes you can grab the brownie mix, and we'll just have a late afternoon tea." Later that night and the next day, I would become so grateful that I had softened.

We got home, and while the brownies baked we decided to go to the park.

"Can I ride my bike there?" Luka-Angel asked.

I was rather shocked at her question. She had seemingly given up on riding some time ago. Her shiny new yellow bike (donated by Heart Kids in Sydney) sat in our garage hardly used. It was just too tiring for her, and pushing her up the hills was getting so hard for me, she was nearly my size now.

Around 5:30pm we enjoyed our very late afternoon tea and then continued on with the housework.

After our 'picnic dinner' in front of the T.V we decided after our mundane housework day we should enjoy some family time around the table and play cards. Saturday was always supposed to be a 'family day', but this one had been more like Mum is overwhelmed and grumpy, let's all do the housework and take some 'family moments' in between.

As we played it wasn't exactly the most pleasant game we have ever played. One of our children even stormed off halfway through the game, unhappy at losing, then sheepishly reappeared to keep playing. In our usual fashion we just pretended like nothing had happened and moved on with the game.

I remember being keenly aware that the kids were swinging on the chairs. This was a habit of theirs I had tried to break over and over again. I had threatened in recent days that the next time I saw them swinging on the chairs, I would write 'Don't swing on your chair' in permanent marker on the wall to remind them it's something they're not allowed to do - I had already penciled it on there some months before. After about the tenth time that night of this continuing (and about the one thousandth time this year), for the sake of shock value I did it. On the inside I was being a little facetious and chuckling at my success in shock value. The kids however were quiet – I think they thought I had completely lost my mind as they watched me with a permanent marker write in large letters on the wall, 'DON'T SWING ON YOUR CHAIR'. I thought that some turpentine would hopefully get it off later. The kids could not believe I had followed through on my threat! I told them calmly that perhaps now they wouldn't forget my message, and it would allow me to stop repeating myself. It was written boldly right beside my little prayer corner, which had four white boards up on the wall (this was a well-used corner). The family prayer posters were there for writing on and titled 'Thank You God For...', 'Pray for Others', 'Help' and 'God Is...' Now above such a beautiful space it read in permanent marker in large letters, 'DON'T SWING ON YOUR CHAIR'.

It had been a long day of hard work and I was tired. The kids gradually went off to bed later than usual. I told Lucas that I wanted to finish packing for our trip to Melbourne. Then regardless of whatever housework mess was left lying around, I was going to sit down in the lounge room with him – and as he had suggested, finish a movie we had started a week before.

It was 10:35pm when I came down the stairs to the lounge room with my mobile phone. I didn't usually keep my mobile phone with me at night. I placed it on the arm of the lounge chair and as I went to sit down, it started to ring. My bottom hadn't even yet quite hit the seat.

At first I turned to Lucas and said, "There's no way I am answering that. I am exhausted and this is my time to relax now." I glanced down and saw that the phone read, 'No Caller ID'. This usually meant work, sometimes meant our cardiac team, and sometimes meant it was from another Salvation Army household or workplace. Somewhere in the back of my mind I knew it could mean something else, but the thought never made it to the front of my mind.

After a lot of rings, Lucas turned to me and urged, "You should get that, it might be important."

I picked it up resentfully, completely unaware of what I was about to hear.

"Hello, Angela," the familiar voice said. My first thought was that our transplant coordinator was ringing regarding our appointments for Luka and Jazz that were due to happen Monday and Tuesday. This thought was very quickly thwarted by her next sentence, "So we have something for Luka." She said it plainly and with no expression.

"What do you mean?" I asked with the most enormous sinking feeling in my stomach. "You don't mean what I think you mean do you? This isn't *the* call-"

"Yes," she interrupted, "this is *the* call. We have booked you on flights at 5:30 tomorrow morning."

"No," I began sobbing instantly, "we can't do this! We are not ready!!! This is not the right time." I knew I sounded incredulous! My mind travelled briefly to the months I thought I was going to have preparing for this, the special times I had imagined spending with Luka… then the fact that I wanted to do today all over again. I wanted to have a real family day, a day where we spent quality time together. A day like we had in family days gone by. Not a housework day with me in a bad mood! I desperately wanted to put Luka-Angel to bed again tonight, and hold her closer and longer. I desperately wanted to look into her soft brown eyes and tell her how much I loved her. I wanted to paint her nails. She had asked me to paint her nails that day, and I had told her I didn't have time! I wanted the time back. I wanted it now!! Every cell in my body screamed so loudly I couldn't hear the nurse's voice properly. I hated what she said. I was instantly angry – how dare she ring us with this news, at this time, at the end of such a busy few weeks.

I suddenly noticed Lucas had somehow moved to the other side of the lounge room. He had slunk against the wall and his head was in his hands. His knees were up as if protecting himself from something. Suddenly he looked up at me with great relief, wide eyes and hope in his voice and said, "Oh – I've just realised, Luka can't have her transplant now!!! She is sick! She has a terrible cough!"

I jumped on his sentiment with utter relief at the realisation and said to our transplant coordinator on the other end, "We have just realised, Luka can't have her transplant yet. She has been sick all week. Jazz was in hospital this week – they are both on Tamiflu medication."

"I know," she informed me, "we received notice from John Hunter Hospital. Does she still have a temperature?"

"No," I said clutching at straws, "but she had a high temperature right up until Wednesday night. She has only been back at school two days. She has a terrible chesty cough." I was aware of Lucas looking at me whilst he now paced the floor, with pleading eyes.

"We can work with that. We have things we can do. Her cough won't matter. We have booked you on flights for 5:30am. I am going to give you the details now, have you got a pen?"

"No... we can't do it." I sobbed down the phone, "It's not the right time. It's too soon. We're not coming, we can't do it, it's too soon, and we are not ready..."

"Angela. Angela, I need you to listen to me." Our familiar team nurse said calmly trying to bring some sanity and reason. "You were booked to fly down tomorrow for appointments weren't you? What time did you book your flights?"

"1:45pm." I responded, thinking she was coming up with a solution.

"When you were coming to see the cardiologists this week, were you planning to take Luka off the list?"

Confused, but then realising what she was saying, I responded with my sobs lessening but my sinking feeling turning to nausea, "No. We weren't planning to take her off the list when we came down." I glanced at Lucas briefly with a tear soaked face.

"Then we need to proceed. Get a pen and I will give you the flight details."

As she gave me the details (including the fact that Jazziah had been booked on the flight as well) I interjected with, "We're not bringing Jazz. Jazz can't come straight away when Luka has her transplant. It's too hard for him, too in his face. We are taking Elijah. Luka wants her big brother there."

She went on to say they need to see Jazz and proceed with his appointment, and the flights were booked anyway. I quickly realised that Elijah had been sick when he went off to bed earlier. He had the first signs of what Luka, Jazz and I had over these last two weeks. I knew instantly he would never be able to come. It could be dangerous for his sister. I wondered how long it would be until I could see him again.

As soon as I hung up the phone I fell to the floor crying so loudly I didn't recognise my voice. I was distraught. "We can't do this, I can't do this, we're not ready, we're not ready. Noooo. This is not okay… we can't do it. I want to do today again. I want to do this week again. It's been such a horrible week…"

Lucas disappeared somewhere and I began my phone calls.

My mum and dad who live on the Gold Coast (eight hours north of us), had just arrived that day to Taree (just two hours north of us) where they were at my uncle and cousin's combined birthday party. I rang them immediately and told them they needed to get in the car and drive here straight away, "I need you. You need to come now." I said firmly. They were in shock too.

Next I rang my sisters, and Pam (my minister) who had been there for me over and over. I knew she was home alone with her husband away and would be running church the next day, but I didn't hesitate at her offer to come over. I was very aware I needed her here. She was my mentor and like a surrogate mother to me at times over these last number of years. I rang several other people asking them to get people to pray and sobbing down the phone with no inhibitions. I have never cried so much in my life!

I walked upstairs quietly, and stared at my sleeping girl. I just needed to see her face. I knew there was no way I would disturb her, that it wouldn't be best for her. It was so tempting to wake her up and ask her to spend some time with me, but I knew her body needed sleep. She was about to embark on the toughest journey and I could hardly comprehend it. I stood close by her bed, praying profusely in my spirit that God would help us. My prayer had no words, I couldn't possibly find any…

By the time Pam arrived I was pacing around the house both traumatised and distraught. I couldn't think straight. Nothing about me felt sane. My head was spinning a million miles an hour. I couldn't even work out what I needed to do or to pack. I just knew I was not ready. I knew this seemed too soon and all wrong. I had no peace whatsoever.

Lucas got straight on the computer trying to find my mum a flight to Melbourne, and looking for the special video we had put together at Luka-Angel's 13th 'Cow' birthday party. It was messages from her friends and family, that we would be playing to her when she was recovered enough to watch it. She knew it existed, but she also knew she wouldn't be allowed to see it until she woke up one day in hospital following her heart transplant.

I found myself grabbing photos of her that I wanted to stare at. Then photos that I thought might help her get through. One of our dogs (it would be months until she would see them), of her brothers and her together, her friends, and one of her dancing.

I found myself looking at some blank cards and thinking it might help her when she was in the ward to be able to write to her friends.

When my little sister Christelle arrived (around 12:30am) I broke down yet again on her shoulder, sobbing loudly like I had never done in front of anyone before. She had left her husband with her three young children, and came straight away, pregnant belly and all.

She was straight into action, "What can I do for you? Do you want me to pack some things?"

I took up her offer as I hadn't yet packed Luka-Angel's things for Melbourne, as I had planned to do it in the morning. "Please don't disturb her though Christelle, she needs to sleep. She can't know about this yet, I have to get myself together before she sees me." I glanced at the piles of folding from our day of washing six loads, and said to her, "Can you please go through that and find her some clothes? They will need to be warm. It's cold in Melbourne."

I watched sitting still on the lounge as Christelle held up different undies asking me, "Are these yours or hers?" I would respond accordingly. I was aware that she only seemed to be packing undies, but I couldn't really think, say or action anything. All I noticed was a suitcase of undies. Lots and lots of undies. My sisters adored their niece as though she was their own little sister. I decided weeks later as I looked at the suitcase, that Christelle must have been in shock that night too.

I would try and drink tea, and then I would collapse again into sobbing, "I can't believe this. I am not ready. We are not ready. I was going to have a season of preparation. This isn't right, it can't be true. It's not the right time. After a couple of hours I noticed my tea was cold, and still nearly full. I have no peace. Pam, I have no peace, what am I going to do?" My hands were throbbing from all of the wringing, and they were tingling at the same time.

Pam would pray with me, or come and hug me. Then I would settle for a minute or two, and then I would start again. My eyes stung so much. It felt like someone had rubbed small red chilies in them like the time when Elijah and Luka-Angel made their chili poison soup.

Every now and then I wondered what Lucas was doing, and each time I found him he was still sitting at the computer, desperately trying to find the special video for Luka I asked him to find.

He told me he had managed to get Mum on the flight with us first thing the next morning. I remember the relief I felt, knowing that Jazz would be looked after and our total attention would be able to be on Luka. I also felt relieved that he wouldn't have to witness our pain and distress as she disappeared out of our sight.

I thought about all the mess around my house. I thought about all the folding, the mess in my cupboards. I thought about the fact that I hadn't been able to shut my linen cupboard for weeks now because it was overflowing and untidy. I wondered how things were going to work here.

I suddenly remembered a little planning sheet we had put together for when the phone call came. I remembered we had discussed who we wanted with us to support us. I remembered that I had written potential people to mind our dogs and house and Jazziah's little bird.

I wondered with deep sadness in my heart how long it would be before I would see my Elijah and Jayjay again. I wondered how long it would take for healing, remembering that the recovery process takes at least three months. I looked at our little birdie Eve and felt so sad that we would all be leaving her suddenly. I wondered who I could possibly get to pack me some more clothes and felt instantly embarrassed about the state of my wardrobe.

I wondered who had lost their loved one tonight and I cried so hard for them.

I wondered if we would lose our little girl, and everything else fell away as if down a large chasm.

Mum and Dad arrived around 2:45am. We talked a little bit, and then I tried to help Mum make their bed. Dad was awfully quiet and his eyes looked deeply sad. I cried on their shoulder, saying yet again, "I am not ready. We are not ready for this."

They told me I should get some sleep.

Just before Pam left, I suddenly remembered the permanent marker on the wall that read, 'Don't swing on your chair!' Sheepishly, I told her about it. Embarrassed and unable to explain myself, I asked if she would mind scrubbing it off. As I said goodbye to Pam, and expressed how grateful I was for her support, she held me, prayed with me and said some encouraging words. I can't remember what they were, but as she drove off, I felt really bad for her that she was going home at 3am to an empty house and then running church the next day.

Christelle offered to stay rather than going home to her three children. "Yes, please stay," I said to her. It made sense for her to look after the boys while Dad drove the rest of us to the airport.

I set up a mattress for her on the loungeroom floor; just needing to do something, then went to bed after setting my alarm for 4am.

Lucas and I held each other and I cried and cried and said there was no way I was getting any sleep tonight. We prayed together and then I recited verses of peace over and over again. 'He will keep in perfect peace, him whose heart is set on him because he trusts in Him.' Isaiah 26:3. Some of the verses I said audibly, some were just on repeat in my mind.

When my alarm sounded just over half an hour later, my first thought was that I hated that alarm and I wanted to go to sleep and then wake up from this nightmare. Then my second thought was a prayer, *'God, give me the strength I need, to be able to do today.'* I turned to Lucas and asked his permission to text a prayer request to some important people in our life and tell them what was about to happen. I knew we needed people to pray for us. I then proceeded knowing that this hour was better than midnight.

I said to Lucas, "Before my feet hit the ground, I need to say that now we are strong for Luka. She cannot see our pain or fear. We need to go in and be strong for her." He nodded knowingly. I knew from the moment I got up, it was all about her, and no longer about my agony. I knew I needed to be the strong adult and her support, not the opposite. As I got dressed in the warmest clothes I could find, I caught a glance of myself in the mirror. I had never seen my eyes look this way. They looked so bloodshot, so red. I realised that she would notice my eyes, and I would have to put it down to sleep deprivation.

Lucas and I walked into Luka-Angel's room hand in hand. I gripped his hand so tightly. I woke her with a kiss, followed by, "Luka, darling, wake up. Luka I need you to wake up. Dad and I have some news for you. We need to know you are fully awake before we tell you something. You must tell us when you are awake properly so we can tell you the news."

Her eyes fluttered and she became a lot more alert having tuned into what I was saying. "What Mum and Dad? What time is it?"

"It's 4:20am," I said, "we have something very important to tell you."

She sat up against the end of her bed as we held her.

"The transplant coordinator rang last night. They have a heart that is right for you. You are having your heart transplant this morning around 9am. We need to leave in 20 minutes."

Her eyes became so big and wide. I had never seen that expression on her before. Then, a big gentle smile came across her whole face.

Lucas seemed quite shocked and said, "Are you smiling? How do you feel about it?"

"Nervous-cited." She said quoting one of her classic made up words. We had heard this word many times since she was in year three at school. Often 'nervous-cited' was a word she used about going to the zoo, performing at a concert, performing in a musical. This word seemed so undermining of this day and what was to come, but being Luka-Angel, seemed so appropriate! It was certainly not in my vocabulary that day.

I told her she would need to get up and quickly pack anything that was very important to her in her back pack. I told her to say goodbye to her room as we wouldn't be back for a very long time. I could hardly believe what I was saying.

"Does Elijah know?" Luka asked.

"No, we are going to wake him up now. He won't be able to come now though, because he is sick."

When we woke Elijah and told him, before we could even say any more than what was about to happen he said, "I know I can't come now mum, I am sick. It wouldn't be safe for Luka."

"Yes," I affirmed with a sad heart. I had always pictured her big brother there. They had journeyed through so much together and he had always cared for her so beautifully since she was a newborn baby. She had requested that he come from the outset of going on the list, saying to me once, "I will definitely need my big brother there."

I wondered why it had worked out like this. It just didn't seem to make sense to me. I thought about how fragile Jazz was, and how sick he had been this week. I wondered how hard this was going to be for him to watch his sister disappear into a theatre and not come back out for hours. I knew seeing her straight up would not be the best thing for him. I wanted to protect him from witnessing his own future. I so wanted him to stay at home so he wouldn't have to go through this. I resigned myself to some understanding that he might provide a helpful distraction when there was nothing we could do but wait.

We woke Jazz and Jayjay. Both were unusually quiet. My mum and dad got up and had a little bit of cereal. "I am fasting Luka. I won't eat until you can eat." I committed. Each time my children had to fast for surgery, I fasted with them. I wanted to support them however I could, and this was an avenue of support I had started a long time ago, when Jazz was only three years old and Luka only six. I loved food, so for me this was a huge sacrifice, but one I never hesitated to make. I wished I could go through it for them, but all I could do was offer to fast alongside them and experience the stomach ache that comes with that. This morning, I allowed myself a last little drink of juice before days of fasting.

As we were about to leave, and frantically grabbing some last minute things from Luka's room, I found myself quickly saying to Luka, "Do you want to grab one of your devotional books for when you are recovering in the ward?" I then found my hand rested upon the 'Encouragement Book' Luka-Angel's older close friend, who was somewhat of a mentor, had made for her 13th birthday. It was a special book from Hannah that I had glanced through once. It had Bible verses, encouraging words, pictures and uplifting quotes. Luka agreed she wanted to take it. We packed it in her backpack, not realising that it would become the book *I* would need, *my* source of strength, and a witness to all of the doctors and nurses who would see it in ICU.

We took one last family photo in the lounge room, all of our eyes revealing the early hour mixed with terrible fear and sadness, and then we walked out to the car. Elijah's, "I love you" spoken to his little sister, hung in my ears as we walked away, and I desperately hoped he would get the chance to tell her again.

CHAPTER 18

LUKA-ANGEL'S HEART TRANSPLANT – DAY ONE

'So do not fear for I am with you. Do not be dismayed for I am your God. I will strengthen you and help you; I will uphold you with my righteous right hand.' Isaiah 41:10 (NIV)

As the engine of the plane buzzed in the background, and the air hostesses moved among the cabin, I observed how sturdy and at peace Luka was and I could barely believe it. I had seen Luka-Angel this way on many occasions, but for her to know what she was about to go through and still show such peace and strength just blew my mind. It was miraculous.

She handed me about fifteen enveloped cards and said to me, "Mum, you need to give these out to each person as you see them." I noted that there were envelopes for nearly every member of our family – aunties and uncles, grandparents, brothers. Then she went on whispering in my ear, "Mum, you are not to be scared, tell Dad too. Don't be scared."

"I'm not." I said to her falsely... "Mum," she said chidingly, "I can tell by your eyes you have been crying. Don't be scared and don't be sad okay?"

We opened Hannah's encouragement book together and stuck our finger in a page. The verse we landed on said 'God is faithful to his promises'. My mind flicked to the moment God told me a few months ago on my jog around the Newcastle beaches as the lighthouse came into sight, "Luka will set up her lighthouse." This would be a promise I would now cling to and was a great hope and consolation.

She then started to say, "Mum, what's that song?" then she sang in my ear so softly, "through it all, through it all, my eyes are on you... through it all, through it all it is well."

I told her what the song was, wondering how she knew that was already such a special song to me. She hadn't been there when I had sung that song as a solo after my message and sharing my story about our children's health, at our church in June. She hadn't known that I sang that representing my part in this journey of kids with a serious heart condition. She had heard me play it and sing it at home, but I had never told her I was singing it in regard to this journey. So it surprised me when she said, "You need to listen to that song while I am sleeping. That is my song. I will be singing that song when I sleep". I knew without any further conversation that she was referring to her time over the next few days.

Luka told me that she had been looking through Hannah's book and that page 27 was for me. "Read it if you need to Mum, while I'm sleeping. That is your page."

Neither of us had any comprehension of just how long she would be sleeping for, or how many times I would need to read that page.

As we got off the plane, I was aware firstly how delightfully cute Luka looked with two braids. I wanted to pick her up again and carry her like I could when she was a little girl, but instead I walked alongside her, holding her hand. My legs felt so heavy I could feel each muscle move as I stepped. My eyes stung so painfully from the sunlight that was now in the sky and it made me want to shut them.

My big sister was waiting for us at the bag carousel with all of our bags.

"I hope I have them all." Karen said. She had caught the first plane out of Sydney and just beat us down there. She had even collected our bags for us before we could reach the conveyer belt. She then went and hailed a taxi van. We were so pleased to have found one that could fit us all in. While we drove to the hospital, Lucas and I facing Luka and Jazz, Karen in the front seat and Mum in the back, I rehearsed the things I wanted to say to Luka before she was put to sleep. I didn't want to forget anything.

It dawned on me that she had always said she wanted to bite my nose and she had told me a few times, that when she was laying on the bed ready for her heart transplant she would say to me, "Mum, can I bite ya nose?" And apparently I would feel sorry for her enough to say, "Yes" and she would finally get to bite it. I decided I would make sure we had that funny moment she had always talked about. I remembered her blogs and I looked for the rainbow that I expected to see in the sky today but I just couldn't see it. I could only see the imaginary black clouds and the lightning behind them. I felt so physically sick but also, so desperate. I was so desperate to find a way to stop this; desperate to run away. Desperate to yell at the doctors and nurses to back off and stay away and that they couldn't touch her perfect body. I wanted to yell at them to take their knives and scalpels away! I thought of her perfect skin, her perfect chest and I realised it would never be the same again.

The adrenalin running through my veins was hard to deal with. I felt jittery and I couldn't think straight. I remember at one point noticing my teeth were chattering. I felt so powerless. My job as a mother is to protect my children, but there was nothing I could do.

I quoted some Bible verses for the kids. Karen leant over the back of the front seat of the taxi as we read a Psalm and then Mum prayed. There was a sense of urgency, we knew from what we had been told that the minute we pulled up at Emergency at The Children's Hospital, the transplant coordinator would be there waiting with a wheelchair. And she was!

As the nurse walked ahead with Luka in the wheelchair, we shuffled along behind with our suitcases desperately trying to keep up. Lucas who knew he couldn't walk that fast, beckoned for me to run ahead and be beside Luka. My mum and Karen tried so hard to push all of our suitcases along so we could keep up. We felt so conspicuous and the suitcases were so noisy on that floor.

I asked the nurse to slow down a bit, so Lucas and Jazz could keep up.

She slowed her pace and Luka looked up at me but seemed more interested in answering the nurse's questions than talking to me. I had nothing I could say that could possibly be summarized into words at that point anyway. All questions or conversation had evaded me. I felt sick, numb and like I was watching us walk to Luka-Angel's impending doom.

I prayed again for peace that passes understanding.

Luka lay on the bed as staff came in, team by team, to talk some things through with her and us. I felt so worried that I didn't know how long this pre-op process would be and feared at any minute they would say, "Okay, say goodbye". I hovered as close as possible to her, every second counted.

We had about half an hour with her, including watching a pathologist take a very large tube of blood. Luka lay still and brave and seemed completely unperturbed.

Watching Jazz and 'Scruffy' (Jazz's security toy) say goodbye to Luka and 'Cowcow' made my heart break some more. I didn't think that was even possible. Luka told me that I had to make sure that every relative that came to visit while she was sleeping kissed 'Cowcow'. Somehow, 'Cowcow' was allowed to feel sad, and would need some comfort.

As Lucas and I escorted Luka's bed down the long corridors to some big plastic swinging doors, Lucas said to me very quietly and so suddenly, "I can't do it! You need to take her in!"

I was stunned and wanted to yell, *'No way! I can't do it either!'* Instead I said, "Really? You want me to go in there?" I had always pictured it would be him. I wasn't very brave with these things. He was better than I at this stuff. I thought about the fact that she hadn't yet had the chance to bite my nose like she wanted to, and so I said, "Okay." Then I said just audibly, "Jesus, give me strength to do this. I can't do this. Jesus, I need you, I need you."

I put on my 'shower cap' and my booties and gown.

Luka was wheeled into a room on her bed, where several staff were all gowned up and waiting for her.

I was aware they were so close to us and watching and listening but I didn't care.

"I love you Luka, so much! You are so precious and so brave and so strong and we love you so much! You are going to be okay." Then I turned my sentiment into something that would be better for Luka and said, "Go on, you can say it!!!" and stuck my wriggling nose down near her mouth.

She said, "Can I bite ya nose?"

I leant down and she bit me on the end of my nose. We laughed and the nurse on the other side of Luka laughed out loud and then quickly stopped herself, no doubt feeling inappropriate. I looked at her and explained with a small smile, "I know that seemed weird. It's okay though, a bit of a private joke."

Then I started some nervous ramble in an attempt to distract her from what was about to take place, "Luka, when you get better from this, you'll be able to dance. You'll be able to dance like you have always wanted to. What do you want to do first? Ballet? Contemporary? Hip Hop? Or maybe netball or basketball? Perhaps you and I can join a team together."

"Ballet and Contemporary." She said quickly.

Then I said her Bible verse, Isaiah 41:10, followed by the psalm she knew so well, "I can lie down and sleep soundly because you Lord will keep me safe."

Then she quietly said yet again, "Mum, you are not allowed to be sad, don't be sad or scared. Tell Dad too, please tell Dad not to be sad".

I told her I loved her with all my heart (and stealing her line) I said, "Soon you will be able to love me with both of yours." She was so brave, so strong and so peaceful. I felt in awe of her.

Then she closed her eyes and the image of her, with the most peaceful face and sweet lips turned slightly up embedded itself into my mind. No writhing, no body movements, just sweetly and peacefully she went off to sleep.

"Jesus is with you." I said audibly, "Jesus is with you and you are not alone." I prayed repetitively, holding my hand out towards her, "Jesus, be in this room. Send your angels. God, surround her." Then I was escorted away from my little girl who was left lying on a bed, surrounded by medical staff and angels. For a second my imagination pondered what the angels looked like. I knew they were all around her.

I felt such peace. I felt God. I felt heaven.

As I approached Lucas who stood just steps from the door, although shivering with nervous energy, I said, "I am okay. She is okay. She was so peaceful." Feeling a little numb, I didn't even feel the need to cry. It was done now, she was in God's hands and all we could do was pray. That was all I had now. So I fell desperately to my knees in my spirit, and I stayed there for weeks!

On this particular day of my life, I could journal nothing. I had no inkling to do anything, but sit and wait and feel.

Nothing was written down, except a quick re-count of the order of events (which I wrote in the notes of my phone not wanting to forget).So I can only reflect and recount some of our story of that day to the best of my memory and from my own perspective. Some moments that day though, of course remain too personal or hard to write about.

After I said goodbye to my little girl, we were ushered to the room where our luggage still sat. We were encouraged to go over to Ronald McDonald House and check in and drop off our bags.

It looked as though we had so much with us, but for me, I knew we didn't have enough. I knew this was all too much of a shock and so I couldn't have possibly packed what I needed for the rest of the year. I recall feeling a brief sadness that I hadn't said goodbye to our beagle Ruby, or our Labrador Zibby or Eve Hope, our bird. The thought brushed past my heart ever so briefly. I felt so far away from my other two sons, although my head was completely in the moment and my thoughts were mainly just prayers. I kept picturing the room my precious Luka-Angel lay in. I kept picturing the doctor's hands. I could only wonder what part they were up to. I kept envisaging the angels guiding the surgeon's hands, and God holding Luka in His strong arms.

We couldn't bring ourselves to leave the parent's room at first. We could only sit. Mum, Karen and Jazz were with Lucas and I, and some of them attempted some breakfast from the parent's waiting room cupboard. A weetbix, a cup of tea, but I had decided to fast with Luka-Angel until she could eat again and food was not even on my radar. It felt like no sacrifice not to eat, I couldn't have, even if I wanted to.

At some point Mum, Karen and Jazz took our suitcases across the road to Ronald McDonald House and we popped over there briefly.

Then we sat in the parents' room at the hospital for hours and hours. Lucas' sister, Tam, who was pregnant, and her husband Morgan arrived in the afternoon. They had got up early with their two year old Ella and driven all the way from Sydney to Melbourne for a two week stay to support us. I knew we really needed them there too, so it was a comfort all day knowing that they were on their way. We sat together, trying to talk every now and then, and praying when we could.

The wait felt like forever. The hours passed, but they felt like days. By the time it reached 4pm and the sky was getting slowly darker, my concern heightened. Any moment now we'll be told she is out. Any moment now. Any moment now…

Why haven't they called us yet?

Why haven't they been in to see us yet?

Lucas and I decided we were not leaving the room.

I remember a few times the realization that Luka-Angel laid just a few walls away from where we sat. If I had inspector gadget arms, I could have reached her, stroked her hair, and held her hand.

It was about ten long hours after we said goodbye to Luka when my mobile suddenly rang. The voice on the other end said, "Things haven't gone as we expected. Luka has been put on the ECMO (heart and lung life support) machine. The new heart isn't working."

On hearing my response, Lucas pleaded with me desperately, "Is she okay? What has happened?" Whilst I still tried to take in what I was being told, my sister Karen picked up on the bad news and quickly ushered Jazz out of the room. We were told someone would be in soon to take us to a room where the doctors would need to speak with us. We would not be able to see Luka yet, as they were still trying to stabilise her. My mum, and Tam and Morgan sat with us, attempting to be strong for us. We all felt confused and this had come as such a shock!

Rainbows in the Storm

I remember twisting my fingers until they hurt, but at the same time breathing a whispered prayer out that sounded like a hoarse scream in mind, "God, save her!!!! Help us!!!!" Then some soul groans. My prayers were hardly like words in those hours, more like feelings and instincts. I knew from what I had read in the Bible and believed that the Holy Spirit interprets our prayers to God. I knew that the Holy Spirit understood my groaning, bringing my deepest prayers before my Heavenly Father who loved me. I felt the sense that those who loved us and loved Luka were lifting us up desperately before our God and I knew because I have been there myself, that in those moments, they would find the words I couldn't find. Besides, I was keenly aware that God is not limited to, or by our feeble verbal language.

It was about half an hour later that we marched hastily down a hallway following the nurse's footsteps to where a room of doctors waited for us. I was grateful my mum was allowed to come with us. The sun had gone down and it was now night time.

One of Luka-Angel's usual cardiologists was there as the initial spoke person. Lucas and I found him to be a man of both great compassion and professionalism.

"Things haven't gone to plan. This is not what we expected."

He went on to tell us that the new heart, transplanted into Luka, currently had *no* function. We were told that this was very unusual, unexpected and that Luka-Angel was now on full life support (ECMO - heart/lung machine, and oxygen). He proceeded to give us a little information on what ECMO was and then explained her chest had to be left open. I squeezed my mum's hand so tight. My first words of response came rushing out, "Can you put her old heart back in? What did her old heart look like? Was it really that bad? Can't you just put it back in?" I truly thought this was a possibility.

It wasn't. Then Lucas said some things. Then I took a deep breath, and with God's peace covering me I recall stating firmly, "It's okay. I *know* she will be okay! She is a fighter! God is with her. I have hope!" Lucas' words were quite different to mine. We were both petrified!! Lucas travelled to the worst case scenario, I couldn't bring myself to, although somehow what we were suddenly facing was indeed nearly the worst case scenario. The only medical hope we had, was that they had a machine to keep her alive.

I have never felt fear or pain or trauma like that before.

I have also never felt peace or hope or strength like that before.

I observed that the surgeon I wanted was the one in the room with us. Luka had the surgeon who told us how magical and miraculous it was every time he saw the transplanted heart spring to life! He was elite in his field. He had won many awards. He was an incredible heart surgeon of great caliber and skill. He looked crushed. He didn't appear to have any words to offer. He looked so tired and his shoulders were slightly hunched over, his eyes never met ours. I felt sorry for him, he had given his best; but I also felt confused – why couldn't he fix this? Why didn't he keep her heart intact in case he could have put it back in?

I sniffed back the tears that threatened to create a flood.

The doctors soon left, and Mum prayed with us. We were so heavy our legs couldn't stand up and we couldn't leave the room. We needed to stay there a while. While Mum went to get Tam, Morgan and Karen, Lucas tried to form words that were simply distraught sentences!

"I *know* she will be okay. I can't even allow any other thought!" I said with hope that was not my own, desperate to convince Lucas, and also determined that there was just no other alternative!

When Tam, Morgan and Karen arrived in the room, we hugged and cried.

"Can we pray?" I asked, and we prayed again together.

The night got longer and longer as we waited to see her.

It became obvious that we wouldn't get to see Luka for hours yet.

Tam and Morgan went home to his sister's house to be with little Ella.

Mum took Jazziah home to bed at Ronald McDonald House. It had been such a long day, he was very quiet and somber and he had already witnessed too much.

Karen sat with us for long hours that seemed like months, years.

We curled up on lounges in the parent's room and I held 'Cowcow' so close, and wet her with my tears. There were no words to utter.

At one point I noticed a prayer book. I never saw it another day in the parent's room in all the months we went back there.

But that day, it sat on the coffee table, just waiting to be read.

I opened it to Psalm 91 and tried to read it out. Karen read some too.

Karen went backwards and forwards to the ICU desk on our behalf, asking when we could see Luka-Angel. We had thought we would have been able to see her by now.

We knew her chest was open. We knew she was on full life support, so Karen asked her medical friend in Sydney (a longtime friend for both of us) for some advice. The suggestion was we look at some photos of ECMO on the internet before we see our girl.

I have never watched a horror movie, I never input gore into my brain, I don't even watch shows like 'CSI'. I didn't know how my brain was going to be able to deal with what I was going to have to see. I recall verbalising something to that effect to Lucas and Karen.

I tried to take a look at a photo online of a baby on ECMO, but one glance and I felt like I could heave. How could I possibly prepare myself to see my precious daughter like this?!

We found out that Luka-Angel now had internal bleeding, and they needed to 'go in' again and seal some things off. I couldn't even imagine what that meant.

Hours more of waiting…

Lucas and I were told that we were the only ones who could visit Luka-Angel tonight. By the time we were escorted hand in hand down the longest of hallways, I was a trembling mess. My stomach churned and yet I couldn't wait to see her. I needed to make sure she was still alive. I was taken back to walking down the long aisle when I was just two years younger than Luka-Angel, to see my seventy-eight-year old nanna's open coffin. I remember feeling terrified. This feeling was so much worse. My little girl was only thirteen years old. This was so wrong.

My reaction to seeing Luka-Angel that first night was traumatic and physical. She didn't even look like my precious daughter.

The nurses in the room were many. They were all moving constantly. They could barely even look up to see us. Their job at that point was to make sure she was kept alive, and transitioned well from the theatre to the ICU room.

Chapter 19

Waiting

'You hold my eyelids open; I am so troubled that I cannot speak.' Psalm 77:4 (Holy Bible)

Journal Entries – Day 2

Today the doctors have advised that nothing eventful will take place today from them. They have said that it is a day of allowing rest, and just observing Luka-Angel and seeing what happens with this heart that won't function. She lies on life support, large tubes protruding from her open chest, pumping blood around her body. The nurses have covered her open chest and some of the tubes with small blankets and a singlet. I couldn't bear to think what her open chest might look like. I was grateful it was covered up. I cannot begin to describe how I felt. I had not slept. I could not eat still. I felt so weary, yet somehow so alert to my surroundings. Machines of blood are visible and seem to pump through strange looking bottles. I have never seen so much blood pumping around tubes before. It is so strange that it is her blood, my little girl's blood outside of her body. Pumping through make shift man made tubes. She looks so peaceful and her hair is still braided. Her skin colour is better today (not so yellow). She looks so sweet and innocent and precious laying there, so still. A tube is down her throat. A tube is also in her nose. There are lines coming out of her neck, her arms in several places. Today I felt like someone had taken my little girl and robbed her of all her life. The tubes that have invaded her body look so out of place on her beautiful smooth skin.

As she lay sleeping I sat and I watched and I waited and I prayed, and I recited verses of hope and peace. I didn't know where to touch her that first day. I didn't want to hurt her, but I so desperately wanted to touch her skin, to hold her hand. I wanted to make sure she knew we were there. She looked so alone, so unlike herself, completely unable to communicate. She was normally so full of life and animation, yet here she lay, completely still and unmoving.

My mind travels back a couple of days to Saturday afternoon when she came on a short bike ride to the park next door with me. I had of course pushed her up the hill on the way. She swung on a swing, laughing and calling out to us as the boys and Lucas and I played soccer. Then she went home and proudly handed out the brownies to us she had made for our very late afternoon tea. Now she lies still, and her body has been invaded everywhere by medical intervention. I feel like they have stolen her from me. I long for her to wake up. I can't even allow myself to wonder what step is next or what might happen if this new heart doesn't come back to life.

Most of our immediate family are here or on their way (Jan, my mother-in-law and Lucas' brother Matt arrived late this afternoon. Tomorrow night my little sister, Christelle, and my son Elijah will arrive. My little sister sacrificed coming straight away, in order to wait until Elijah was a little better to escort him down. I am so grateful. We feel our family's support and we wouldn't want to be here without them. I am sure Lucas desperately misses his dad at a time like this. My dad and brother will arrive in a couple of days. I feel like I really need my dad here. I rang him last night to tell him to forget getting our house in order, that I have people in place who have kindly offered to help me with that. I need him here. I feel so sad for Lucas who can't have that. Just having people we love to come back to when we walk out of her ICU room is so important.

We made a promise to Luka that we wouldn't leave her alone, and we are following through on that. Our family are taking turns (with us) to rotate in and out of her room, making sure we are there for her in case she can hear us. Sometimes I don't want to leave her side, but I also recall how much she loves our wider family, and think she would be uplifted knowing they are there for her too. It is hard to know where to touch her. She is covered in tubes and she looks so fragile. The nurses are amazing and they never leave her side. She has a minimum of two nurses at a time at the moment, and often there are more. They are constantly working on the machines and the many medications going into her, keeping things balanced and making sure things are working. It looks like such an exhausting job!

Journal Entry – Day 2 Post-Transplant (morning)

Sitting in a room surrounded by people, some we love, some we don't know.

Waiting.

Waiting.

Waiting.

I have never waited like this before. I don't feel irritated like I normally do when waiting. Just empty, nervous and still.

As I wait and chatter buzzes around me, I find my inner voice screaming, crying, and praying incessantly.

I pick up my phone and go to 'Notes' with the need to give this voice an outlet:

2:24pm

Make her well God, make her well, make her well, make her well. Make her well.

Heavenly Father may you cover her with your mighty protecting hand. May you shield her from anything untoward, may you embrace her mind, her heart, her body, her spirit with your pure love. May she have perseverance beyond measure. May this heart be made completely new and whole and strong. May it meld perfectly with her body.

Cover her with your angels. Cover her.

Shield and rampart, protector, strengthener, bring healing El Rapha.

Chapter 20

Full of Hope, Full of Faith

'He is able to do immeasurably more than ALL we ask or imagine, according to His power that is at work within us.' Ephesians 3:20 (NIV)

How could I possibly begin to put into words the journey we have been on? So many days I have flashbacks and am taken back to a time of the rawest emotional roller coaster I have ever been on. The shocks, the trauma, the sadness, the deep pain in my heart, the joys, the miracles, the sense that I touched heaven as I watched and waited for my daughter to arise from her death bed. I have found out over these last nearly 8 months that words just can't seem to convey the journey.

Memories are deeply embedded, but they mostly come in pictures, not words. Over the journey of Luka-Angel's heart transplant I experienced trauma and pain that I didn't know were possible. I also experienced joy, peace and strength that I never knew were possible. I had faith that I never knew I was capable of. I had *hope* instilled fast, deep and strong within my very soul that I believe God gave to me and I am so grateful. I felt heaven like I never have, and God's presence was in the room. I could almost see his very hands, holding onto Luka-Angel's new heart, shaping it, molding it, healing it and making it her own. I felt the support of family, friends and strangers like I have never known it. This was a new space in life that I have never been in before.

On the day after Luka-Angel's heart transplant, my sister gave me a journal to write in over this time. The front of it says 'Embrace the Journey'. As she gave it to me, she apologised and offered to buy me a new one. She feared the words on the front of the journal were insensitive at such a significant time and particularly since things had gone so badly. As Karen handed it to me she said, "I'm so sorry. I thought it said 'The Journey', there was a sticker over the front of the book and I didn't realise that under the sticker it said, Embrace the Journey." I said it was fine and thanked her. Little did I know that 'Embrace the Journey' would be a message that would embed itself within my spirit.

Journal Excerpts – Day 2 Post-Transplant – Night time

Yesterday was so, so tough. Tonight however, with the encouragement of the Holy Spirit, the very real and joy-bringing presence of Jesus – I will embrace the journey. I will embrace the journey to my daughter's healing. My daughter's great testimony of what Jesus has done for her. I will embrace the journey of learning to trust. I will embrace this journey of experiencing peace like I have never understood it. I will embrace the journey of seeing people all around the world unite in prayer for our girl.

Thousands of people have acknowledged they are praying for Luka-Angel through our church website! I will embrace the journey to my daughter's fully restored health. I will embrace the journey of an ever-deepening faith and heavy reliance on my God who flung stars into space, who carries me in his hand.

I will embrace the journey of keeping hope alive and thriving! I will embrace the journey of becoming stronger and braver.

> Psalm 46:1-2 'God is my refuge and strength. An ever present help in times of trouble. Therefore I will not fear, though the earth gives way and the mountains fall into the heart of the sea.'

HE IS HERE:

My shield and rampart

My fortress, my strong tower

My refuge and strength

My ever-loving Daddy

My Saviour

My Redeemer

My healer

Our healer

The great physician

My comfort

My stronghold

My foundation

My peace

My strength

El Roi, the God who sees.

> 'Through it all, through it all my eyes are on you.
>
> Through it all, through it all it is well.
>
> Through it all, through it all, my eyes are on you
>
> And it is well, with me.
>
> So let go, my soul and trust in Him.
>
> The waves and wind still know His name.
>
> It is well with my soul, It is well with my soul.
>
> It is well, it is well with my soul.
>
> FAR BE IT FROM ME TO NOT BELIEVE –
>
> EVEN WHEN MY EYES CAN'T SEE.
>
> AND THIS MOUNTAIN THAT'S IN FRONT OF ME,
>
> WILL BE THROWN INTO THE MIDST OF THE SEA'. (Bethel song: 'It Is Well')

In Jesus Name!

> 'He is able to do immeasurably more than ALL we ask or imagine, according to His power that is at work within us.' Ephesians 3:20 (NIV)

Angela Flemming Cairns

The Lord is with us…

Lord of our lives

Lord of light

Lord of love

Lord over creation

Lord of the heavens

Lord of the earth

Lord over sickness

He is the PRINCE OF PEACE!

(I believe God just whispered to me, 'You have every reason to HOPE!')

Chapter 21

Moments of Joy in the Storm

'He will yet fill your mouth with laughter and your lips with shouting.' Job 8:21 (ESV)

Day 2 – Post-Transplant (late at night)

Karen and I had put ourselves on the shift of staying with Luka-Angel overnight. I had spotted two beanbags in the hallway at the end of ICU which happened to be just outside Luka-Angel's room. Naively thinking they were there for the parents, I informed Karen that when it got too hard to sit up beside Luka, we will just go and sleep in the beanbags outside her door. We rugged up for the long haul, knowing it would be an uncomfortable night, but also knowing there was no way I was leaving my little girl's side.

The nurse asked us around 11:30pm, "Are you two planning on staying here for the night?"

"Yes," I said naively, "and when we get too tired, we'll just take turns sleeping in the beanbags out there," I said pointing to the end of the hallway.

She appeared shocked and both nurses stopped what they were doing and looked up at us.

"Sorry, where?" One of the nurses queried, confused.

"In the beanbags, just out there." I said pointing out the door of Luka-Angel's room thinking it was a normal thing and that the beanbags must be there for parents. Lucas and I had spent parts of our day in them, and no one had told us to get up.

"Oh no, you can't do that. Sorry," said the nurse matter-of-factly, "you are not allowed to sleep out there. The beanbags are there for the patients who are starting to recover."

It came as a bit of a shock and we were quite surprised, but also felt quite silly for assuming this was something we could do. I guess being a children's ICU and having many rooms leading onto that same hallway, it all made sense that some random adults couldn't just sleep in the hallway for the night.

As Karen's head began to nod off about half an hour later she whispered to me, "Oh, those beanbags look so nice and comfy." Glancing outside the room she followed it with, "I wish I could just turn into a ball of fluff and roll down the hallway and land in one."

I looked at her realising the delirium lack of sleep can bring. Many nights we had known this delirium in worlds that seemed so long ago, so far away. At camps as teenagers, sleepovers where we stayed up all night - even in our roles as Salvation Army Youth and Children's Coordinators we had known this intentional sleep deprivation. We also knew that it can bring all kinds of weird and wonderful comments, or sometimes late night dares being carried out. This always unfolded into hysteria. Usually I was the one who couldn't stop laughing. Karen seemed at times to have a little more self-control. It seemed the most unlikely setting, but it suddenly hit us hard.

I turned to her and responded, "Yeah, a ball of fluff. Me too, I wish I could turn into a ball of fluff and land on a beanbag too," with that, we were gone. Quiet hysteria unfolded. Tears rolled down my cheeks. We tried so hard to stifle our giggling, it just seemed so inappropriate and how the heck were we going to explain to the nurses who were just across from us why we were in stitches! It just wasn't even that funny, but somehow in the moment it released a whole lot of pent up emotion.

We decided Karen had better leave the room, otherwise I could feel I was going to keep laughing and it just felt so ridiculous and somewhat embarrassing! My heart was broken into a thousand pieces, and yet I could laugh. The thought crossed my mind that Luka-Angel would find us funny, but probably also rouse on us a little. My giggling often embarrassed her. She had quite the knack of pulling a funny face behind a doctor, or whispering something funny in my ear. She would often silently laugh when their back was turned, but then manage to pull it together just before she would get caught. I, however, often had trouble pulling it together, once I had started. She would take the role of adult and tell me to stop laughing, but would often do things to make me keep going. I knew if she could see us now, she would be doing the same thing.

Karen whispered to me that she would sleep in the parent's room just outside of ICU, and when I found it too hard to keep sitting on the hard chairs of ICU, I could text her, and we could swap. I was so grateful for my big sister. She had been there for me so often from the time I was born. She was my second mother, my best friend, my confidante and I could always be very real with her. Here she was journeying something so significant, by my side and even managing to help me laugh.

It was around 1:15am when the head ICU doctor just came to check on Luka-Angel. She took one look at me and started to lecture me. "Are you going to get some sleep tonight? You need to look after yourself."

"No," I said firmly, "I am staying here." The seat was so uncomfortable. I had noticed that in the ICU room with so much going on, there was no possibility of a pull out lounge or bed for me. Sitting upright for hours was getting so painful, but I went on, "I am not leaving her side."

The compassionate doctor tried to convince me for some time that I need to look after myself and get some sleep and nutrition. I affirmed again, "I am not leaving her. I am very determined!"

She gave me a little smile at the tenacity I showed, shook her head and gave me gentle eyes. Then without knowing anything about me, she spoke my language, "This is a marathon, not a sprint. She still has a long way to go. You will need your energy. You will need rest."

It floored me. It was as though she had known that I was a passionate runner. My eyes were so heavy but my spirit was strong, and I was a mum who wanted to keep my promise to my daughter. The thought of walking back across the road to Ronald McDonald House was too full on. I needed to be at least a few steps away from her. There was no way I was going to desert her.

After the doctor left the room, I apologised to the nurses and told them I am sorry if I was in their way. I said that I had told Luka we would stay by her side, and if they really needed me to leave I would.

One nurse kindly turned to me and said, "No darling, you are not in our way at all. I have a twelve-year-old girl. I just can't imagine this. You are welcome to stay; the doctor is just concerned for you. This will definitely be a long road."

At 1:25am, I looked up from the book I had been reading and was blown away by what I saw. The nurses had not stopped working or fussing over Luka-Angel – they were constantly walking around, measuring things, putting medicine in tubes. The nurse who spoke with me had taken a moment, moved into an awkward position and had carefully lifted Luka-Angel's head. She was braiding my little girl's hair, ever so gently and tenderly, picking up one strand after another.

Tears filled my eyes and all I could do was whisper, "Thank you."

"Their hair gets quite messy and knotty when they lay on it all day," she said kindly.

Within an hour of that, I got up and went to the parent's room just around the corner, and was greeted with a flustered sister. "Quick!!" she said flinging her hand in a signal. "Come in quickly before he sees us. Don't talk!!" She put her hand up to my mouth as I tried to ask her who we were hiding from.

She went on in whispers to explain to me that the security guard had caught her lying on the lounge in the parent's room (where she was waiting to tag team with me in ICU, and determined to stay the night to support me all the way through). The security guard had insisted she was not allowed to stay in there for the night. It was supposed to be locked at 10:30pm and no one was allowed in there. It was a safety issue. She had simply put on her charm and begged him to let her stay there, explaining some of our situation.

"I could lose my job," he had explained, then relenting compassionately, "oh, okay. You can stay, but I am turning a blind eye and you *must* not let anyone in this door. I will lock you in, and you can't leave or let anyone else in."

Suddenly we heard footsteps and I dove behind the lounge, with the two of us giggling stupidly. It was nice to have a moment of crazy with my sister yet again, even in amongst this mess.

Chapter 22

The First Big Miracle

'I will remove from you your heart of stone, and give you a heart of flesh...' Ezekiel 36:26 (Amp)

It was the third day after our daughter's heart transplant. My 'rest' on the single lounge of the parent's room was hardly 'sleep'. I hadn't slept for days and was exhausted. It was 6am when I ducked back over to Ronald McDonald House and took a quick shower. It was just too hard to be away from Luka-Angel. The water of the shower felt so refreshing and soothing, I hoped that somehow it could wash away the reality I was currently facing. These last few days felt like months. I hadn't eaten since Saturday night and I hadn't been drinking enough water. It was as though I forgot that my body needed certain things. My focus was completely on my Luka-Angel. I just needed to see her turn a corner. I needed to see that things were going to get better. I hoped for it and believed she was strong enough to beat this. But somewhere deep inside I knew this was not her heart that wasn't working. I knew her body was strong enough but I just couldn't know if the new heart was strong enough to keep fighting. Nothing had changed since Sunday and she was still only surviving because she was hooked up to the heart/lung machine. Her breaths were being generated, her pulse was being generated, and her blood flow was false. I wondered if she was aware of any of it. The heart/lung machine had its own risks. I wondered if she was visiting heaven. We had so many people from all over the place (including strangers) message us and talk about seeing Luka bathed in light, and surrounded by light. There were also many messages about her being 'prepared for her future' or God's hands holding her heart. The consistency of all of these messages was so encouraging and helped spur me on with the hope I already had. It was hard though, and words cannot even begin to describe the depths of trauma this was for us.

After my shower, I put my lighthouse jewellery on (every day Luka was in hospital I wore jewellery she had made to raise funds for her future dream). It made me feel closer to her, and reminded me she still had a great purpose to fulfill on this earth. I went into ICU where Lucas and Jan were on their early morning shift. They were present for an Echo the medical team did on Luka, and it was explained that there was a large shadow across her heart. Possibly a clot but they weren't sure what it was. Some more doctors were coming to have a look. I could see that this was something to be very concerned about.

We were asked to leave the room, and I sat down outside the room in ICU and looked out of the wall size windows to a beautiful view over parklands. I could see the vastness of the pale blue sky, and the tall trees that provided a beautiful foreground. I started again to pray and worship God and beg him again for healing for Luka. I knew that he could see exactly what the problem was. I decided I wanted to read some messages that I had been sent, and for the first time scrolled through a few (our family had read us a few, but I hadn't yet looked myself). I was absolutely blown away by the amount of messages I had received on my Facebook page. I came across a link to a YouTube clip of a song sent to me by a good friend. I started to watch the song, and then Lucas came back from briefly seeing our family in the parent's room and sat down beside me deflated. We had no words to exchange, it was impossible to know what to even talk about.

All of a sudden when the song I was watching on YouTube finished, another song I had never heard before came straight on. It was by a completely different artist. Its words were nothing like the song I had just been watching, it was just a random song that came on by itself. I knew straight away it was both a gift and a message from above. Every word spoke directly into our situation, and I began to weep. I said to Lucas, "You have to listen to this song. It just came on by itself! It is for us. She will be okay Lucas, it's another sign."

> '...you're shattered, like you've never been before. The life you knew in a thousand pieces on the floor...Tell your heart to beat again, close your eyes and breathe it in. Let the shadows fall away, step into the light of grace. Yesterday's a closing door, you don't live there anymore. Say goodbye to where you've been, and tell your heart to beat again...Love's healing hands have pulled you through... Your story's far from over, and your journey's just begun.' ('Tell Your Heart to Beat Again' by Danny Gokey).

This was to be a new season. Oh how my heart grieved for her old heart. That made no sense to me, but it just was. I missed her old heart. I was saddened that she now had a different heart inside of her. We were saying 'goodbye' to yesterday, to days where she couldn't run or do sport, saying goodbye to the heart she had been born with, and now in this new season she would live with a new energy and safety, but she would also live with no immune system. There were shadows they had just discovered over the heart just minutes before, and here this song was speaking out, *"Let the shadows fall away, step into the light of grace."*

Unbelievable!

Through that moment in time, of hearing such a poignant song, a new strength surged within me. We had to once again leave our little girl as life-saving surgery came to her. We were told this surgery, that was expected to take about four hours, was exploratory and they were hoping to discover what the shadow was. They thought it could be a clot, I wondered ever so briefly, if it was the shadow of God's hands. We were told she would still be on life support for a few days and her chest would remain open.

Back at Ronald McDonald House, as some of the family got much needed sleep, I lay face down on my mattress on the floor and began to plead. I knew by all the messages I was seeing, that many people along with me, were praying from a distance for a miracle for Luka. I saw myself at the throne of God in heaven pleading with him, "Make her heart beat God, make her well. Make her well. Fix it. Fix this heart God." I prayed like I have never prayed before. I could not stop. I began to thank God for all the things I could thank him for, his great love, his saving power, a great country, a hospital that was amazing, doctors who could help us, and I began to feel his presence and his peace so vividly my hands shook! I felt him speak to me. He told me she would be okay. He told me she would tell her story.

I knew without a doubt that she WOULD live to tell her own great story!

I believed people would believe in God because of the miracles he was going to give her. I knew that people's faith would be grown through this, and I kept thinking, 'We just need to endure this. At least she is asleep and at peace, this is for us to endure right now. When she wakes up, she will have much to go through but right now, she is at peace.' I believed completely that God was molding that heart to fit Luka-Angel's body and making it her own.

I felt driven to share some of our journey on my Facebook page. It was so unlike me to do so, but all I could think was that if this isn't to help and grow other people in their faith, it is for nothing! I also desperately wanted as many people as possible to pray. So I put up some posts. One of them said in amongst other things, 'I believe', 'I choose hope.' 'Will you hope and believe with me?' To see some friends and strangers start to respond with, 'I choose hope' or '#prayingforluka,' gave me great strength.

I woke Lucas up and said to him with great excitement having experienced the power and presence of God, "Lucas, she is going to be okay! I believe God has told me that she will tell her story. She can't tell her story if she doesn't make it. I believe God is going to do a miracle!"

"When?!!!" Lucas responded with skepticism, and was naturally distraught.

"I don't know. But I know he will, I really do. He told me. We just have to endure this and be patient. There's a miracle coming..."

Just as I finished my sentence the phone rang, Lucas answered - my journal records this within the very same sixty seconds I had spoken with Lucas about my new found hope.

The surgeon told Lucas that Luka-Angel's surgery went really well. They found a large clot in her heart that they believed had developed over the last couple of days whilst she was on ECMO. They removed it. They went on to tell him that during the operation, out of the blue, the heart muscle had begun to function! Although she still needed temporary pace makers and they couldn't yet close her chest, things were looking so much better, so they had taken her off ECMO. We had not long been told she would still be on ECMO for a few more days. This truly was a miracle! I pictured God's hands pumping that new heart during this operation, and getting it started again. It felt to me at the time, almost as if this heart had been grieving for its original person, but now was ready to be the vessel to give my little girl new life.

I ran into the lounge room where Lucas' brother and Mum were. I jumped up and down crying and laughing and saying, "We have our first miracle! We have our miracle!"

We made our way back to the hospital immediately.

After briefly meeting a staff member from our kid's school who had come out of his way to give us a very special gift and card from the staff at Luka-Angel's school, I literally ran across the bottom floor of the hospital to where my mum and sister, Karen, were. I was jumping up and down with excitement saying, "We have our miracle! I want to dance!! I am so happy! God told me he would heal her! We have our miracle!"

My mum said, "If you want to dance, dance!" So I spun in several circles, my arms in the air and danced a joyful dance. I didn't even realise anyone else was around me. To me, my little girl had been given a miracle. God had heard the prayers of the thousands and I was rejoicing!

We received another call that they were going to get rid of some of her sedation, and start to wake her up. I was shocked! I just couldn't wait! I couldn't wait to see her again! They were going to try and get her to eat this afternoon. It seemed that all of this turn around had happened so suddenly. It was so hard to take in, but my heart was leaping for joy! I decided to eat again, and Mum rushed to the closest café asking them for raisin toast (my favourite breakfast). I remember hearing her gush, "She wants raisin toast. Her daughter just had a miracle. She needs raisin toast!" The guy apologised that they don't do raisin toast in the afternoons (no doubt confused by the demands and the excitement). I came behind Mum smiling broadly and said, "It's okay Mum, forget the raisin toast. I'll just have a pink donut!" It was my afternoon breakfast after days of fasting. The fast was broken.

I got into the lift with Lucas and found myself beaming. The lift was completely full and I just couldn't help myself so almost shouting to those around me, I said, "We have a miracle! My little girl got a miracle!!!"

Later, on other days when I caught that same lift, I occasionally reflected on that moment in time, and thought how strange it must have been. How odd I must have seemed. I was truly filled with an uncontainable joy! The kind of joy that one cannot keep in, the kind of joy that needs to be shouted from the rooftops! My little girl was back! My little girl would live! Hope had become a reality! One woman in the lift that day grabbed my hand as she got off on floor two and with tears rushing to her eyes, she said, "That's so wonderful darling. I wish I could stay and hear all about it…just wonderful!!"

I felt impatient as Luka began to wake up. I wanted to hear all about her journey, all about the things I imagined she may have seen or experienced. I had to be patient. I had to choose to suppress my questions, and just allow her to get better.

Although still seriously ill, the first request she had later that afternoon besides, "Ice," was a whispered, "chocolate milkshake". Every word she said felt like her first word. Every little thing she said meant she was with us, she was okay.

My mum was always one to want to give her grandchildren yummy and generous morning and afternoon teas when we visited. Hospitality is one of her gifts. So at Luka's first request, we decided to call my mum, who was waiting in the parent's room, to have the privilege of buying Luka what she had asked for. Mum had rushed straight out and bought two chocolate milkshakes. One just didn't seem enough that day!! I'll never forget the over-excited expression on Mum's face as she came to the glass door of Luka's ICU room. She held those two chocolate milkshakes up in the air like they were a trophy, her face beaming with the broadest smile! It didn't even matter that day that most of the two milkshakes went to waste, all that Luka-Angel could manage after days of not eating or drinking, were two sips.

Chapter 23

You Make Me Brave

'He will bring me safely back from the battles that I fight.' Psalm 55:18 (GNT)

Journal Excerpts & recounts - Day 5 & 6 Post-Transplant

Day 5 - morning

'Bless the Lord Oh my soul

Oh my soul, Worship His holy name

Sing like never before, Oh my soul

I'll worship your holy name…

Whatever may pass and whatever lies before me

Let me be singing when the evening comes.' (10,000 Reasons by Matt Redman)

Angela Flemming Cairns

Day 5 - 2:33pm

She has turned a corner...

The song for the day is "You Make Me Brave" (by Bethel Music).

I listened to it this morning and then put it on Facebook today as a sign of the journey we are on.

The ventilator is finally out!! Hallelujah! Thank you Jesus!!

She has wanted that thing out ALL DAY today, putting her hand up and whimpering, trying to pull at it but not having the strength.

We are supposed to try and wake her up a bit (they have taken her off a lot of sedation). She is finding it hard to come around. I have asked Luka if she wants to listen to music, she said "yes," and whispered, "Brave".

I called Elijah who was elsewhere in the hospital, and I put him on speaker (her eyes sprung open when she heard her big brother's voice). I asked him what song she sang with her friend Jasmyn at school at a recent assembly so I could play it to Luka (I had thought that was the 'Brave' Luka meant). "Brave, by Sara Bareilles...," he said. Then quoting some lyrics, "Say what you wanna say..." Luka, who until this point, had hardly uttered more than a word, whispered with a furrowed brow, "no... You Make Me Brave, You make me Brave".

"You don't want Brave? You want You Make Me Brave?" I had asked. She mustered strength to slowly nod her head.

So I put on 'You Make Me Brave' by Bethel music, and held it up to Luka's ear as she closed her eyes and fell back asleep, while the lyrics played,

> *'You make me brave, you make me brave. You call me out beyond the shore into the waves. You make me brave,*

you make me brave, no fear can hinder now the love that
made a way' ('You Make Me Brave' by Bethel Music).

2:40pm

Echo showed her heart function looks better than yesterday – this new heart is getting a little stronger every day.

Day 5 – Night time

Well, my God told me yesterday morning, "Wait patiently for the Lord. He has already won the victory!" I absolutely believe that Tuesday was an incredible spiritual battle. God the King won in that theatre room, as the heart muscle function suddenly came to life for the first time, and Luka came off ECMO. Now we trust him who won, he who holds her heart and as the psalm says, 'He will bring me back safely from the battles that I fight'. Luka's progress today has been phenomenal.

She is no longer intubated, no nasal feeding tube (as she quietly demanded through signals and the occasional whisper to the nurse that if they would take it out, she would do her best to eat). She has been sponged bathed and is relaxed, calm, and at peace.

I am so, so proud of her.

Rest sweetly my sweet girl with two cute braids! Rest and know His love, and His hand that holds you.

Christelle and Matt left tonight to go back to their families. Karen left tonight as she is doing my cousin, Natania's wedding. I remember as a young teenager, visiting baby Natania after her big, open heart surgery. Now she is getting married. Lucas and I had been working on a song to sing her down the aisle. The wedding is this weekend so we can no longer make it. I have insisted to my mum that she should go to the wedding as all of her siblings gather together. So Dad, Mum and Mike leave tomorrow. God has given me such hope. I just know Luka-Angel will be okay.

Having our family has been incredibly special.

Thank you Lord for family!

7pmish (Recount & Journal Excerpts)

Tam comes out of Luka's ICU room as I tag in, and tells me Luka has said some 'funny things' and that I should ask the nurse about them. Tam tells me her and 'Nurse S' have had lots of good conversations. Tam tells me she's been telling 'S' all about Luka. As Tam leaves and I go into the closed doors of Luka-Angel's isolation room in ICU, apron and gloves on, 'Nurse S' tells me how wonderful my family is. She tells me she's had a good conversation with my sister-in-law. Then she goes on to smile and say, "Your sister-in-law tells me that I should tell you some funny things Luka said...," then she hesitates. "But I don't want to cross a line, I don't want to offend you in any way." "No, that's okay", I reassured her, "tell me, I'd love to know."

"Well," 'Nurse S' says with a smile, "She asked me if I was the right nurse. So I told her that I am on the roster, and I am supposed to be here so I must be the right nurse." Then she said to me, "As long as you're not trying to kill me".

11pmish

We were kicked out of the ICU room, told we could not stay as they needed to do emergency heart surgery on the little baby across from Luka's room there in ICU. As I left, my mum consoled me and told me that at least with no choice from staff but to leave, it would be a good opportunity for me to finally get a night's sleep.

11:20pm

My body is so very tired and exhausted. It's hard to walk. I cannot think of eating, but occasionally make myself eat a mouthful or two just to get my body by. It's even hard to remember to drink water. I have hardly showered over these last few days, so the hot water running over my body tonight felt like a luxury I remembered from a long time ago. Lots of tears shed in the shower tonight. I am so weary. Some moments I feel like I am floating and this isn't real. I haven't thought about anything but Luka-Angel for days and anything that used to enter my mind seems long gone. Everything is about Luka getting well. My thoughts are all in these moments. Our family being here gives us a sense of safety. I feel no inhibitions, I am just in every moment, every raw emotion I feel, displayed. I find myself desiring to tell any nurse who will listen how amazing my Luka-Angel is; how strong, how brave, how loving, and how kind. I find myself talking about her to them quite often – desperate for them to know who she is, so they will fight for her life. So many of them have told me how amazing she sounds and how they can't wait to meet her. I know that her life has impacted so many lives already.

Chapter 24

Mighty To Save

'The Lord your God is with you, he is mighty to save...'
Zephaniah 3:17 (NIV)

Journal Entries - Day 5

11:30pm

I went into our shared room with no floor space where Elijah and Jazz were already asleep, (Lucas was in the shower) and Jan (my Mum in law) was sitting on her bed about to climb in. She patted the bed beside her, beckoning me to come and sit down and pulled out her Bible. "God gave me a verse earlier today Angela. I felt it was the perfect one for you today." She said she wanted to share it with me. As she flicked the pages of the Bible telling me she couldn't remember where it was, but she would find it and it was something about "God being with you, and being mighty to save." I exclaimed, "Zephaniah 3:17! I love that verse, but you turn to it and read it to me in case you read a slightly different version to what I know." She turned to Zephaniah 3:17. This was a verse I had recently put up on my fridge at home.

Jan read, "The Lord your God is with you, He is mighty to save. He will take great delight in you and will rejoice over you with singing." Zephaniah 3:17

11:43pm

Going to bed on Psalm 92 'Singing praises for the work God's hands have done!'

Just Before Midnight

I was just dozing off on my trundle on the floor of our Ronald McDonald House room when Lucas climbing into his bed says, "Ange, are you still awake?"

"Yes…just…" I mumbled.

"Do you want me to read you the 'verse for the day' (from his phone app)?"

"Yes." I said.

"The Lord your God is with you," Lucas read as my mind awakened, "he is mighty to save…"

Sitting up fast I exclaimed, "Did you hear your mum before?" (knowing full well he had been in the shower a couple of walls away).

"No?" He said questioningly.

"She read me that verse just before she went to sleep!" I said excitedly, knowing it was no coincidence. Little did I know at that point in time, how important that verse would become over the next few hours!

Journal Excerpts & Recount – Day 6 (My grandma & Lucas' aunty's birthday)

2:11am

I was suddenly and sharply awakened by my mobile phone ringing on the pillow I was sleeping on. Scrambling I grabbed it, "Hello, this is Angela speaking" I muttered sleepily.

"This is 'Dr T' the head doctor from ICU. Luka-Angel's external pacemakers just failed." She said in her heavy accent as I sat bolt upright, now fully alert and my heart racing, "We have just finished doing CPR, she is critical and we are stabilising her".

"Can we come up straight away?" I interrupted, expecting to hear that we wouldn't be allowed to.

"Yes, of course. That would be a good idea," said 'Dr T'.

Jan had already flicked the lamp on and Lucas was sitting up looking at me as I said in a panic, "Quick get dressed!"

Together in the small lounge room we talked as we got dressed and I looked at my husband and for a second thought he looked quite pale and sick (no doubt from his tachycardia) and said, "Do I have permission to run?! Can I go ahead?!"

"Yes!" He emphasized, no longer caring that I would be going out and across the parklands by myself at 2:20 in the morning, "Run!!"

I called my mum's phone as I ran and she didn't answer.

Onto my big sister's phone, "Karen," I panted down the phone, "Call Mum and Dad, tell Mum to come to the hospital! Luka has just been resuscitated. I won't talk now, I'll talk later."

Feeling all of the adrenalin coursing through my veins, I wondered who I could get to pray. My instinct told me to call many to action, my head told me just to wait on some more information, and my heart told me, "Text Pearl". Pearl (a girl from my youth ministry in Tweed who I had mentored years before), was not someone I had contacted on this whole journey. It felt strange to me to text Pearl now, but it just seemed right, and her name wouldn't leave my mind, so I did. I slowed my run to a fast walk long enough to text:

(Day 6 - 2:30am)

Confidential: highly!

Emergency right now.

Please pray Pearl.

Pearl's response just minutes later: "I am praying right now"

Thank you.

Very scared.

Very, very scared. By myself

Waiting for Lucas.

Pearl: 'God is with you Ange and with Luka. Is Lucas far away? Call me if you need. I am praying. Awake and praying with you.'

I arrived at the security guard's office around the corner from emergency and told him my daughter had just been resuscitated and I needed to be taken to ICU. I told him my husband was coming but might be ten more minutes. He said he would take me up straight away, and then bring Lucas up when he arrived.

As we walked what seemed like the longest hallway ever, and got into the lift, he said to me with a caring glance, "How old is your daughter?"

"Just thirteen years old," I said with glassy eyes and a trembling lip. He continued to walk me down the long corridor, expressing concern and saying he hoped that everything would go well. "Thousands of people are praying for her," I said with confidence, "she'll be okay, she'll just have a big story to tell".

On arriving at ICU the nurse said I couldn't see Luka yet as they were still sorting her out, but could I wait in the meeting room. She explained that the doctor would come and speak with me shortly. "Is she alive?" I asked, fear pulsing through my veins. Her brief response was, "She is critical, but they are stabilising her now."

"Don't call the doctor to speak with me yet," I said. "My husband has a heart condition and is still walking here, he can't run. I ran here. Can we please wait for him?"

The nurse escorted me into a cold room with a few soft chairs. I had only sat in a room similar to this on the other side of ICU when the doctors met with us post-transplant and told us things had gone poorly. I wasn't a big fan of sitting in these rooms. They seemed only for bad or complicated news. As I sat completely alone in the meeting room, at first I felt completely alone. It was then I received Pearl's text straight back, "Awake and praying with you." I no longer felt alone. I felt peace descend, and it was as though I sensed Pearl kneeling on the floor beside where I sat, taking my hand.

My mind flashed back to a time when I mentored a young teenage Pearl. She was so quiet. I saw the stage at the church at Tweed Heads Salvation Army and the first time I saw her speak on the stage at youth church. Those kids meant the world to me! That particular night at youth church, I had asked a few of the girls to share their favourite Bible verses. With confidence and authority this quiet teenage girl who hardly spoke (and especially not on a stage) said from memory, "Zephaniah 3:17, 'The Lord your God is with you, He is mighty to save, he will take great delight in you and rejoice over you with singing". My heart swelled with pride! I was shocked! I could see her faith in that moment, and knew God was working in her life. I reflected on that verse – the first Bible verse I had ever heard come out of Pearl's mouth and thought how God must have led me to text her tonight over everyone else in my life. Because it suddenly dawned on me as I sat alone in that room, that in my mind, in a quick 'flashback' memory, I saw her saying the very verse God had already given to me twice in the last two and a half hours. This verse had become so real to me, right when we needed someone who was mighty to save! At the same time I trembled. I could hardly believe that both of Luka's external pace makers had failed. No one knew why. I couldn't believe that for a moment her heart had stopped beating. I wondered what was next.

I withheld the notion within me to panic, and instead chose trust. I chose to open myself up to God's great peace. I breathed deeply as I prayed, and I saw Luka telling her story to many people and I saw this story being even more amazing now that Luka had 'come back to life'. Just like Jairus' little girl in the book of Luke (I had tried to memorise this story just eighteen months ago, reading it over and over until it was firmly in my mind). Jairus' daughter was twelve years old. At the time this story got into my heart, Luka-Angel was twelve years old and I wanted to hear from Jesus what Jairus had heard, "Don't be afraid, just have faith and she will be healed" (Luke 8:50). I wanted to see what Jairus saw – when all hope was lost and someone said, "Don't bother the teacher anymore; your daughter (once very ill) is now dead." (Luke 8:49) And yet, Jairus chose to trust, and follow Jesus who walked into the room of his dead twelve-year-old girl and stared death in the face and told it to be no more! Jesus had said, "Little girl, get up!" (Luke 8:54) and that is exactly what she did! Here I was in the midst of my own story, which was not so dissimilar. She had been brought back to life and I could hardly get my head around it. It had seemed that she was turning a big corner today, and now she was back on life support, her life once again, hanging in the balance.

I sent out another text to a few more people:

"Praying people, highly confidential – no social media please. This is a call to action.

We have had an emergency. Please pray. Luka's temporary pace makers failed tonight. She needed compressions. She needs emergency surgery. The surgeons were here until midnight for someone else, so they have her in a kind of 'safe zone', she will be first off the rank in daylight for emergency surgery. They will need to put in a permanent pace maker. Pray, pray and fight this with us. God has a big calling on her life."

Back at our little room at Ronald McDonald House, Lucas' mum was sitting in our lounge room in the early hours of the morning with Elijah and Jazziah, desperately praying for Luka-Angel. She noticed a little devotional book that someone had given us to give to Luka when she woke up. Praying, Jan opened it randomly and it fell straight on the page that was titled 'Lord, Guard My Heart'. The devotional was never meant to be taken literally, but the words in that little book on that particular page could have been written for Luka's literal heart at that time. Jan began to pray these words over her granddaughter, "Lord, guard Luka's heart". It seemed to have been given to her, at the perfect time.

Jan also wrote in her diary about a moment that she witnessed earlier while Luka was in ICU. She had been praying for healing for Luka. All of a sudden a gentle wind entered the room where Luka lay. Jan saw the wind come down from the top of the room, across Luka's hair, and down her bed across her body. Then it was gone. It was so real, Jan looked up to see if the window was open, and realised suddenly that the window did not open in that room. It was a permanent glass fixture in the wall. It seemed that the wind of God's presence, had revealed itself in that moment. In her journal Jan wrote:

> *Hebrews 1:7* (NCV) *'God makes his angels become like winds'!! You sent an angel – thank you Jesus!*

During that morning we know of several people who were woken up within minutes of resuscitation time and prompted to pray for Luka (knowing nothing about the emergency). One such lady was someone from the church we used to be part of in Tweed Heads. She had woken up with such a strong impression that she had to pray for Luka right now, so she prayed for hours. She rang my mum as soon as it was a reasonable hour and asked her, "What has happened to Luka? How is she? God woke me up at 1:20am to pray for her." Mum was able to share with her what had happened.

Another lady had a dream of a person who had a heart transplant, was on life support and the heart wasn't working. She believed the dream was God-given and began praying for this person to be healed. From the other side of the world, she wrote that dream to her friend in New Zealand and asked if she knew anyone who was in this situation. This lady's friend was a teacher, and that morning their staff had gathered to pray for this little girl called Luka who was in Australia.

My aunty, who is a head nurse at the hospital in Taree (nearly two days drive away from our hospital in Melbourne), had visited the hospital chapel to pray for Luka-Angel. As Aunty Janine sat praying for her great niece, she suddenly noticed that the Bible at the front of the chapel lay open. It wasn't uncommon for my aunty to visit this chapel on the hard days of her work, but the Bible was rarely open. Aunty Janine felt compelled, drawn to look at the pages. To her amazement the Bible had been opened on the story of Jesus raising a twelve-year-old girl back to life. Jairus' little girl. Aunty Janine had no idea how important that story was to me.

Letter to Luka

6am

Well Luka-Angel, I want to let you know it has been a rough night, but God is with you! The scripture verse just came to mind,

> 'God is within her
>
> She will not fall;
>
> God will help her at break of day.'
>
> Psalm 46:5 (NIV)

(I have been draped across you gently for hours, praying, quoting scripture, getting out of the way every time the nurses needed to check you – they have fussed over you all night long. I have played music, sung to you, prayed for you and clung to the patch of skin on your arm that is not covered in tubes).

I know <u>great</u> peace, comfort and HOPE! So much hope – because I know God is going to use you so much in the lives of others.

The doctors have done their best – but not by any fault of their own, it's just not enough – which means God will do the rest!

He holds your heart within his hands.

Tonight at 2:11am I was suddenly woken with a phone call from a doctor in ICU. Luka, sweet girl, your temporary pace makers had stopped working. Your heart stopped beating. 'Nurse S' was with you. You were no longer heavily sedated and you had pointed to your neck and indicated that your neck hurt. She had noticed your neck was swollen all around the line (tube in your neck), and had just finished calling the head ICU doctor and staff. While the staff were at your side looking at your neck and noticing the air under your skin, you had pain in your chest. While they were in the room, your temporary pacemakers suddenly stopped working...

...and your heart stopped beating!

They were in the right place – right over you – and began CPR within seconds of the flat line on your monitors. As the head ICU doctor was compressing your chest, she said you came to and you were looking at her as she did compressions. She asked you how you were feeling.

You said, "I am not afraid!"

After CPR, they sedated you, put the breathing device back in (tube down your throat), and put some temporary pacemakers back in place to keep your heart beating.

When the doctor called, I got dressed and ran all the way to the hospital (Daddy told me I could go ahead, because he could only walk over of course).

Security let me in and walked me up. I waited in a meeting room on a lounge by myself and texted just a few people an emergency message to pray for you.

I felt God's peace and presence.

The doctor told us sixteen people had run into your room in the emergency when your heart stopped beating. Sixteen people!!!!!!!!!!!!!!!! (One exclamation mark for each person).

As I write Luka, you sleep soundly, your colour looks good and Nurse S and another nurse work very hard beside you.

The doctor said you need emergency surgery to put a permanent pace maker in.

As the doctor talked to us, I held Nurse S's hand so tight I think I might have broken her fingers!!

I know you told us, "Not to be scared, and not to be sad," but Dad and I admittedly feel very frightened.

The surgeons were here until after midnight doing someone else's surgery in ICU, so they are sleeping for a few hours before they come and do your emergency surgery. The doctor told me it would be too dangerous for them to come in now with no sleep.

I was allowed to come to your bedside around 2:45am, and I played worship music to you (from my phone). I said Bible verses over and over and prayed out loud. I felt so much PEACE, like heaven was actually in the room where you and I were. (Dad waited downstairs with Grandma watching over him and praying for you. Grandma caught a taxi here at 3:30am!).

A song came up on YouTube by itself, straight after I had played another song. It came up as a simple amateur PowerPoint, and a verse came up on the screen right before the song played :

Zephaniah 3:17 'The Lord your God is with you – He is mighty to save'.

AMAZING!!!!!

4 times in 4 hours!!!!! God is here, and he is mighty to save!!

Grandma and I sit here now.

Nurses and doctors are continually checking on you. Two nurses don't leave your side.

You look so very sweet and beautiful – especially with those two braids outlining your pretty, pretty face.

So tonight my sweet, precious, amazing daughter – you were resuscitated at 1:40am!!!

Nurse S has told me all about it, as I have asked her.

You were able to squeeze her hand after CPR and answer some questions before they put you back to sleep. You were awake before your monitor flat lined, then you came around during compressions – you may remember the doctors and nurses all around you and the pressing on your chest.

I have no doubt my girl that God has the most incredible plans for you – even greater and more amazing than we originally realised! You are very special and I feel so privileged to be called your Mummy.

Xo xo xo

6:45am (Letter to Luka continued)

Taking a break from writing to drink the coffee this kind nurse called Rebecca just bought me from a café downstairs.

PS: Nurse S seemed amazed at the events that had taken place and said about the doctors around you just 'happening to be there,' when your heart stopped:

"There are just some things you can't explain. I am scientific, but I hear you, I hear your prayers, your verses and there are some things that just can't be explained. For some things we have no answer. The fact that the right people were in the room at the right time..." (Grandma told another nurse about the thousands of people who were praying. The nurse commented, "and that's the X-factor").

I have prayed over you so, so, so many times and read so many Bible verses and played beautiful worship music to you and sang to you. As I saw you through the rest of this morning I played some of our favourites...

'You Make Me Brave'

'Mighty to Save'

'Healer'

'Cornerstone'

'The Stand'

Chapter 25

Break Every Chain

'The Lord will fight for you, you need only to be still.'
Exodus 14:14 (NIV)

Letter to Luka (Excerpt)

Early this morning, when Dad and I had to say goodbye as you were about to be whisked off for emergency surgery, I held it together and smiled at you. Then I turned to the nurses and staff, trembling and with tears about to flow, I demanded, "Fight for her!"

As our family gradually arrived over the next hour or so and we pulled together, I said, "We need the thousands praying". I truly felt in my heart that this was again, a spiritual battle, that your life & destiny were at stake, and we needed to get as many people praying as we could. Our family (of about ten) gathered together in the foyer of the cardiac waiting area in a circle and we prayed unified, asking for healing and help from our Heavenly Father. Then we sent out our texts and social media calling for prayer. I remember the message that I got back from Terri from our church after she had looked at the church website:

> 'I want to encourage you, the thousands are praying!
> People are praying for you EVERYWHERE!!'

Having to retreat by ourselves as I needed a place to bawl my eyes out, I remember feeling the turning point in my heart. I had been stretched out on the floor in the privacy of the mother's breastfeeding room – laying down intentionally before God for the first time in my life. Seeing myself lay at his powerful throne, I begged and pleaded and prayed, "God you can do this – give us a miracle, come on God, come on!!! Break the chains, break the chains. Look after her, help us, help us; you say you care, so help us. Save her life God..." I had shouted and pleaded. Getting up from my sorry state, I remember being washed with peace and joy, and knowing things would be okay. I turned yet again to music and played the song: 'Tell your heart to beat again'. All of a sudden another song came on YouTube, all by itself: 'Break Every Chain' (by Jesus Culture). As I watched the clip and saw the lyrics, it was as though they had been written for this moment in time. I had never heard this song before. Once again I believed at just the right time, God gave me a song for this very moment in time! With it he spoke life, hope, and the fact that we weren't in this alone and told me there were more miracles to come. I had no doubt again my Luka-Angel, that he held you safely in his hands.

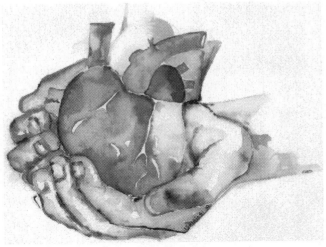

'Heart in His Hands' by Fred

The song lyrics said, "There's an army rising up." People were praying everywhere, our Salvation Army, our church, our family, our friends, God's people all over the world! I was receiving messages from people who had dreams and visions of you Luka (not even knowing your story), people writing their prayers, recording their prayer and sending it to me, people committing to pray.

'Break Every Chain' the lyrics of the song played repetitively...It felt as though there were chains over your heart. I saw your new heart in chains, and knew God was breaking the chains. He was releasing your heart to beat as it should.

In the video clip of this song, there was even an image of a glowing heart with God's hands around it - your heart. So many people had talked about God's hands being wrapped around your heart. People had seen it, I had felt it.

The lion even came across the screen. The lion Aunty Tam had seen, the Lion Deb had talked about, the Lion Aunty Karen had worn – representing our protective God.

Journal Excerpt - Day 6

Feels like the longest day ever...

The only thing I can reconcile is that God wants to use this to bring people to their knees and bring people closer to him and bring salvation.

I said to God 'If this is for people to see you are real, I can deal with this - with our hope coming through at the end. I can endure this Lord, I need my hope though (of Luka coming through this) – so I tried to get the message for prayer out. I turned only to scripture – reciting, reading and praying.

I turned to Hannah's Encouragement book she made for Luka-Angel's 13th birthday as I had many times over the last number of days. I came to page 28 and saw the word in large letters 'UNAFRAID'. I decided that this was Luka-Angel's page. She knew peace. She knew courage and bravery, and she was unafraid. I suddenly noted that the page Luka-Angel had told me I had to read while she slept was right opposite it. Page 27 read Isaiah 43:1-4. 'Do not fear for I have redeemed you. I have called you by name, you are mine. When you pass through the waters I will be with you; and when you pass through the rivers they will not sweep over you.'

Journal Entry – Day 7

When I am broken

My God sustains me

When I am hurting

My God sustains me

When I am helpless

My God sustains me

You Lord are my help

You Lord are my shield

You Lord are my refuge, my strength, my joy, my song.

Journal Entry – Day 8

'But the Lord stood with me and strengthened me...' 2 Timothy 4:17 (NASB)

Without you I could not have done this Lord.

Without you holding me up, I could not have stood.

Without you carrying me, I could not have walked around.

Without you giving me hope, I would have only felt despair.

Thank you.

Journal Entry - Day 8

Luka is awake! Her room is brighter; the tube is out of her mouth. She looks frail and has lost a lot of weight. She couldn't communicate through words today. Just with a whiteboard at times, and with great effort a little scrawl with her texta. Her eyes were very downcast. She looked very low.

Having waited so patiently for two days now of her being a little awake but unable to speak, I asked her what she remembered about when she slept.

Hannah's book was on the bed. Luka could hardly even move her hand she was so weak, but she ever so slowly moved her arm while I patiently waited to see what she was doing. Her hand travelled down to Hannah's book which I had put by her side on the bed. With just one finger stretched out and me holding the book she had indicated she wanted, with great effort, she slowly but carefully, flicked through each of the many pages. I didn't know what she was doing but I could tell she was being purposeful.

She flicked to page 28 and with that one finger stretched out, the intravenous line in her hand revealing some of her journey, she pointed markedly to the word on page 28 'UNAFRAID!'

I said to her, "That is you?"

She gently nodded, her eyes engaged and soft but without her usual twinkle.

Then I pointed to page 27, the one she had told me was for me to read 'while she was sleeping', and I said, "That page, was for me, the one you told me to read."

Again, with great effort a slow little nod.

AMAZING!!

I didn't know at that time that she wouldn't remember telling the head ICU doctor, as she was having compressions done following cardiac arrest, "I am not afraid". It would be words that will mark me for the rest of my life. Words straight from the Bible when people were in terrible situations, or when people saw angels, words I have very recently seen in a Disney movie, words I have never heard uttered out of my daughter's mouth but seen in her every move, and perseverance over this time. Words that some people I know have now made their own motto. Words that would lift our eyes to remember the one who makes her unafraid! Unafraid! I can be unafraid because he gives me peace that passes understanding, I can be unafraid because he holds me in his righteous right hand, I can be unafraid because he is with me and I am never alone, I can be unafraid because he will never forsake me. I can be unafraid and *'be strong and take courage,'* because the Lord my God is with me, wherever I go (Joshua 1:9). I can be unafraid because even when faced with death, and resuscitation, my little girl could lift her eyes to the one who holds her. I can be unafraid because my girl could look the head ICU doctor in the eyes, whilst that doctor was doing compressions on her chest to keep her alive, and confidently whisper, "I am not afraid!"

When Jesus called Peter out of the boat onto the water he said, "Do not be afraid." When Jairus knew his daughter was dying, Jesus said to him, "Don't be afraid". When Mary was met by the angel who was to tell this young innocent teenager of her out-of-wedlock pregnancy to the Most High God, the angel said, "Do not be afraid".

I have many mountains ahead of me.

I have two more transplants to go through of those nearest and dearest to me, unless we get a miracle. May it be my story too, that I can shout from the roof tops, because I am held by my Creator's hands, and sheltered underneath his wings, "I AM NOT AFRAID!"

Chapter 26

Somewhere Over the Rainbow

'On the day I called, you answered me; you made me bold with strength in my soul.' Psalm 138:3 (NASB)

I'll never forget how fragile my strong girl was as she started to come around. Up until then, she had been lying on her back, unable to move, unable to communicate. Oh, how I missed her smile so much in those days. Oh, how I longed to hear her voice, hear her laugh and hear her speak. I wondered how much she knew of this journey we had all been on while she slept. I wondered how shocked she would be when she found out that thousands of people had been praying for her. I wondered if she remembered anything after the moment I walked her into theatre for her transplant.

Here she was frail, weak, fragile, awake now, but unable to walk yet, or even feed herself.

When they told me on day eight in ICU that today would be the day the physiotherapist would come and see her and get her to sit in a chair, I thought it would be a breeze. No one had explained to me how long or slow recovery is after six emergency operations and being asleep in ICU for so many days. I somehow thought that when Luka woke up I would get my little girl back, my very energetic, spirited little girl.

Such patience it took for me to sit and allow her to do things as she could. It took me so much patience not to ask her everything under the sun when we hadn't talked for so long. So much patience required to not tell her everything that had been going on while she slept.

The day they came into her ICU room to get her into a chair, I was excited. As they gradually moved her body, got her to try and lift her legs up and try to move her arms, I became aware that this would take some time. About an hour and a half later she was finally reclining in her 'chair' (more of a big, cushioned, upright bed than a chair). She was very downcast. It was a look I had never really seen on my Luka-Angel before. A look that if I had ever seen it, had only crossed her face so briefly it could hardly even be labeled an expression. Of course, I had seen her cry, but this expression was different. Her face revealed a long hard journey, her body was so weak. In contrast to this, when the 'Starlight' visitors (special entertainers and support for hospitalised children) came her eyes changed. A little light reflected from them again. She scrawled on her whiteboard with the fingers she could move, that she would like them to play her the song 'Nightingale' by Demi Lovato. They said they didn't know how to play that on the ukulele, but went to the effort of pulling out an iPad and getting it to play for her.

As the song filled my ears, my thoughts drifted to about ten months before. There she was, sailing and dancing on an aerial hoop. She was the most graceful in the room. The day we had seen the circus come to town on our holiday in Forster – I could have predicted what actually happened when we got back in the car, "I WANT TO JOIN THE CIRCUS!" At first I thought this was impossible. Because of her heart condition, Luka had never been able to do any such thing! Jazz chimed in with great gusto that he wanted to join the circus too. They decided they would run away with the circus! I wasn't yet ready for them to leave home, and so I started to investigate if there was anything in Newcastle that might be suitable for them.

I figured that even if they could join the circus to juggle, at least that was something they could have all for themselves. Something unique, somewhere they could shine.

Months on, when Luka started showing great interest in the Aerial Hoop (an acrobatic hoop suspended from the ceiling by a rope), I wondered how she would be able to do this. The instructor explained to me that it shouldn't put her heart rate up too much, but would be a good strengthener. It was a low cardio, low impact activity. I remember recalling at the time that Lucas' Dad had to do gym work before his transplant to strengthen his upper torso. I thought this could actually be a great help for Luka's eventual transplant. So here she was in December 2015, dancing on the aerial hoop to her song of choice 'Nightingale' by Demi Lovato. She looked like a graceful bird, flying through the air spinning around in her aqua coloured leotard and her braided hair. It was the first dancing she had ever been able to freely do. Her movements flowed and bent and swayed with the music. She was so strong. No one in the 100 plus audience could have possibly guessed that this little girl couldn't dance on the ground, couldn't allow her heart rate to go up and would soon need a heart transplant. No one except for the crowd of sixteen supportive friends and family who had come just to watch Luka & Jazz in their Circus spectacular end of year performance.

The track finished and I was back seeing my little girl, her hair braided, but no aqua leotard; this time a white gown, sitting, unable to move in a big hospital bed-like chair. My eyes overflowed and I quickly swallowed up any salty water hovering, waiting to spill.

"Would you like us to sing a song?" The beautiful Starlight girl known as 'Captain Unicorn' asked.

Luka nodded and scrawled on her whiteboard, 'Somewhere over the rainbow'. The lump re-entered my throat.

When they asked her if she was too old for bubbles, my sweet girl whispered hoarsely 'bubbles are refreshing'. It seemed that every word she wrote or whispered made me want to jump up and down with excitement. Ever so slowly I was seeing glimpses of the Luka I knew so well, and once again, music was bringing us healing and joy.

As I sat on the windowsill of my corner of the ICU cove, I looked out to the trees and the beautiful big sky and thought about the rainbow Luka-Angel had written about in her blog. I thought about all the rainbows God had provided for me in the sky, right when I needed them, to remind me that he keeps his promises. I saw how broken and bruised her body was and thought about the fact that she died briefly just two nights ago. She was unable to do much yet, but she was alive! Now she was requesting a song I had never heard her request or sing, but a song that meant so much, 'Somewhere over the rainbow'.

The sweet 'Starlight' girls strummed their ukulele and sang her requested song, as I slid further and further down my bench seat to be out of view of my angel whose spirits were being lifted as they sang. I couldn't allow her to see my pain. The tears overflowed fast down my cheeks, so I got up and disappeared around the wall to grab some tissues to hide my sniffles. She had enough to go through without seeing her mother's hurting heart. At this point, she didn't even know all that had happened. All she knew was that she had had her heart transplant, she felt very unwell and weak, and there was a long road ahead.

It was only a day later when again some 'Starlight' visitors came to her isolation room at ICU and asked if they could play her a song. Again she whispered 'Somewhere over the rainbow'. This time to my surprise, the nurse sang along confidently, with our starlight visitors, singing as loudly as them. Luka hardly had any voice left from all the intubation, so her attempts were thwarted. They invited me to join, but as I tried to sing the words, the poignancy of the song again washed over me. One of the starlight girls then went on to paint Luka's nails (and she requested little rainbows be painted on each one). I was witnessing another miracle, a rainbow in itself – my little girl could smile again.

Letter to Luka – Day 8

Psalm 138:3

'In the day when I cried out, you answered me and made me bold with strength.'

(A letter to Luka from my aching heart)

My Beautiful Girl,

You look better today than yesterday. I know it is hard for you to just lay there, with your body so tired and having gone through so much. It will just take time to heal.

You seemed so sad yesterday and today.

I have been told that is normal for patients after a big operation.

Your joy will come, my Luka-Angel...

You have been through a lot!

Call out to God to provide you with strength. He will help you.

'The name of the Lord is a strong tower; the righteous run to it and are safe'. Proverbs 18:10

Chapter 27

Getting Better Every Day

'Be strong and courageous! Do not fear or tremble before them, for the Lord your God is the one who is going with you. He will not fail you or abandon you.' Joshua 1:9 (NET)

In amongst the darkness, trauma and unknowns of Luka-Angel's rocky transplant journey, rays of light always shone through. There was something so sacred and beautiful about her room, about the journey. The warmth and peace and presence of God could be felt like nothing I have ever experienced before. This cannot be underestimated and words don't do it justice. The joy of who Luka-Angel is, her courage, her strength also helped me feel strong.

We were also held fast by the thousands of people praying for us and sending us encouraging messages and love. We were completely blown away by those who gave up their time to bring people together in prayer, especially in those first few days of the unpredictable and unexpected. We felt peace and comfort from those praying. It was described by my husband as a feeling of what God's Kingdom is like, the unity and love of people coming together. We felt so grateful, so uplifted and so blessed.

We also were surrounded by most of our family and although perhaps they didn't realise how much it meant, their support and physical presence with us kept us feeling safe and secure. When my sister-in-law Tam had Bible verse posters printed for Luka-Angel's ICU room, I didn't grasp how much they would mean to me or how much they would hold me fast. We had them posted around Luka's room, and some days when she was awake for brief moments, I would put some at her feet hoping she could read them. One poster said, *'God is within her, she will not fall. God will help her at the break of day.'* Psalm 46:5 (NIV). The background was a ballerina. These words really strengthened me some days, as I knew them to be true. In the corner of the room was a painting Luka had done for me that said, *'All things are possible for the one who believes.'* Mark 9:23 (ESV). A polaroid photo of Luka and her big brother Elijah at her 13th birthday party, was up on the wall. In it she beamed a great big smile and looked stunning in her '60's style', cow print dress.

Among the posters there was one with a strong lion in the background and the verse from Joshua 1:9, *'Be strong and take courage for the Lord your God will be with you wherever you go.'* As Luka-Angel lay in ICU kept alive by life support, my sister-in-law Tam had a vivid image one morning. She was hesitant to name it as a definite vision from God, but it was a picture she visualised. I believe it *was* a vision from God. There was darkness all around Luka-Angel and she was lying completely still (as in ICU). A strong, protective lion was standing over the top of Luka-Angel when suddenly it roared wildly into the darkness as if protecting her from something. The same afternoon that Tam told us of her experience, a close friend came to visit us. Deb told us she kept seeing Luka face to face with and protected by God in the form of a lion (she likened it to Aslan and Lucy in the book/movie Narnia). This for me was no coincidence.

The first night in the ward, after being moved from ICU, Luka-Angel whispered to me, "Mummy, can you please move that Bible verse right in front of me, I want to see it all the time." We had transferred all the Bible verse posters from her ICU room to her ward room. There were at least ten posters up on the walls of her room. When I asked her which one she wanted moved she said, "The one with the lion on it. I want to see it at all times, it makes me feel safe." (I had been waiting for stories of heaven and wanted to ask my girl so many questions, but I had decided just to wait, to be silent. I knew in time, she might have stories to talk to me about. This patiently waiting thing was so hard for me, and out of my usual character. This felt like the first glimpse I got into her inner journey). I asked her, "Really? Is it the Bible verse that makes you feel safe?"

"No Mum, the lion. I have been thinking God is like a lion. If I was in a dark alley, and a bad man was coming to get me, God would not be just like one lion, but like a thousand lions, protecting me and keeping me safe."

Luka had *never* spoken of God as the lion before! I found this astounding!

Whilst Luka-Angel was still in the ward, my sister Karen gave her a few jumpers. One of them had the face of a lion on the back and the word 'Conqueror' on the front. Karen had worn a similar top to this, on the day Luka-Angel had her transplant. Luka-Angel's face lit up as she was presented with this gift and her mouth dropped open and she put it straight on (with some help). Every time Luka had to do physiotherapy, or have a biopsy, for the months following, she would wear her lion jumper to remind her she could draw on God's strength to help her, and that through him she was indeed a conqueror.

One day, a couple of months down the track of her recovery, Luka painted the best painting I have ever seen from her. This was something she had painted in the hospital school classroom. It was the face of a lion. His expression personified him, revealing gentleness, doting love and kindness. His rainbow mane flowed from his face and down his neck. This painting now hangs framed on our lounge room wall as a reminder of Luka's journey and our protective, present God.

I firmly believe that as Luka was sleeping, there was a fight for her life. I sensed that darkness was trying to rob her of her life but God kept reminding me he was stronger. He would tell me words of hope and remind me she would tell her story one day. I knew he was holding her.

For me, hope was like a spotlight in the darkness. I remember saying a few times to my family, "She will be okay. This is not her pain right now, she is sleeping peacefully. This is for us to endure, soon she will wake up and then it will be hard for her." I am so completely thankful that my God instilled peace and hope into my heart and I never doubted how her journey would turn out. Besides the first day, I never for a second imagined we would lose her even though perhaps all the science pointed that way. For that hope, I am so incredibly thankful!

Many things helped me get through such a difficult time, and I am thankful that I had little reminders of hope every day. I have a ring that is formed into the word 'hope'. Even though this is not sentimental or valuable, I wore it every day so that there would be a reminder on my hand of *hope*. I also wore Luka-Angel's own handmade jewellery each day. She had created her 'Lighthouse Jewellery' line to raise money for her future dream of setting up her 'Lighthouse' centre for the homeless and I wore her jewellery proudly.

As she lay still, I took pride in who she is, and declared to anyone who would listen just how amazing she is! I wanted every doctor, every nurse, to fight for her. To understand she was no ordinary girl, and this precious child had big dreams to help other people. I guess in a way, I knew if they saved her life, they would save many lives. I knew God wanted to use her in this world to help others. Wearing the jewellery she had made became a must and it opened up many conversations! Each new day, I would put a different item on. It felt as though by wearing it, I was declaring that she would live out her God-given destiny. She would set up her centre for the homeless.

I have never forgotten the day approximately four months before Luka-Angel's transplant, when I pleaded with God for a sign or a word that Luka-Angel would be okay. I already had a real belief that God told me that Jazz would grow up. I desperately needed some hope for Luka. As I rounded the corner, down the hill at Newcastle baths, I came to a sudden halt as the Nobby's Beach Lighthouse came into my view. I had run this route many times. As my eyes landed on the lighthouse, I heard God's voice whisper, "Luka-Angel will set up her Lighthouse." It was so strong it literally stopped me in my tracks. That was it. Tears of joy filled my eyes as hope filled my heart. All would be well. This is what I needed to hear.

A few nights later, I received a phone call from my close friend who lives in Uganda. Leah rang me and told me about a Christian prophet that she and her husband Rob had met. The prophet was a friend of a friend who knew nothing about them. He started telling them all kinds of things that were completely right, things that Rob and Leah had shared together, but told no one. She said he was correct with everything he said about them and she felt blessed for the encouragement and knowledge she had received. She started quietly praying in her heart that this man would be given a word from God to encourage us. Leah had been praying for us, knowing that soon Luka-Angel was to be listed for transplant. Mid-sentence, as if reading her mind, he stopped and said to Leah, "You have friends with heart conditions. There are a few people in the family with heart problems."

"Yes!" she said amazed!

He went on to tell her, "You must tell the mother her children will not die. Her children will live! Tell the mother!"

This came just days after my lighthouse run. It was all the assurance I needed. Suddenly the fears I couldn't shake for Luka-Angel were dispelled. I knew deeply, strongly that she would be okay. No matter what happened, no matter what difficult days ahead we had to face, I now knew without a shadow of a doubt, my little girl would grow up!

The day we were told Luka was to be moved from ICU to the ward, another beautiful, big rainbow appeared outside Luka-Angel's window. As much as I was completely excited, this came as no big surprise to me. It seems that God uses rainbows to remind me he keeps his promises, at just the right time, over and over again.

When the rainbow came up in Luka-Angel's window (this second time in ICU) I pulled out my camera desperate to capture the image. We even managed to get Luka, lying in her bed, in the foreground of the photo.

I had never really thought through that Luka would have to learn to walk again. Her new yellow leotard hung in the hospital room and her second-hand ballet shoes were on display in the corner (given to her by a professional ballerina who was a friend of Elyse). Luka-Angel used to say to me, "Mummy, one day, when I have my heart transplant you will be standing at the end of the bed and holding up a yellow, glittery leotard, and that's how I will know that my heart transplant is over, and soon I will be able to dance." I thought it was the quirkiest and funniest little thing, but I also thought it was 'very Luka'. So when I expressed my disappointment in not having time to have found a leotard that was yellow, my sister became determined to make that happen for her. Karen's friend Linda went to great lengths to get this thing made (staying up all night) and sent off in an express post envelope so that Luka-Angel could see it as soon as she woke up. We didn't know that we would be waiting days. Several times I thought she was 'awake enough' and I would hold up her leotard at the end of the bed, and smile at her as her eyes fluttered. She was still ventilated and heavily sedated, and each time I tried, she would nod straight back off not even seeing me. The nurses must have thought I was a little insane as I never really got the chance to explain myself to most of them about why every now and then I would stand at the end of her bed smiling and holding up a long-sleeved, glittery, yellow leotard.

I naively thought she would be up and walking soon, and that within a few weeks of physiotherapy, she would be ready to dance.

When the physiotherapist came to visit her room and set some goals, one of her major goals was to cartwheel. She couldn't even sit up yet. I loved her goal! And they took it seriously too. I thought about her broken, bruised and battered chest, the burns that were there from the defibrillator pads, the drains (still in her chest), cannulas and lines still in her veins, and tried to imagine her being able to cartwheel. Sure enough though, it became her goal and she was determined to achieve it!

Luka's whole body hurt, and the sensations she had from medications were both strange and uncomfortable. Yet when the nurse offered her Panadol she would say, "No thank-you." I always knew she was very brave and had a pain tolerance that spoke of a persevering and strong mind. I was quietly so very proud of her strength, independence and bravery.

Physiotherapy was difficult for her at first. Some days she told us that she didn't want the physiotherapist to come to the ward. She didn't want to do it as it was so hard for her particularly at first, but her determination took over. She would put her lion jumper on, and I would watch amazed as she, despite her weariness and with tears in her eyes, gave her best. She would turn to me, with determination and say, "The quicker I get better, the sooner I will be able to dance!" Simple things like lifting her legs out of bed or taking steps, or showering, once so easy, was now so difficult. So many operations and a few weeks on her back had affected her muscle tone and physical ability greatly. A moment that surprised me was when Luka was able to take her first assisted, slow steps to the bathroom. As she turned on the tap to wash her hands, tears filled her big, brown eyes and she exclaimed softly, "Running water!" Then she asked the nurse if she could stand there a while and let the warm water run over her hands. She told me later she had forgotten what that felt like. She hadn't felt running water for three weeks and for her, the sensation was incredible!

Chapter 28

The Cup of Tea

'But whoever drinks the water that I will give him will never be thirsty again. The water I give him will become in him a spring of water welling up to eternal life.' John 4:14 (ESV)

In the first number of days of being awake, Luka-Angel barely had a voice. All of the intubation had damaged her vocal chords. More than a week after being moved to the ward, she turned to my sister and I and said, almost pleadingly, "I would like a cup of English Breakfast Tea." It was yet another milestone and I couldn't contain my excitement. I wanted to be able to serve her, I wanted her to feel happy again. Whatever she wanted, I was determined to make happen for her (within reason). She explained to us through a hoarse voice that she was in fact *desperately* craving English Breakfast Tea.

With the nurse's permission, Karen and I put Luka in a wheelchair and took her to a little café downstairs for some English Breakfast Tea. Having her out of the ward for the first time, I was so keenly aware of germs. I felt like holding a sign up and telling everyone to back away and keep their germs to themselves because my girl had just had a heart transplant and had absolutely no immunity at this point in time. In my mind it seemed right that everyone should get out of the café so we could get this girl the English Breakfast Tea she truly deserved! I saw little green germ monsters everywhere. Aware of the fact that her immunity would now always be suppressed, I wondered if this would be my new normal.

Karen helped me wipe the table, and the cup that the café gave her.

I was so disappointed there was no teapot. I felt on such an occasion as this, that her English Breakfast Tea should have arrived at the table in a pretty little teapot, with a colourful tea cosy on top. It should have been brought out on a silver tray, with a little old fashioned floral tea cup and saucer like the one I got from my nanna's collection when she died. Bone China was in order today! Instead, it arrived in a cardboard, throw away cup, just plastic and paper. "She deserves a teapot!" I whispered to Karen who nodded fiercely in agreement, as if already reading my mind.

As she sipped her tea quietly delighting in each mouthful, Karen and I felt the preciousness of this moment. "She's drinking tea," I excitedly whispered to Karen with tears filling my eyes fast! Karen nodded with similar enthusiasm and joy in her eyes.

Every moment Luka did something new was a milestone. It was like celebrating the first steps of a toddler, yet somehow, for her sake, I had to contain myself. I felt like I could literally jump up and down and scream and cheer and hold a big handmade banner up every time she did something new. But instead, I treasured it in my heart, and at times when that was not enough, my journal.

One night, a week or so after being moved to the ward, Luka-Angel drew me a picture. It was a simple picture of a little house on the beach. It was the first moment she had been interested in doing something creative. Considering she was usually creative, I thought this was a great new leap forward. I commented on the beautiful picture and thanked her.

"It is your house on the beach in heaven," Luka told me.

I was shocked! One day, years before, I was praying and seeking God, and I felt he told me that he had a house on the beach for me that awaited me in heaven. One day I would live there. I had tucked my little encounter deep in my heart.

"Have I told you about that?" I said confused, and in awe.

Luka looked at me with a bewildered expression.

"Told me about what?"

"Have I ever told you that I felt God tell me years ago, he has a house on the beach in heaven for me?"

"No." Luka said with certainty.

"What made you draw that?" I asked Luka curiously, wondering if she had seen my one day home in heaven.

"I don't know. I just did."

I could hardly believe it. Although she has no actual memories of heaven, I really believed that she had seen God. This house in heaven (I believed God had told me about years before) was something that often gave me joy and hope. This was something tucked away in my heart. Luka was still finding it hard to even sit up in bed and certainly hadn't been writing or drawing until this moment. Now she had drawn a picture so significant. This was more confirmation God had been with her, preparing her for many things that are yet to come in her life.

Luka had a new purity, sweetness and innocence in those weeks in hospital. She really shone. There was a sense of heaven around her and within her. God's presence was shining through her and she seemed 'untouched by the world' and literally 'touched by heaven,' similar to that of a newborn. Untainted. Pure.

As the days went by and Luka was recovering, we heard all kinds of things from her. Whilst sleeping in ICU, Luka-Angel had many dreams. Some were quite strange and some amusing, like the one where Elijah was playing his electric guitar too loudly in the 'old peoples' ward, and Luka demanded several times that I tell him to stop playing his guitar so loudly in the middle of the night. Others were quite poignant and amazing.

One such repetitive dream was of homeless kids by the hundreds living in tents in the park beside the hospital outside her room. Some had come to take up residence in her ICU room and hallway. The dreams were so very real that it took her well over a week after leaving ICU to accept that they weren't actual happenings. She had explained to us that at times in her dreams, she herself had been living homeless and cold in a tent at the park. To this day when we visit the hospital she can point out the area of the park where the homeless kids were staying. It seemed to me that she was being prepared for her future. Her dream of setting up a centre for the homeless was very real and something she had been fundraising for since she was eleven years old. Her plans were all mapped out and she had even drawn up the program she would be running for those who sleep rough, from education, to counselling, to 'learn to swim' classes. This vision of hers that had been held fast in her heart for a few years now, helped me remember that God had so much more for her to do here on earth yet.

It was exciting in some moments to imagine who she would become, and the incredible ways in which she could bless the world.

Chapter 29

Out of the Blue – Another Miracle!

'I will answer them before they even call to me. While they are still talking to me about their needs, I will go ahead and answer their prayers.' Isaiah 65:24 (NLT)

Journal Entry – Day 10

8:45am

Luka-Angel's face looks beautiful and well. Her vitals are all good. Pacemaker doing the job it needs to – God has told me to 'wait patiently' and He would 'see this through to completion'. I believe He will. I can do this patient waiting, because she is safe for now. The initial patient waiting when she entered ICU with no heart muscle function and no heart electric function, only temporary machines keeping her alive was 'patient waiting' like I have never, ever known. I thank God for how far we have come and that she can lay there and talk to me now. Each night as her discomfort disturbs her desire to sleep, we watch movies together. Usually dance movies. Then when we finally close our eyes, this is followed by being interrupted all night by Luka-Angel's discomfort and pain. I am tired, hardly get a wink of sleep, but so relieved to have my daughter through the worst.

9am

WE HAVE OUR FULL MIRACLE!!

We just heard from the doctor following a few tests whilst she lay in her ward bed that ALL electric pathways kicked in overnight. Out of the blue, they have all started working. Her heart is beating on its own for the first time. Lucas just heard the news and he is so emotional and so relieved. He launched his arms around me in a big hug. In a sense, I feel he is back now too, it was comforting to see him smile again. When Dr J told me about the test results, that the electric pathways are now all working, I asked him with a little bit of excited cheek, "Can I please have that in writing?!" I was simply amazed, but not shocked, for I knew it was coming! God had assured me. Our God is a miracle working God – He is able to save. He has held that heart within his mighty hands and gradually, carefully, been molding it together. Renewing it.

Three times on one day I received the Bible verse 'being confident of this, that he who began a good work in you will carry it on to completion.' Philippians 1:6 (NIV). I had received the verse in a text from a Salvo Officer friend, in a message on facebook from another friend, and in my own reading that day. I had thought it might be months, years, but he has chosen to demonstrate his power, in his timing, now, with thousands watching, so that people may see he is a miracle working God who hears our prayers!

Chapter 30

A Well Deserved Trophy

'Grey hair is a glorious crown; it is found in the way of righteousness.' Proverbs 16:31(HCSB)

Letter to My Sisters

(Date: Approximately four weeks post heart-transplant)

10:43pm

Dear Sisters,

As I glance in the mirror these last days, I see the toll the last 4 weeks have taken on me. The lines have increased so much. Bemusing though that one thing reveals the stress more than any extra line or bag or sag on my face.... The one white hair that has dramatically presented itself in amongst the other brown hairs around it! One stand out, wiry grey hair! Right in the middle of my left eyebrow!!! The first time I saw it I got such a shock... 'Do eyebrows go grey??!!!' I questioned. Then I

thought of nearly every older person I have ever known...
Yes... Eyebrows do generally go grey!

Guess I'm on a new path of maturity! I do believe that small wiry, white hair is representative of the stress I have been under and somehow, amidst my horror, lies a certain acceptance and honour of it! This grey eyebrow hair is indeed a trophy... so I haven't plucked it out. I have decided that for the time being, it deserves to stay! My first white eyebrow hair.

Love,
Ange

Chapter 31

A View from Above

> 'He's the one who comforts us in all our troubles so that we can comfort other people who are in every kind of trouble.' 2 Corinthians 1:4 (CEB)

Approximately a month after being in hospital, Luka was discharged to stay across the road at Ronald McDonald House in the isolation room. Her ward stay had been filled with long uncomfortable days, getting used to taking copious amounts of medication, struggling with her lack of taste and having no appetite, sleepless nights, daily blood tests, many specialist visits, migraines and physiotherapy. This was softened by kind and caring nurses who always went the extra mile, and some very special visitors from far away. Some particular highlights for Luka were catching up with some of her best friends from school, some special videos (including her school class singing the song 'Brave' for her), a visit from her cousins, aunts and uncles, Great Nanna all the way from Queensland and other relatives from Sydney, along with the hospital 'clown doctors', who seemed to have the same zany sense of humour as their bed-ridden audience!

Much to her sheer embarrassment, when we pushed Luka in a wheelchair out of the hospital and over the road to Ronald McDonald House, we couldn't even see her. She wasn't embarrassed of being in a wheelchair, but of the fact that we took up the whole corridor. The eight large, rainbow coloured helium balloons, several bunches of flowers, presents, craft bags, toys and suitcases surrounded her frail body, hiding her red face.

Our stay at Ronald McDonald House was filled with nights of movies, late night dessert runs by me, and a feeling of isolation and loneliness. Mum and Dad were looking after our three boys in a little house away from the hospital. Lucas rotated between there and RMH. Our family was split between two residences and even though only a half an hour drive from each other, the weeks were long and taxing, and it just felt like we were worlds apart.

Journal Entry - One Cold Lonely Night:

Sometimes I see myself from above as if from another perspective, and I feel sorry for all the sadness and the hardship I go through. Life is hard. Life has so much pain.

Tonight as I walked across the park back to Ronald McDonald House alone, I saw myself again from a different perspective. I ached from the pain I have gone through, from the pain I go through and the pain I will go through. I hurt looking at the mum who does life differently. For the mum who has the pain of watching helplessly as their children suffer. I considered the pain of my daughter, her life that is so abnormal, and the fact that I have to go through this all over again with my son and my husband.

I thought of all the parents who were just sitting at McDonalds within the hospital that I had just passed. The parents who have a forlorn look on their faces, many of them just like me a few months ago, taking a quick desperate break from the walls of their children's small ward room to shove down some sort of 'nourishment' at McDonalds. Parents, who then go back up to watch helplessly and wait for their child to get better. So much waiting!

Never in my life have I sat around so much. I'm always on the go. It's usually very hard for me to stop! It takes incredible self-discipline for me to sit still, to hold still and to sit around. Yet these months, that's what I have had to do over and over, sometimes for weeks. It's interesting when the pain is completely intense and the outcome unknown how there is no impatience in the waiting. It is a different kind of waiting. In this waiting, there is only pain, reflection and hope. I held hope so tightly in those days. Without hope, I would have crumbled. Hope was the only thing that held me rock solid. The hope that Luka-Angel would fulfill her dreams. The hope that she would one day dance as she always planned to, that she would set up her 'Lighthouse' for the homeless. The hope that this was happening for some God-known, important reason, and we would come out the other side and she would live a long fulfilling life.

Sometimes the ache I feel when I see what I carry makes me start to cry. Usually I have to swallow that lump and quickly brush away my tears. Luka hates to see me cry. She doesn't understand my tears. She doesn't cry for herself. She has never, not one day, in all these years of not being able to do sport, go on walks, or dance, cried for herself. She has only ever enjoyed the life that she has, and towards the end looked forward to the one that is to come. She is amazing. This is a mentality I aspire to learn.

As my heart aches for myself, watching myself walk across the darkening park at 8:37pm, alone, sad and reflective, I then begin to ache for all the other mothers in the world. The mothers who helplessly watch as their children starve, the mothers whose children were stolen from them and placed into slavery, the mothers who will never know what happened to their children, the mothers who can't find clean water for their thirsty children to drink, the mothers who have no hospital to take their chronically ill child to. Oh how my heart aches. My heart feels broken. Yet here I am back at the door of Ronald McDonald House. I swallow my lump, deciding I don't have time to call anyone, even though I am desperate to voice this pain. I blink back my tears, and brush away the ones that started to come out of my nose when blocked from my eyes. I use my little access card to get into my bedroom door and the first thing my very observant daughter, pale face and her black 'CONQUERER jumper' on says is, "Mum, have you been crying?"

"No darling," I respond quickly with a smile, "It's cold and windy out there and it affected my eyes."

For tonight, she moves back to her TV screen satisfied with my answer.

Chapter 32

The Lady & the Blue Bracelet

'Religion that God our Father accepts as pure and faultless is this: to look after orphans and widows in their distress and to keep oneself from being polluted by the world.' James 1:27 (NIV)

It was about ten weeks after Luka's transplant when we decided to go and visit my Uncle Peter and Aunty Mary and cousins who live in the beautiful Dandenong Ranges.

Luka had just been the master of ceremonies for a very special event, a short film festival, written, produced and acted by patients from the children's hospital. We were now on the road. We stopped reluctantly at Hungry Jacks on the way as our children were feeling hungry and it was lunch time.

As soon as we walked into Hungry Jacks, Luka grabbed my arm and pointed out a woman in the line. She looked about her mid-late 60's.

"Mum, I feel so sorry for that woman. She is lonely."

I was very curious and wondered what Luka could have possibly seen, since we had only just walked into the restaurant.

"How do you know? Was she sitting by herself?" I asked.

"I just know Mum. I can feel it." I wondered about this gift of empathy, and was quite fascinated.

As we sat and waited for our food and the lady still lined up, Luka turned to me with a sense of urgency. "I feel like I need to give her my bracelet Mum. I *really* need to give her my bracelet."

I looked at the bracelet newly on her wrist. Luka had been given some beautiful blue glass beads from a friend of mine and had carefully constructed this bracelet. She was very proud of this bracelet and had put it together just that week.

My words went against the awkward feeling within. I too, had had moments like this. Honouring the potential gift of empathy and the possible leading of God, I looked at my daughter who so recently had been through so much, and been surrounded by God's presence in a place I have never gone to, and I said, "Okay, so let's pray for the right opportunity."

As the lady came and sat behind us, I whispered to Luka, "Do you want to go sit with her? I will come with you."

We got up quickly from our seats, much to my husband's confusion, and I said to the lady who was now sitting by herself, "Do you mind if we sit with you a few minutes?"

The surprised lady agreed that would be okay.

"My daughter would like to give you something."

Luka took the bracelet off her wrist and said to the lady, "I made this, this week, and I feel like I really want to give it to you. Would you like it?"

The woman put her hand out and accepted the bracelet her eyes filling with tears.

Over the minutes we sat there, her story unfolded. She lived by herself. Her husband had died. Her only son lived far away and hardly got to see her. She had bought the second meal that was in front of her for her dog who was waiting in the car.

She went on to tell us as we saw her naked wrists and fingers that someone had recently broken into her house and stolen *all* of her jewellery including her engagement and wedding rings and many sentimental items.

"I only have my dog as company," she went on.

"You are such a beautiful young girl," she told Luka, "so beautiful!" She asked if we lived in Melbourne and it felt appropriate to share Luka's story for the first time with someone we didn't know. "Is it okay if I tell her?" I asked Luka. Luka nodded.

Naturally the woman was very touched and her eyes filled with tears again. "You are so strong and brave and such a beautiful girl!"

I told the woman that now she could remember that a little girl cared, that a little girl had seen her loneliness and I believed God had urged this little girl to give her the bracelet, because he knew her, and deeply cared about her and loved her.

I told her we believed in Jesus and we would pray for her.

We sat together and ate our lunch together for about half an hour.

When the lady got up to go, it was obvious she could hardly believe what had unfolded.

She pointed to her bracelet and said, "I will treasure this. It is now my only piece of jewellery."

Luka-Angel and I walked back to the car that day with full hearts and our heads buzzing!

"Wow Luka, you knew didn't you! You were right! God whispered to you, and you were bold enough to follow through on what you believed! I am amazed, and touched and so, so proud of you!"

Chapter 33

'Little Dude' & Finding our New Normal

'Blessed be the Lord – day after day he carries us along.'
Psalm 68:19 (The Message)

When we finally moved from Ronald McDonald House to the little house in Preston, temporarily provided for us by our employers, The Salvation Army, life became about daily hospital visits, weekends of adventuring around country Victoria, Op shopping and home schooling. We had decided to make the best of a hard and isolating time. We had a roof over our head, our cupboards were gradually getting more clothing than the few items we had brought down (due to all of the Op shopping), and we were trying to find joy in the little things. The boys enjoyed skating in the carpark behind us and although they missed their friends desperately, I was so glad they had each other. We joined the local library for the first time in our lives and the boys would ask to go there every day! They felt like they were shopping, but for free! It was a short walk from our house and was so convenient. We all tried to stay positive and be strong, even though things were different so suddenly. We regularly enjoyed our local Italian pizza shop that only charged

$10 for a family size pizza, enjoyed little trips to get Pho Soup from a street full of Vietnamese restaurants and tried bubble tea. The Preston Markets were around the corner and became a place I loved to walk through, and find some distraction from our reality. We hadn't really lived in city suburbia before as a family. Something about the smell of rotting fruit and the shouting and heckling of the market men, felt distracting and fun. I would go and buy my fresh fruit and vegies and feel like I had some sort of a 'normal life'. I often wondered if anyone could tell I was still coming up for air after such a difficult couple of months. It wouldn't take much for my eyes to fill up.

One trip to the markets, I sat at the big old piano in the courtyard that was there to be played by anyone who wished. I sat and played and sang my 'go to' of old, 'Time After Time' (by Cindi Lauper). I sang my heart out and my eyes were slightly watery as I played and sang to my boys, realising one child was missing (and was at her usual daily hospital visits, but this day her dad was with her). My teary eyes spilled into tears of shock, embarrassment and laughter as I noticed my ten-year-old Jazz had taken his 'grandpa hat' off while I was closing my eyes and singing and placed it on top of the piano. People were stopping and listening. "Mum," he whispered, "you could make some money busking!" I am not sure how many minutes the hat was there, but I quickly grabbed it off the piano before anyone could throw their money in. Elijah, Jazz and Jayjay had been busking together before, and knew it was a good way to make a quick dollar. Jazz's little entrepreneurial spirit had kicked in again that day.

One market trip, Jazz was desperate to buy his sister a little, overpriced, knitted toy made in Mexico. It was small enough to fit in one's hand, the brightest fluorescent green with large eyes and little arms and legs. It looked a little bit like a baby crossed with a frog. He called it 'Little Dude'. "Mum, that little guy is begging for me to buy him for Luka. He feels sorry for her, and he told me his name is 'Little Dude' and he wants me to buy him for Luka. I just *have* to buy him for her. 'Little Dude' looked at me Mum, and then he said 'please buy me for Luka?'" I looked at the $15 toy and declined Jazz's pleadings. "I will pay for him with my own money Mum." Jazz begged with what he calls his 'puss in boots eyes'. Knowing Jazz had all of $15 to his name, I talked to him about impulse buying, about the large cost of this 'Little Dude'. Then we walked away from the markets for some thinking time. Days later as Jazz came to me with coins filling his hand and pleading again, I softened. He told me that he'd had some thinking time, and he wanted to spend all of his earnings on his sister.

Together we snuck off to the markets early in the morning. We walked (and scootered) with purpose, back to 'Little Dude' who was still waiting to be purchased by the little boy with blonde hair and blue eyes. Handing over his precious two months of earnings, Jazz lovingly took 'Little Dude' to his face and kissed him- apparently 'Little Dude' had thanked Jazz for coming back to buy him. He then scootered home so fast I could hardly keep up with him. He went straight into his sister's room and explained that 'Little Dude' had begged Jazz to buy him for Luka, as if giving this little toy the credit. She took 'Little Dude' straight up to her face, fussed over how cute he was, and kissed him. These two had shared a love of stuffed toys (I am not allowed to call them 'stuffed', as every toy is a 'real' being) for years now. Something that growing up, I refused to own. I had thought stuffed toys were for 'wussy' 'girlie' girls. Not 'tough' tom boys like myself. Turns out stuffed toys can bring comfort to the bravest kids in the world. Many a cuddly toy has provided a voice through which my son would share his feelings, and then there are some like 'Cowcow' who have seen a little girl through thick and thin. 'Cowcow' has been by Luka-Angel's side since she was one year old. This wise old cow (who apparently is forever about a three-year-old in Luka's mind) has seen Luka through every hospital visit, doctor's appointments, needles and more. 'Cowcow' has been the companion that has helped her when I couldn't. Now 'Little Dude' was to join the many friends that took up most of Luka-Angel's sleeping space on her bed. He had been generously bought with precious earnings, from a little boy who saw his sister as a hero! 'Little Dude' will forever be special, apparently we didn't choose him, he chose us.

Another day during our time of living in Preston, I walked into a beautician's booth (to deal with the neglect of my overgrown unsightly legs) and here God provided for me a Sri Lankan sister. She asked me how long we had lived in Melbourne and from there our conversation unfolded. The beautician began to weep as she started to tell me about her year of grief. Her parents had been visiting from overseas earlier in the year for a few weeks. Her father had hit his leg on the suitcase as he was packing to return home and after septicemia, he suddenly died. She was suffering such grief. Together we shared our pain and it was like I had met a new soul sister. We met together several times, and her generosity and care for me was invaluable. She absolutely refused to charge me for appointments, and further to that, she sent her hairdressing husband over to our house to give our three boys a haircut. More than that, she was a very caring, listening ear, a devout catholic and had become devoted to praying for healing for Luka-Angel and Jazz. She was absolutely God's provision of a friend to me at a time when some days felt so lonely. She often rang me even for months afterwards to see how Luka was going.

It was also during that time, that Luka-Angel discovered a new home. Her struggle of being so far from home was becoming very real and difficult. The isolation and loneliness she felt at that time was inconsolable. It was so hard because I couldn't help her. One day, while shopping at the nearby Woolworths with the little old lady trolley Jazz had bought me at the op shop, Luka became determined not to leave Woolworths. It was one of the first times she had been out and about, as due to her suppressed immune system, we had to protect her as much as possible.

"I am not leaving!" she demanded, tears filling her eyes, "can we stay here?"

I was so confused. It took me a while to ask the right questions. She was sniffing the air and looking around and she said to me, "This feels like my home. It makes me think I am at the Woolworths near home and I don't want to leave."

From that moment, any time I went grocery shopping, she would beg to come along with me. She could hardly walk the two hundred metres from home to Woolworths and would become so breathless (later we were to find out that her new heart couldn't go over 80 beats per minute, some lasting effects of the initial trauma post-transplant), so most of the time I said she couldn't come because it was too taxing on her to walk that far. I was also worried about what she might catch every time she was out. She would wear a mask most of the time, and it amused me so much when this sweet, kind girl of mine told me that when people stared too much, she would stick her tongue out at them from under the mask because they couldn't see it anyway! It made me laugh so much when she had revealed to me her secret response to those that stared.

She would beg and beg to go to Woolworths, and although it was the strangest thing, it made so much sense. It got to the point that she asked me if it was a 24hour Woolworths as she wanted to move in there.

One Friday her Physio appointment was cancelled so we decided to go on a long weekend to Phillip Island. We were so blessed to be able to stay at my cousin's holiday house. We had the most freeing and adventurous weekend of family walks, op shopping, movies and a couple of beach visits. As we walked around Nobby's Lookout for the second time that year and the second time in our lives, it was amazing to see the difference for our family. Luka-Angel conquered the stairs this time, all on her own. Not only that, but after we went on an off track adventure down to an isolated beach we discovered hundreds of penguins in the wild hovering in their burrows. It was so exciting to see them. Getting back up the steep hill to the car, I walked behind my daughter by some metres. This was the first time I had ever seen her conquer a hill unassisted! It was truly miraculous and amazing! She stood at the top and spread her arms wide taking in the view and her new ability. She was so proud of herself. My heart was filled with joy seeing her achieve in this way. Never could I have imagined this in my wildest dreams, Luka walking up a hill all on her own. This was the first time I could see outside of hospital walls her new capabilities.

The next day as Luka-Angel and I cartwheeled on the beach together I was inwardly jumping for joy! She had more than achieved her goal of cartwheeling. She could do several now in a row and not be puffed. She could jump off a sandbank and then run straight back up it and jump off again. She was even somersaulting in the air off a sand dune, then getting back up and doing it all again. Although no words were spoken about it, I watched as her three brothers joined her with similar moves and a whole lot of laughter. They all were having fun together, in a way they never had been able to before in their lives! No one was having to help Luka back up, she could do it all by herself!

However, in the background of my mind, I wondered how Jazz felt, now that his sister who had always journeyed with him could do things he couldn't yet do. One day as we walked along a path on a country cousin visit to Emerald, a bittersweet memory was etched forever into my brain. I had been pushing Jazz along the path on his skateboard so we could walk to the local markets from where we parked our car. Jazz then got slightly ahead of me and another incline was suddenly in front of him. Before I could skip a few steps to catch up to him to help, I watched as Luka raced ahead and placed her hand on his lower back to push him along the path. Bittersweet tears filled my eyes. She knew what it was to struggle. She knew what it was to have to be helped. He didn't even have to call out or stop. She was already there, right at his back, reaching out to help him before I could even act. She was now able to not only help herself but able to help her brother and she understood completely, what it was like for him.

Luka-Angel helping Jazz, five months after her transplant, on one of our many visits to the hospital in Melbourne.

Chapter 34

A New Day

'...weeping may last through the night, but joy comes with the morning.' Psalm 30:5 (NLT)

It was on our 17th Wedding Anniversary that we attempted to walk up to the pub on the corner for lunch. It became apparent on this walk that things with Luka-Angel were not quite right. She was extremely pale, short of breath, had tingles in her hands and feet and felt her heart rhythm was all over the place. She kept saying she felt 'extra heart beats'. Lucas and Luka got so far behind the boys and I on the way home, and I remember thinking I could no longer ignore the fact that she couldn't walk very far still. It seemed on that particular day, that not much had changed. Later that night we started to feel really concerned about her as the sensations still hadn't completely subsided. This began a few weeks of further investigations including extra tests, exercise tests, pace maker checks, halter monitors etc. Finally we had an answer! It turned out Luka-Angel's new heart could not go above 80 beats per minute. This meant any time Luka-Angel exercised, her heart couldn't lift its rate, and her body would not get the oxygen it needed. This meant Luka-Angel couldn't go home in the timeframe we had expected.

After changing the settings on the pace maker, and various monitoring, we were released to go home for just a few nights for her last day of school. This had been Luka-Angel's goal, to get back to school for at least the last day of the year, the boys had already gone home with Lucas for some awards they were receiving on presentation day. Luka was so excited as we went to the airport she could hardly contain her smile. She had to squeeze 'Cowcow' extra hard on the plane to release her nervous energy. The minute we walked in the door of our home and I saw our little bird Eve Hope, I burst into tears. The last time I had seen this part of my house, I was leaving on a plane for my daughter's impending heart transplant. I didn't actually know if we would all be in this house together again. All six of us. I'm not much of a dog person, but after holding our little cockatiel and telling her how much I missed her, I ran outside to the dogs and cuddled them as they leapt for joy. Luka-Angel had already done so and they seemed to be celebrating the fact that she was home safe. I knew they had missed her. Zibby had always been Luka-Angel's protector. Especially at the beach when they swam together. She would panic if Luka ducked under water even for a moment.

The next day as we walked into school we were met with an experience I can hardly put into words. Luka-Angel's friends were already waiting for her with a couple of teachers, in the front office of the school building. I had pictured their usual loud selves, I had envisaged this moment, and I had imagined loud cheering, laughing, jumping and excitement. Instead, I was met with probably the most sacred moment I have ever witnessed.

They were friends who had been through so much, friends who had been on their knees for my girl, friends who had cried so many tears their pillows were soaked. Friends who had stood by my girl from a distance, even one friend who had written her a letter for every day she was away so she could 'catch up' on what had been happening. The moment was completely, uncharacteristically, but perfectly, *silent*!

Luka stepped through the door, tears filling her eyes, the friends ever so gently gathered together in a circle of hugs, heads on shoulders, and wept almost silently (only their sniffles could be heard). A few teachers and some office staff stood slightly at a distance, quietly taking it in, and for some of them, silent tears filled their eyes. The hug was sacred, special, fitting for a moment such as this. This was not a girl returning from a great holiday, this was a girl who had lost her life, and then regained it again. This beautiful school God had led us to five years before, had supported us financially, prayerfully, and sent us a photo of the whole school in a heart formation with the hashtag '#prayingforluka'. Luka had even received a letter of encouragement from every member of her class. She had received little presents, and even a giant stuffed cow imported from America from one of Elijah's friends. In the sight before me, as the friends held each other, I sensed angels in the room; I could *feel* the presence of God. This was a fitting celebration!

Returning to Melbourne didn't seem so hard after the welcome home party Luka-Angel's friends threw for her, or the special times she had with each of her best friends. We returned to Victoria not knowing how long we would be there for, but somehow it seemed more manageable and the end was in sight. Finally, the day came when the doctors said they could release her. We made presents for all of the medical team, and Luka painted special paintings for them; each one so personal and unique, with her own meaning behind it. The painting Luka did for the cardiologist who had been her main doctor through the last few months, was of a tree with colourful finger print leaves. When Luka gave it to Dr J he said surprised, "I recently got married, and we had a big tree painting that our guests were asked to put their finger print on to make the leaves, it was quite a lot like this one!" We hadn't seen Luka do a painting like this before.

As we moved around the hospital saying our goodbyes, we knew this would always be another home to us. We knew we would be coming back regularly anyway. The day we were released, we wanted to take a celebratory photo of Luka. The photo we took of her would never show all she had been through except for the scar peeking out the top of her dress. She leapt with all her might off a retaining wall, just below the ward room she had stayed in, and into the blue sky before landing onto the ground. No one witnessing the photo at the back of the hospital that day could have possibly been able to tell that just four months before she had gone through so much!

Journal Entry 4 Months Post Transplant - 4:50am

As we drive away from our little, white, picket-fenced home contrasted to its concrete city surroundings in Preston, Victoria, streets of rubbish, dirty footpaths and graffiti are in my view. The smell of international food and rotten fruit from the local markets are my scent. Luka and I shout out the window at the top of our lungs, "Goodbye Preston!!" My early morning voice goes hoarse and I cough. As I reflect on the season that has been, I recall the early days of terrible grief and sadness, fear and hope, joy then sorrow, then joy again, then sorrow, then joy. Hours and hours and days of waiting! Then weeks then months. Desperate prayer, fragile vulnerability pleading for help in prayer, not caring any more who knew our story. Needing the world to beg our Creator God for the light of Luka-Angel to stay in this world. Mostly for us but also for the greater good of others – her big dreams driving me to hope.

I recall the beautiful nurses and telling them all about our Luka. I told them about our God who sees, who cares, who loves. The God who weeps with us, who brings us comfort, our God who can heal. So many beautiful people around me, other mums in agony, their child in ICU. Other mums who brought me food and told me I needed to eat. Our family standing with us, tag teaming, 'holding up our arms', helping us walk when we couldn't, washing our clothes, loving and caring for our boys. Lots and lots of sitting! I don't usually sit. I usually run, walk, clean, dream, think, list accomplish, DO! All I could do, was BE. All I could do was pray, pleading desperately. Music was my comfort and hope builder. Music my remedy for bringing my precious Angel comfort. So many songs of hope played in her sleeping ear, so many whispers of Bible verses, 'God is within her, she will not fall'. Bible verses said for me, 'You are my hope, my refuge, my fortress an ever present help in times of trouble'. 'Have mercy on me O God, have mercy on me for I come to you for safety. In the shadow of your wings I find protection until the raging storms are over.' 'He who began a good work in you will bring it through to completion.' Kisses on her hair as she lay sleeping, too afraid to kiss her skin in case I contaminate her. She looked so fragile. I see her sweet and innocent face lying there so still. Nurses so busy they never stopped! Beautiful nurses! A small blanket covering up her deepest physical wounds. Big invisible hands encompassing her new heart, slowly, slowly bringing new life. Remolding it, remaking it just for her. The pulses in her veins beating so strong in her frail body. It seemed to beat right out of her skin. The beats generated by machines.

More waiting.

Finally, slowly, breakthroughs.

Bit by bit.

Patient waiting, rewarded.

First the muscle began to work (the electrics still false).

Then we lost her.

Then we got her back, before we even knew we had lost her.

Pelting legs and heavy breathing as I ran across that park at 2am. Sprinting by myself, not my usual frightened self (wondering who was hiding in the bushes to grab me), just determined to get to my daughter's side.

The security guard who made us coffee.

Walking back into the room and seeing her all rigged up again. Ventilator back in. More tubes. Watchful eyes. Saying goodbye to her again as the sun came up and she returned to theatre.

Pleading with the world and the God of the heavens 'fight for her!'

More waiting.

Gradually, getting her back again.

Finally she was safe. Muscle functioning and now the pace maker in! Still praying for the electrics miracle.

Every little step forward, creating in me the feeling of joy a mum receives witnessing her baby's milestones. She said, "water!" She said, "milkshake!", "She is sitting up!", "She is speaking!"

As 'Somewhere Over the Rainbow' played, and the rainbow visited the sky outside her window within hours, I knew God had put that there for us! A reminder that He keeps His promises!

Every little step forward the greatest joy! "She laughed!"

Then ten days after our first day, the electrics miracle. All heart electric pathways activated! Out of the blue!

Weeks and weeks of hard work, waiting, watching, blood tests, medications, physiotherapy, perseverance, pace maker checks and adjustments, family time, hospital school, home school, creating, painting, jewellery making, weekends exploring the outskirts of Melbourne, more tests, biopsy's.

Now she sits in the back of the car, surrounded by all of her new fluffy friends with 'Cowcow' as their leader, and we are driving away!

Maybe just for two weeks at this point in time, but for now it feels like another big win! Home in time for Christmas!!

"Goodbye Preston, 'bye Woolworths, 'bye Two Dollar Shop, goodbye Cash Converters!" Luka-Angel and I spontaneously shout alternately with our windows down at 4:50am and darkness hovers around us ready to lift at any given moment!

We quickly shove the excess rubbish in the bin on the street. The bag we couldn't fit in the bin of the house we just finished packing up. Empty house, full bins, a full car and trailer (my feet only finding a place on the dash board). Time to move home.

Sunrise is nearly here, and I can sense it!

A new day is on the rise!

Chapter 35

Sheltered From the Storm

'Be merciful to me, O God, be merciful, for I come to you for safety. In the shadow of your wings I find protection until the raging storms are over.' Psalm 57:1 (GNT)

(Five Months Post-transplant)

Still on monthly visits to Melbourne (and sometimes fortnightly), we were now home in Newcastle. Things seemed to be normalising, although in some ways with Luka-Angel's now suppressed immunity, we had to find a new normal. The afternoon looked a little gloomy. A patch of blue sky still called me to go ahead with my jog to the local duck park. I could see in the distance some very dark clouds threatening to open, potentially a storm brewing. I couldn't deny it might hit at any moment but my body called me to run despite the rain that might come.

As I ran and the sky got brighter and bluer I felt a false sense of security that the rain would hold off. I had made it to our local duck park and began to take in the sight of the expanse of water and sky. My heart sang and my feet pounded. I always felt 'at home' when running. I processed some of the pain in my heart, started to pray and then found myself trying to embed the scripture Psalm 91 in my mind. I really wanted this one to stick. So far I had only managed to memorise the first few verses and part of the last verse: 'Whoever dwells in the shelter of the most high will rest in the shadow of the Almighty. If you say of the Lord 'You are my refuge and my strength, my God in whom I trust...' And the last verse 'with long life I will satisfy him and show him my salvation.'

As I ran I reflected on the time months back, when I had sent a text to some friends. I had decided it was time we tell them that we had made a decision to allow Luka to be put on the heart transplant list. Every day at that time I had been praying the verse Psalm 57:1 'Have mercy on me O God, Have mercy on me for I come to you for safety. In the shadow of your wings I find protection until the raging storms are over'. The dark clouds hung fast in the sky every day at that time. They threatened to open up, to overwhelm me, to hit me with hail, lightning, thunder and anything else they could throw at me. Each day I prayed this verse many times, and particularly when I went to bed. The night always held such darkness and fear for me. I would wake sometimes thinking I had heard myself scream. I would wake with my heart racing and everything in me wanting to scream at doctors, "Leave her alone! Don't you touch my baby girl!"

My counselor, (who I secretly named 'Princess Fiona' because her beauty, green dress and red hair had reminded me of the human version of Shrek's Fiona)... had said to me, "Allow that voice. That voice that wakes you screaming, that voice that yells at the doctors in your mind is your protective mother's instinct. Let her scream. Tell her it's okay to feel that way. This voice is natural; it's a good voice, the voice of a mother wanting to protect her child. Soothe her. Tell her it's okay and then go back to sleep. Don't suppress or stifle her. Tell her she's right to feel this way."

As I was running, I was reminded of the first time I had really paid attention to Psalm 91. I had started writing in my text to some friends (when I informed them we were putting Luka on the list) a verse from Psalm 57 that I had been praying for months. As I went to write the last part: *'in the shadow of your wings I find protection until the raging storms are over'*, I deleted the verse and decided not to write it. I don't know why.

My friend Jess had responded initially with something along the lines of being too busy to respond properly, and wanting to take time to pray before she responded. Later that night I received a long text from Jess. Jess had been praying for Luka-Angel in light of my informing her we would be listing Luka, and had seen visions of Luka grown up. She also wrote Psalm 91 in the text and said she saw a vision of our house with my family of six tucked inside. Over every inch of the house were God's wings, protecting feathers. Not a place of our house was uncovered, his feathers covered every corner. Jess said she believed God's wings were protecting us and he would continue to protect us and bring Luka-Angel safely through.

As I read Psalm 91 in Jess's text, it felt like the answer to the prayer I had been repetitively praying, *'Have mercy on me O God, have mercy on me for I come to you for safety. In the shadow of your wings I find protection until the raging storms are over'* (Psalm 57:1). I hadn't ended up writing my verse in the text. So Jess's response was confirmation that God was hearing my prayers. I received Jess's text as our family was driving home in the dark. As I got home that night, it looked different. I could see and picture God's wings over our house. Not a space uncovered by his feathers. I pictured his angels filling every space and holding on to us. Our house looked more peaceful than ever before, a safe refuge.

As I ran and reflected that day, months after transplant, I contemplated how I had never really told Jess how much her text meant. How much those words held me fast while Luka slept. How much those words gave me hope, security and comfort. Her words were yet another offering of prophetic knowledge that God had a future for Luka-Angel here on earth. This was another hope to cling to during our toughest hours, days, and weeks ahead.

As I ran around the duck park, in and out of reflection and pondering, I felt thankful the rain had held off. It seemed to have disappeared. I stopped for a moment and took in the sight of the water on the dry rocks. I thought about the time I stood there last June, noticing how dry the rocks were right where sometimes I had seen rapids. Not a drop of water to be found. I felt God share with me that I needed to invite him into every dry place in my life and he had resources that could flow and wash over me. As I allowed him to do that, he would overflow abundantly into the lives of others around me. I prayed in response that He would fill every dry place within me to overflowing. That he would pour himself in me, over me and out from me. Love, joy, peace, patience, kindness, goodness, gentleness, self-control, courage, strength... all that his beauty entailed. The next day following that one in June, I had run past these rocks and they had looked completely different; a stream, flowing with water pouring fast from the large body of water above, flowing into every crevice between the rocks, flowing over the rocks and making them beautiful. The water flowed quickly to the base of the rocks and out into a large body of water that lit up the neighbourhood with its beauty. I felt God tell me that this is how it can be when I ask him to fill me, when I open up every place to him.

Now months later, as I stopped briefly, I noted there was only a little water. It seemed to fill the crevices between the rocks, but not be overflowing or abundant. I prayed again that God would abundantly pour into my life.

I paused just a moment at the top of the next hill and took in the view of the sky and water. Suddenly, out of nowhere, the sky went dark. So dark it looked like night, although it was only 6pm on a daylight savings Monday night. It wasn't usually dark until 8 o'clock. As the sky went dark, a harsh, strong wind blew up then the pelting began. I continued my jog home (I had no choice) the rain stinging my skin. My clothes were absolutely soaked. I looked for the lightning that seemed inevitable and tried to work out what I might do out on this open footpath when the lightning came. I tried to find a place of shelter, but it seemed there was no choice except to remain in the pelting rain. I wondered if it was hail it felt so hard, but there were no balls of ice on the ground to indicate such. I wondered if my family might come looking for me in the car. I wondered if someone might come to 'rescue' me. No cars drove past and I didn't have the courage to knock on the door of a stranger.

As I came up the next hill, my eyeballs stinging from the rain, I noticed a building with a dry patch of concrete. Under the roof awning in one part of the 'Grace Church' car park, there was shelter. I wondered whether I would be better pressing on through the rain, the discomfort and the pain, or whether choosing to seek refuge for a few minutes might be helpful. I made the choice to take the shelter. As I stood sheltered by 'Grace' (church), hearing and seeing the storm around me, and seeing the water flood down the gutters, down the footpath and into the drains, I kept safe and felt a moment of refuge in Grace's shelter.

My mind travelled back to the hallways and white rooms of the Royal Children's Hospital. I recalled the storm around, the wind, the pelting rain, the thunderous sound of hearing that my only daughter's transplant had not been successful. I remembered the first night, laying on a chair and howling. It was a sound I hadn't heard out of myself before. I remembered my sister Karen reading scripture over me, patting my hair and her calming voice as my heart broke into a million pieces and every cell of my body ached. I remembered being soaked by the rain, my skin stinging from the hard rain coming in from all angles. I also remembered the moment I decided to rest in the shelter of 'Grace.' The next day, grace held me fast, held me close, and encompassed me as I chose to rest in his hand, in his shelter. I remembered the storm remained around me, the rain continued to pelt, and the darkness fell solidly around me, but I had found shelter. I didn't have to press on alone in the rain and the storm anymore. There was a place I could find refuge, comfort and safety. I recalled how I had chosen to dwell there, and how it felt warm. It felt dry and I could still see and hear the storm and the rain, but I was safe. I was held. I was protected.

After minutes of dwelling under the shelter of the 'Grace' church roof, which felt like hours of reflection, I came out from under the roof and faced the rain again. I arrived home and to my slight dismay no one had been worried about me. I stood on the doorstep calling out with laughter – I looked like I had jumped into a pool, disappointed by the very little attention I received as the T.V provided distraction for some of the household. I contemplated how I was going to get upstairs without soaking the floorboards. No one brought me a towel, so I decided to drip my way through the house to my shower upstairs, announcing to each person to be careful not to slip on my puddles. When I reached the top floor of the house I noticed another set of wet, puddled footsteps. Then the hugest puddle at the bathroom door. I called out 'Who is in the shower?'

"It's me," Luka-Angel called out.

"Oh," I said a little frustrated, "well, I am soaking! I need a shower, I am going to jump in our shower so don't be too long because as soon as I turn it on it will take some of your hot water." I shouted through the door.

Looking around me at all the water already on the floor, I called out to the boys downstairs, "Who has put wet footprints all through the hallway?" No response. "Who has been playing with water?" All the boys made clear it wasn't them. There was a LOT of water, and it looked as though the boys had enjoyed a water fight! "Someone is going to slip over – whoever did it needs to clean it up." I called out.

Suddenly the voice from inside the kid's shower called out joyfully, "It was me! I dripped the puddles through the house. I was dancing in the rain Mum!! I saw the rain, and I couldn't help it, I ran outside to dance in it!"

My heart overflowed with joy. Whilst I had sought refuge from the pelting rain during my jog under the 'Grace' church roof, my delightful daughter had come outside of the refuge of our house, and taken an intentional moment to joyfully dance in the rain.

This felt strangely familiar.

I contemplated those white walls of the Royal Children's Hospital again, her body didn't work but for machines. Her expression was still and revealed nothing but peace. Her spirit had been dancing in the rain; dancing in the rain with her Creator God, soaring in his presence, delighting in the light around her. Meanwhile, I had been taking shelter in his Grace from the storm that blew fiercely all around me.

Chapter 36

The Burden & the Cartwheel

'Feed the hungry and help those in trouble. Then your light will shine out from the darkness, and the darkness around you will be as bright as noon. The Lord will guide you continually, giving you water when you are dry and restoring your strength.' Isaiah 58:10-12 (NLT)

Journal entry:

Yesterday it was six months to the calendar date of Luka-Angel's heart transplant.

Due to a week of some extra symptoms including extra beats and shortness of breath, we were called to Melbourne for a week of tests. I wasn't particularly concerned and assumed it was something to do with the pace maker. So here we were yesterday, waking up in the same room at Ronald McDonald House we have stayed in many times before over the last seven years – room 38.

We started our day by catching the taxi to the Rose Street Artist Markets just off Brunswick Street in Fitzroy.

We realised as we arrived at the markets that we didn't have any money, so we walked about three blocks to Coles to get some cash out and a couple of bottles of water. On approaching Coles, we couldn't help but notice the lady bowed down on the footpath. A piece of old cardboard provided her seat and another piece her sign. There was a little loose change on the sign which read that she needed help.

Luka-Angel when she was about six years old first came face to face with the issue of homelessness. She would cry as she read the hand written cardboard signs of those living homeless in Melbourne and tug on my arm telling me I couldn't just walk past and we had to help them. I remember thinking as we passed so many, and she wanted to give to every single one, how was I going to keep this up? We bought one man a sandwich from the 7-11 shop he sat out the front of. I came to know that I needed to bring change in my pockets whenever we flew down for our Melbourne Hospital visits. The first time I saw Luka bring change from her own pocket money really shocked me. She gave all she had, telling me that she had everything she needed anyway, so she could give her money away.

So here we were outside Coles on Fitzroy, when to no surprise, Luka turned to me and said, "Mum, can we please buy her some food?"

"Sure," I had replied.

Well, as we walked around Coles, one thing led to another. More and more was being put in the basket. At one point I said, "Luka, I think this is enough now! We have to remember she will have to carry it."

"Mum," she said to me both angry and shocked, "how would you feel if you were homeless? Of course she needs a toothbrush and some toothpaste too. Food is not enough."

Luka insisted on buying her a bag to make the things easier for her to carry. We chose a bag with a little dog on the front as the lady herself had a dog beside her. Delighted with our purchases and looking forward to presenting them, we walked towards the exit.

"Excuse me." The young man's voice from the table in the corner called.

I looked over initially frustrated that he had called for my attention. I hadn't seen him call to the several people who had walked in front of me. He went on trying to get me to help his cause. I told him repetitively that I would love to give a one off donation and I was not interested in a monthly donation as I was already at my maximum of monthly donations to some other causes. 'Mr Salesman' continued the conversation which really was quite a good one. Although somewhat irritated I reconciled that at least we had nothing to do today other than please ourselves. I watched the little dog of the homeless woman through the front window – then his little furry face was out of sight again. Finally on getting away, we made for our exit, our heavy yellow bag with the picture of a dog still in my hand.

As we came out the doors it was clear straight away that she was gone. We were so disappointed!

'What was the point of all that effort?' I thought. I felt sort of silly and a little annoyed at the woman for moving. We wondered where she had gone in such a short amount of time? We decided to walk across the busy road and see if she was down the dirty old alley in front of us. Walking down the very run down alley was unnerving coupled with the off-putting pungent smell of urine. Strong, stale, concrete embedded urine.

We realised we would have to carry the bag around until we found her. As we walked back towards the Rose Street Markets I felt rather annoyed. I recalled unpacking my handbag that morning at the Ronald McDonald House unit, taking out anything unnecessary so I could walk fairly freely on our market trip. Here I was holding a heavy grocery bag. It then hit me that the burden the homeless carry every day far outweighs the burden of me carrying a grocery bag for the day. The burden of not knowing where to sleep that night, not being able to hang on to or accumulate things as there's nowhere to put them, how to stay safe, what food will they eat the next day, where will they wash or go to the toilet, what if they get sick – how will they see a doctor, let alone the root causes of why they were there in the first place. Then of course the burden my daughter carries for the homeless. From the six-year-old girl who would cry for them, to the teenager who now takes the action and even scolds me if I don't. The thirteen-year-old girl, who has been through so much herself, yet thinks about others more than her own pain and dreams constantly about her 'Lighthouse' Homelessness Centre.

We walked around the Artists' Markets and Luka-Angel seemed to point out everything that was a heart, keenly aware of it being her six month anniversary. She found two necklaces side-by-side, hand made by the sweet older lady behind the stall. One was a little boy with a hole in his chest in the shape of a heart; the other was a little girl with brown hair, holding out her heart. Side by side they sat. For a long time Luka held them together, touched them and looked at them.

She looked up at me and said with great sparkle, "Mum, it's the donor and the recipient".

After moving on from the markets, we made our way to the zoo as Luka was desperate to see the lions. On getting there we found out the lions had died a month ago.

On our walk home, I delighted in the fact that she could walk home. Previously, this would never have been a possibility.

As we approached the large parklands with the hospital providing the backdrop, Luka-Angel cartwheeled and did split leaps over the grass. We *stopped long enough to contemplate that just six months before, Luka lay in one of the rooms in the distance, on life support.*

As she frolicked and danced and laughed and ran, I could barely believe where we had been, or where we were now.

Chapter 37

Finally Able to Dance

'You have turned my mourning into joyful dancing'.
Psalm 30:11 (NLT)

It doesn't seem so long ago that I was in this street for different reasons. Luka had spotted this dance studio on one of her visits to a local doctor. She had watched the ballerinas walking into their academy and longed to be able to do the same. That was a tough day for her, so we had decided to walk into the studio, so she could take a look. She took a business card and said to me with great determination and hope, "Mum, this will be my dance studio after I have had a heart transplant." Then she went home and framed the business card and put it on her bedside table.

This day, as I watch the back of Luka, perfect little bun, black leotard, pink tights, ballet shoes in hand, casually stroll into the dance academy doors as if she's been doing this her whole life, I can hardly comprehend we are at this point in time. My daughter, finally able to dance!

I cannot help but interrupt this thought to give you a glimpse into my diary. For the above written moment, there were a few lessons to learn in Luka-Angel's first season of dance. I feel compelled to let you know some reality of a mum of four with a busy life, so here is a glimpse into my journal on Luka-Angel's first day of dance.

Journal Entry

January (Five months post-transplant)

It suddenly hit me as I scrambled and rushed through Kmart looking for the pink tights that I suddenly remembered were required. Determined, I became aware I was marching along, nearly bowling over anyone in front of me. My thirteen year old waited in the car so I could go a little faster to purchase what we needed. Climbing back into the car twelve whole minutes later with no success of getting the ideal thing... I threw her the thick, apricot, stirruped leggings on this 41 degree day.

My usual modest daughter got completely changed in the front seat of the car as we drove. Throwing a beach towel over her, we giggled every time the lights went red, matching her face.

This was not the way I had pictured we would prepare for her first proper dance class. I guess we didn't really look into exactly what would be needed. I was still getting my head around the whole back to school thing, having had several months off. I hadn't even thought about the pink tights. I had searched high and low through my usual shops to find the leotard the day before, and found one a size too small deciding it would have to do. The white stockings she had found at home and popped underneath it revealing her undergarments were just not quite right. The thick white stuck out like an eyesore from beneath her leotard lines. I had pictured a more graceful and special departure for her first ballet class. A more reserved and pondered trip...even perhaps accompanied by a photo shoot or something. Her three brothers would wave her off loyally at the door as she gracefully waltzed down the stairs and into the car, dressed in her perfect ballet outfit, her hair so neatly in a bun. Instead, clothes flew, and

I may have even broken the speed limit in places as the old beach towel became the change room and time was not on our side.

Luka had done a few weeks of ballet lessons when she was six years old but it had been too difficult for her. At the time I didn't understand it was because of her heart. I recall my frustration as she refused to get out of the car one day, just weeks into the term. She was crying that, "It hurts and it's too hard!" I had already paid the term's fees in advance! I never knew then it wasn't just too hard for her, it was actually dangerous for her to participate. So beyond that short few weeks, this was her first ballet class!

Luka was finally dressed, and as I pulled up at the studio I was squealing and ranting, and raving with excitement! "I can't believe you can finally dance Luka! Can you believe it?" Luka turned to me with a now firm face of maturity and said, "Mum, STOP! Keep it together. Don't do that in there will you?!" In obedience, I got out of the car like a 'normal' dance mum and casually walked my daughter in. As they whisked her off to her first ballet class while I tried to peer after her, I soon realised I wouldn't be allowed in. So I slunk back to the waiting room to sit and imagine what Luka dancing freely might look like.

As I sat down to fill out the insurance forms, the mother next to me smiled saying, "Is this your daughter's first time here?" "Yes," I beamed, and couldn't help but go on. I was thankful for a moment to proudly share a short part of my very determined daughter's story.

The mother simply smiled back with tears in her eyes. I welled up and responded "This is a very poignant moment for her." She nodded as I swallowed my tears...

I recall a time not so long ago, when my little girl, convinced she was 'born to be a dancer', would clear the lower floor of our house, put on her music and dance outfit, even though she couldn't even get through half a song. She would end up bent over on the old blue lounge, head down, holding her breath as she gasped for air. Often I would remind her to not get to that point, but she would say to me in a frustrated tone, "Mum, I want to dance!" For her, one minute of slow movement to music, was worth the minutes of chest tightening, tachycardia and breathlessness that would follow. She would get up again minutes later, and it would be a repeat story, until she was just too weak to keep trying.

It seemed the more she couldn't dance, the more she would try.

I remember telling her one day that she could perhaps focus on 'preparing her body' for dancing in the future after her transplant. I advised her to do some stretches and increase her flexibility. Little did I realise she would be stretching and increasing her flexibility nearly every waking moment (at home anyway). I remember the day she managed to do the splits. I could hardly comprehend her determination. I remember trying to get myself to the splits around the same age. I never quite got there. Here she was, just months into trying, and already achieving the splits. However, she didn't stop there. She learned how to cartwheel perfectly. Every reaction her body had after a cartwheel was comparable to someone who had just run kilometres as she faced breathlessness, exhaustion and tachycardia. Next she learned to do bend backs.

The day we got the phone call that changed our lives I was so busy with the work to be done around the house. I was therefore so grateful later, that when she had said, "Mum, come watch this," as I passed the lounge room briskly getting on with my work, that I had backtracked. My first response had been, "I can't stop Luka, there's too much to do". Then all in a second I remembered our mandate that every day counts, and I had reversed my brisk walk a few steps and said, "Okay, show me. I only have a couple of minutes." To my shock she had done her first one handed cartwheel.

Here I am today, driving off from the dance academy, dwelling on the journey it has taken to get here. Just five months ago, Luka had to teach her muscles to walk again. Now she is back to doing the splits, standing on pointe, and finally able to dance without stopping!! As the other ballet dancers come in and out of those doors, I wonder if they could ever dream of the determination and challenges it has taken for my Luka-Angel to get to the point of being able to attend dance classes. This was surely a journey many could never possibly imagine. The part of her scar that surreptitiously peeks out from the top of her leotard, tells a portion of a story that no one there knows yet.

Chapter 38

The Choppy Seas

'God is our refuge and strength, an ever-present help in trouble. Therefore we will not fear, though the earth gives way, and the mountains fall into the heart of the sea, though its waters roar and foam...' Psalm 46:1-2 (NIV)

I have just been on a run along the Bar Beach Anzac walk around the headlands. The wind beats strong today following a cyclone up north. There were times on my run when I was pushed into the fence alongside the cliff, my feet involuntarily being lifted in slightly the wrong direction. This run was uncomfortable, more painful than usual, and took over-and-above endurance.

As I stopped at the top of my favourite cliff top and looked out over the ocean that extends so far, I noticed how incredibly choppy the water was. To my left, the waves crashed so hard on the rocks and shoreline that the spray reached the cliffs. To my right, the waves were white, strong and larger than I have seen here. I noted how the waves seemed to reflect the turbulence I feel inside today. Today, I can't put words to all the swirling, choppy feelings. The anxiety, the fears that sometimes surface, the disappointment in myself as some ugly thoughts were captured in my mind.

I remember as I write, a time about seven years ago, when I went running just before a big storm hit the coast at Coolangatta. The waves were some of the largest I had seen. At the end of my run, I had sat down on some rocks, thinking about how large the waves were and how in awe I was of their power. I remember God whispering to me, "Sometimes, my child, the waves in life are rough, powerful and scary, but underneath those waves out there, there are dolphins. Underneath even the roughest and choppiest sea, dolphins can still be found." I knew instantly that the dolphins represented 'peace'. I knew instantly that underneath the roughest of seas I have to face, that there is peace always available to me. It won't always be obvious. I can't always see it, but I can know confidently that it lies there, it hasn't disappeared. Just like the dolphins, even the waves can't chase them out of the sea. I can always recall that peace is available and I can ask for the peace of God to be revealed to me, to wash over me, even in the hardest of times.

After I had just finished hearing God speak those years ago, just finished recognising what he was saying to me, he made that illustration visually and beautifully embed itself in my mind. A pod of dolphins arose out of the rough waves, sailing peacefully in them, through them, rising to their surface just beyond the crashing of their white froth and I was amazed!

Today, I need to remember this.

Today the wind blows so hard against me it literally hurts my skin, and pushes me in directions I don't want to go. Today I am facing some of the demons of my past, some of the pains in my heart, some of the anxiety of my family's future. I remember though, that in amidst this weather, and the choppiest of seas, as I continue to push forward, I can call on the peace of God. Oh, how I need to know that peace.

> *'The men were amazed and asked, "What kind of man is this? Even the winds and the waves obey him!"*
> Matthew 8:27 (NLT)

Chapter 39

Home is Where the Heart Is

'A sweet friendship refreshes the soul.' Proverbs 27:9 (The Message)

As I watch my daughter sitting on the floor of this hotel room on a yoga mat, laughing and calling out as she replicates the yoga moves on the yoga channel, I can hardly comprehend what we've been through and how we got here. As she twists her body into the strangest positions, pushing her flexibility even further, she chats away with joy! This will be the first specialist visit where I expect good and smooth results. This is also the first visit we have ever brought her friend to. We finally feel in a 'safe zone'. The last few months have been the best she has ever had in terms of health and physical ability, and most days, the worries for Luka stay at bay.

Last Friday I watched as for the first time in her life, my daughter got to 'walk around with friends'. It was the school's cross-country race. The upbeat music was pumping loudly through the speakers on their stands, and a buzz was in the air. Students lined up and ran. As I waited under the shady tree for Luka to pass by, I reflected on my joy that Luka was able to participate in her first cross country. After years of waiting, she could finally walk around with a group of friends. In past times, when the school went to the local oval for sport, Luka had to be driven, on the year six social event everyone had walked to the bowling alley, Luka had to be driven. As the four friends passed (covered in paint – it was a colour run), the laughter and the camaraderie was beautiful. Four friends walking together may not seem so out of the ordinary to the average eye. For Luka though, this was a first. Never before had she walked around with friends (for a significant amount of time). An experience she only got to have for the first time at nearly fourteen years old!

Here we are though, back in Melbourne for the fifth time this year, on this very cold April day. The wind whips at the windows and the temperature outside is fourteen degrees. Just the temperature takes me back to seven months ago. As I look out the hotel window, just 20 metres from where I sit I can see the footpath that reminds me instantly of the 2am morning on the 9th September when I ran to see my little girl who had just been resuscitated in the Intensive Care Unit. My heart is reflective every time we arrive back here at the Children's Hospital. I joked to Luka back in February as we had a monthly hospital visit, that seeing this place again felt like coming home, instantly following with, "Well, they say home is where the heart is." To which we both laughed! Many times since Luka has pulled out this little joke. I have observed that interestingly there is a certain attachment that comes with the heart. This organ is no ordinary organ. This is the organ we refer to about all things beautiful, all things to do with feelings, all things we are passionate about, all things we love. 'He has my heart,' you might say about someone you love, or, 'she broke my heart', or, 'do it with all of your heart.' This is no ordinary vessel, out of the overflow of it, the Bible says, the mouth speaks. We say we 'accept Jesus into' it, when we make a decision to become a Christian. It is our life source; it is responsible for keeping us alive. This is no ordinary organ. This organ appears to represent the very core of who we are.

I remember the day about twelve months before Luka was transplanted. She came to me and asked me what would happen to her heart when they take it out? She was crying and said she felt sorry for her heart and needed to know what would happen to it. Concerned, I had asked her if she was truly ready to hear the answer. She said, "Yes". So I explained that I couldn't be sure, but I imagine they would incinerate it. She had quietly nodded and walked away. Often she confessed she felt sad for her heart and was so proud of that little guy for trying so hard to keep her alive and well. On feeling frustrated at some issues she was having a few months post-transplant, I once referred to her new heart as being a bit 'dodgy'. Luka instantly jumped to defend her new heart and said, "How could you say that Mum? This is my new heart now and I love it." It is bittersweet to try and understand that someone lost this heart. Some family long for their person, and know that somewhere out there, his or her heart is still beating, but within someone else. Such a difficult thing to comprehend or reconcile. My gratitude for this incredible gift cannot be put into words. This gift brings my daughter life she could never have known. This incredible gift can never be valued. It truly is invaluable!

Somewhere in the midst of writing this the storm clouds brew over in the distance. This journey is not over for us yet. Every time I gaze into my ten-year-old son's face, every time I see him bent over, short of breath and tachycardic, every time I see that he can't keep up with his little brother, or try out for the soccer team, or jump on the trampoline, or ride a bike up an incline, or go for a walk or run, I see the dark clouds. They hover every day, threatening wildly to break loose at any given moment. They hover every day and often make me shudder; usually late at night when it is quiet, distractions are gone and my defenses are down. Those clouds send my heart racing several times a night, to which I quieten my fears with verses on God's peace that passes understanding:

'He will keep in perfect peace him whose heart is set on him because he trusts in Him' (Isaiah 26:3). 'My peace I give to you, my peace I leave with you. I do not give to you as the world gives; do not let your hearts be troubled or afraid.' (John 14:27)

These clouds hover on the sunniest of days. My precious boy often arrives home from school with joy on his face as he rushes to his precious cockatiel, 'Evie', and instantly I see the colour of his pale skin, the dark circles around his eyes. I cup his face in my hands and say, "Jazz, do you feel well today? You don't look very good," and my heart sinks.

Tomorrow my daughter will wake up early, go down to pathology and put her arm out for tubes of blood to be filled up and tested to make sure her medications are balanced well and there is not too much toxicity. Her 'normal' is far from everyone else's normal. Since she was a cute little blonde six-year-old, it has been her normal to visit doctors every few months (and now monthly), have blood taken, lay still for Echos, ECGs, blood pressure and have the occasional cardiac catheter or exercise test. This is also the normal Jazz has known. They do life with a smile, Echos with compliancy and blood tests with bravery. They have courage I couldn't possibly replicate or even know how to resource. I am in awe of how God has made them, and the way they embrace life. They urge me to do better, not get caught up in the little things, and to be more courageous. Their circumstances make me stronger, more resilient and create in me a perseverance that I couldn't possibly achieve without my Creator strengthening me and upholding me.

As I sit here yet again on the eve of more tests and clinic visits, and reflect on Luka's blue face at cross country the other day, I see past the blue paint covering her smooth skin, and see a smile that beamed so big it almost reached the corners of her eyes. I reflect on the laughter that accompanied the sight before me, and the strength of friendship, these friends that in the last seven months have been through more than most adults. As I sit in my second home, Ronald McDonald House, hearing the chatting of my daughter and her best friend in the background, my heart is warmed. So thankful we don't have to do life's ups and downs alone.

Chapter 40

Snakes & Adders

> 'He will command his angels concerning you to guard you in all your ways. On their hands they will bear you up, lest you strike your foot against a stone. You will tread on the lion and the adder, the young lion and serpent you will trample under foot. Because he holds fast to me in love, I will deliver him. I will protect him because he knows my name.' Psalm 91:11-14 (ESV)

I am amazed at how many times I have seen God save Luka-Angel.

There are so many times that come to mind for me, when I have been sure that Luka was only saved by our great God and the miraculous has taken place. I am also sure there have been other times I have not seen when God sent his angels to protect Luka or my family.

Some occasions have been very dramatic and memorable, and other times haven't been as shocking, but simply times where I could not possibly explain what just happened.

One such time was when Luka-Angel was about two and a half to three years old. She loved being pushed high on the swing and would always ask to go higher. This particular day I let loose as she called out delightedly, "Higher, push me higher!" Her smile revealed her joy as she soared through the sky above the ground below. At the peak of one of her heights, all of a sudden Luka-Angel fell off the swing and turned upside down her head aimed straight to the hard ground below. It was so quick, all in a breath, and I remember hearing my involuntary scream. At the last minute, right before my eyes, Luka-Angel's body flipped the right way up, just centimetres before hitting the ground, and she landed on her bottom instead of her head. It literally looked like someone invisible had grabbed her body and made it do a very quick half somersault just in the nick of time. A slightly bruised backside was nothing compared to what could have been a broken neck or severely bumped head.

I remember turning to the family member with me and saying, "How did that happen?! How did her body turn like that?" I decided it could only have been an angel. The way her body suddenly spun, just before she hit the ground seemed physically impossible!

It came as no surprise considering her history, when Luka-Angel encountered another such experience just a few days ago as I write.

A canoe trip and camping in the bush might have seemed a silly decision, just seven months post-transplant, and with Jazz and Lucas' health issues. However, with our mandate to 'live life to the full', the idea of the camping trip in the middle of nowhere that came out of a discussion with our good friends, seemed perfect! A chance to celebrate Luka-Angel's new fitness, get away, have an adventure and embrace life before Jazz goes on the heart transplant list. I remember a family 'voice of reason and wisdom' saying to me that she didn't think it was the best idea. The remoteness of what we were doing, coupled with the exercise just seemed quite foolish to her. I felt very at peace about going, and that is always enough for me. There will always be a reason not to do something, that doesn't mean we shouldn't. We were very tired, and several times I heard Lucas say, "Let's just cancel." I could see his point, we were all tired, but I was driven to follow through on this, for all of us. I felt that an adventure was in order, and we needed to embrace the moment!

We knew we would be camping in the bush, and that facilities would not be available. We knew we were canoeing to get there, and that takes time and energy. We understood camping in the bush can be uncomfortable but we needed to take the bare minimum. We also knew that in the bush, there can be all kinds of critters, so we packed our first aid kit and snake bite kit over luxuries like mattresses or pillows.

What a camping trip it was. Getting back to nature always makes my heart full. Just seeing the open sky, the water, smelling the bush and being surrounded by God's beauty brings me closer to him.

Our campsites much to our surprise had the bonus of a pit toilet. Here we were thinking we would have to dig a hole or use the open ended bucket Lucas had brought, so a smelly pit toilet in the middle of the bush, a walk away from our campsite, was a great surprise and bonus for us girls! The first night walking through the complete darkness of the bush to get to the pit toilet was really quite a sight; lots of tussling between my sister and I and Luka, to get the middle position. The sound of cracking in the bush making our already nervous bodies jump and voices squeal, but lots of laughter at our own silly behavior trumped it all. Several times I had to drop to the ground as I was truly busting and standing at a time like that just didn't feel overly safe! Aunty Karen, Luka and I tussled and walked, with arms linked all the way to the toilet on that first night. On the way back, a big jump scare from a very satisfied crew of kids with

Elijah as their leader, made the experience all the more memorable. I recall shining my head lamp straight at him, before I could laugh, to make sure it was just my boys (and our friend Serenity) and not some strangers waiting to pounce on three victims.

Another day of canoeing landed us at another beautiful campsite. Once again, we were met with the surprise of another pit toilet a walk away from our tents. When our friend Samuel suggested a sunset bushwalk, I jumped at the chance. As we beat our way through the thick scrub up the hill, and were met at the top with more thick scrub and dense bush I asked, "Where is the track?" Samuel was a little confused by my question. Having grown up and even lived for a time in the bush on his own, he didn't really do tracks. My biggest concern was my daughter, with no immune system. Walking through thick scrub land in the Australian bush, to me, was playing with fire. Some of the foliage was shin deep. I kept looking for snakes, believing they were there somewhere, watching our every move.

As we followed Samuel, I became aware that my feet behind his, were matching his footsteps. Where he trod, I wanted my foot to go. I knew that if there was a snake, it would hopefully flee where his foot had already gone. As I looked not ahead, but down, at each footprint of Samuel's, it dawned on me that this is what I have been doing for the last fifteen years of my life. Not looking ahead, but carefully endeavouring to place my feet right in the footprints of Jesus. I could not see the future, he could. I couldn't look ahead and have my future mapped out, but Jesus knew everything. He knew what my future held and he knew how to get there. He knew the dangers that lay waiting to trip me up. As I trudged steadily in Samuel's footprints, I recalled years earlier when I had been praying one day at a youth leader's conference, and I saw a vision of Jesus in front of me. He had a beautiful warm and gentle smile on his face and he was looking back at me eagerly, his eyes calling me to come forward. His hand was outstretched for mine. Just after I grabbed it he started to run carefully ahead, almost a skip in his step, and with anticipation, joy, adventure and gentleness in his eyes he kept looking back at me with a smile. I kept trying to look around him to see what was ahead, but instead all I could do was land my eyes on him in front of me. He said, "Follow me, keep your eyes on me," and the impression I had, was that I could trust him fully and there was adventure ahead.

As it got dark on our bush walk, my fear overtook my feeling of fun and certainty. Finally though, we made it out the other side of the bush, down the hill, through the thick, sludgy reeds, and back safely to camp. No snakes, no snake bites. Though at times I was terrified I still enjoyed the adventure so much, but I recall finally being able to breathe out, that Luka-Angel was safe, and we were back at our campsite.

Not more than two hours later, (it was completely dark), Luka needed to go to the toilet. As I contemplated whether Karen's Kmart headlamp would provide enough light for us, Lucas insisted I take his good one. I said I didn't need to, but he insisted it was a good headlamp and placed it on my forehead, despite my protests. As Luka and I proceeded, I was so aware of the difference of this headlamp to the cheap Kmart one I had been wearing on the other nights. I could see at least twenty metres in front of me. Luka and I were marveling at the light shining so far ahead and Karen was catching us up from behind. I don't recall really looking down at our feet at all, as I was so fixated on how far ahead this light could shine.

Suddenly, I saw the snake right in front of Luka's raised foot. It felt like slow motion as I wacked my left arm backwards slamming her behind me and saying, "SNAKE!!" As Karen scurried up on my right, my right arm held her back (knowing how curious and daring she is) and again I yelled, "SNAKE!" I had prepped my kids in the car on the way to our trip saying "If you see a snake, you must stand completely still, everything within you will want to run, but you MUST STAND STILL!" Then checking in with them again that they remembered the drill I repeated, "What do you do?" Jazz and Jayjay would chant, "Stand still!" Ironically in this moment, with the snake right in front of us, the next word out of my mouth after, "SNAKE!" was, "RUN," and we did!! As we took our first step backwards, the snake launched into a strike, striking near Luka's raised foot! I had seen it's very wide open mouth, its fangs, and its neck snap sharp, and fast!! I had only ever seen a snake strike before on T.V. Keeping my head lamp fixed on the snake as we ran backwards, Karen called for Lucas and Samuel. We wanted that thing gone otherwise we were back to shovels and squatting!

As the men approached, I panted, "It looks the colour brown, I am not sure what it is though, it doesn't really look like a brown snake, it's a little fatter." The men got closer, and Samuel exclaimed with excitement, "It's a Death Adder!"

In that moment I knew that this was quite incredible. I had been reading a book on Psalm 91 having had it become a very important psalm in our journey to transplant, and then during Luka-Angel's time in hospital. Just a few days ago, I had been reading a story of a young boy whose mum would pray Psalm 91 over her children. Her son had been bitten by a venomous snake and needed anti-venom. The boy was fine. I had been praying Psalm 91 over our whole camping trip. I had even dwelt on the verses, *'For He will send his angels concerning you to guard you in all your ways. On their hands they will bear you up, lest you strike your foot against a stone. You will tread on the lion and the adder; the young lion and serpent you will trample underfoot.'* (Ps 91:11-13)

I knew this is exactly what had happened. Another reminder that God's protection was over us, his angels were guarding Luka-Angel. The fact that it was her foot, not mine that the death adder had struck at. The name of that particular snake felt reminiscent of what had happened, Luka had already faced death, and been revived. Here she was again, face to face with potential death, somehow without even intentionally looking, I saw it waiting, ready to pounce, hiding slightly under the sand, in the dark. I had intended to have no torch. Yet, Lucas had put his best brand headlamp on me, only on that particular walk.

Even though a little unnerved by the whole event, I felt God was reminding me firmly he had everything under control. Death Adders may come ready to attack, but God and his angels are one step ahead!!

Any wonder a few nights ago as Luka-Angel and I were in the car, she said to me with a big knowing smile, "I think God has a great purpose for my life Mum!" "Why do you say that?" I asked, wanting to hear from her. "Because of all the times he has saved me. Like the Death Adder that tried to bite me the other night (pause)... and the night I was resuscitated." "Yes", I said to Luka, "I think God has a great plan for your life!"

Chapter 41

King of our Hearts

'The cords of death entangled me, the anguish of the grave came over me; I was overcome by distress and sorrow. Then I called on the Name of the Lord "Lord, save me!" The Lord is gracious and righteous; our God is full of compassion.' Psalm 116:3-5 (NIV)

8 Months Post Heart Transplant

I was at the band rehearsal in my church tonight as we learnt a new song. We had just enjoyed an hour or so around the fire pit at the front of church, and been led in some worship under the stars on a crisp May evening. I shared a little blanket with the two girls either side of me. My friend beside me had been weeping towards the end of worship about a teenage boy she knew who suddenly died just four days before. He had a pre-existing condition, but this had come as a real shock! I silently put my hand on her shoulder and prayed for the God of all comfort to be close to her, and to the boy's family. She didn't tell me why she was crying, but I knew, so I prayed the Holy Spirit would help her in her grief.

Now we were inside, a little warmer and working on a new song 'King of My Heart'. This song wasn't so new to me. I recalled immediately the first time I heard it, and it took me straight to the ICU room and the cold hard seat I sat on, next to Luka-Angel. She was lying still on a bed, with tubes protruding from places all over her body. I pictured the many machines and flashing lights around her, and the pungent smell of sanitizer and alcohol wipes.

The next time I heard the song suddenly came to my mind, and the words hit me hard. I was transported back to a moment just about five months ago.

Lucas and I were in a space of still doing the recovery journey with Luka-Angel day to day, with most days at the hospital, which was very tiring. We were also still reeling from the shock of what we had been through and we were doing the journey alone at this point in time. Lucas seemed at that time to be covering his sorrows with the distraction of the TV and movies, and we were hardly talking together about what we had been through. I guess it seemed too poignant, and with kids around all the time it was just too hard. Most nights while Lucas watched TV, I would take myself off to bed, and crochet, journal, cry or pray before I fell asleep. This had never been a pattern of mine before, to lie in bed and do something. It felt strangely spoiling and comforting, but also very unusual for me.

This particular night (the second time I heard the song 'King of My Heart') I had felt especially isolated and very, very alone. A darkness and deep sadness had overcome my spirit. The visitors had stopped. Luka was starting to really struggle herself with isolation and loneliness, and although I completely understood it, I couldn't fix it. We were so far away from all we knew and loved. All six of us were trying our best to do life as 'normal' as possible, but everything in truth, was completely new and out of the ordinary.

There was nothing 'normal' about our days of one parent taking Luka to the hospital, and the other one staying home to home school the younger two, while our fifteen-year-old tried to teach himself. Nothing normal about the suburban city street we lived in or the little white house that we were temporarily calling 'home'. Nothing normal about the concrete backyard or the strong smell of Asian food and squashed old vegetables from the city markets around the corner. Everything around us seemed foreign, as we pretended to normalise it as much as possible. Someone had sent me a link to the song 'King of My Heart' yet again, and as I lay in my bed I played it.

In my dimly lit bedroom, the feeling that this was not over yet (knowing Jazz and Lucas would eventually need heart transplants too), and Luka-Angel still not completely well, was very real, and frightening.

As I watched my little phone screen and Stephanie Gretchen sang 'King of My Heart' with no inhibitions and some incredible improvisation and anointing of the spirit of God, tears streamed down my face. The words calmed me, fed me and lifted my spirit up. Over and over I heard, "You're never gonna let, you're never gonna let me down."

I was completely aware as the music played and I felt God's arms around me, that although I may have thought I was doing this leg of the journey alone, I wasn't. Loneliness gradually faded that night, as I felt the presence of my Heavenly Father fill my room reminding me he was good, he was with me and he would never, ever let me down. He was the King of my heart, the King of my little girl's new heart that up until this point had still been having lots of rhythm issues. He was the King of Lucas' hypertrophic heart, the King of Jazziah's restrictive heart.

The presence of my large, invisible God fell on my room, my spirit and on my heart reminding me that he was faithful!

As my mind gradually eased back into the music rehearsal I was at, I snuck away to take a 'moment'...

The mix of grief and assurance once again filled me, as I walked towards my door of escape to the background of the beautiful music of our church band: "You're never gonna let, you're never gonna let me down. You're never gonna let, you're never gonna let me down, you're never gonna let, you're never gonna let me down."

> 'The Lord is close to the brokenhearted and saves those who are crushed in spirit.' Psalm 34:18 (NIV)

Chapter 42

Not Alone

'So be strong and courageous! Do not be afraid and do not panic before them. For the Lord your God will personally go ahead of you; he will neither fail you or abandon you.' Deuteronomy 31:6 (NLT)

As I read through many past diary entries, I read over and over again where I encountered great loneliness in this journey of sickness, heart conditions and hospital visits.

It seems that every time I was feeling the worst of it, God reassured me by giving me images of thousands of people gathering around us and praying for us. One diary entry I believed God had said to me when I told him of my loneliness in all this, "If only you could see…" Then I instantly had an image of angels all around us, and thousands of Christians with hands outstretched on us and towards us, praying for us and upholding us in prayer.

I am amazed now, eight years down the track from some of those many diary entries that I have now seen it! It is exactly what happened. After Luka-Angel's transplant went so wrong, the thousands began to pray, then the tens of thousands. God knew. He already saw it all those years ago! I am sitting here just amazed having read these journal entries for the first time in years and seeing that he knew, and he even gave me a picture of it back then!

During our time of transplant for Luka, there was no doubt of countless supporting people. There were people walking up and down their hallways pleading, some on their knees before God, a friend who stood outside looked up at the sky and demanded, "She is one of your own – heal her!" Prayer meetings were held, a whole camp of Salvation Army children took time out from their schedule to write prayers for Luka, church groups everywhere prayed for Luka. Not just in Australia, but even as far as Uganda, Kenya, Ireland, New York, Canada, New Zealand, the Philippines, Switzerland, the U.S.A, South Africa, the United Kingdom, Papua New Guinea, Sri Lanka, Japan and Sweden. I am still amazed and touched at this outpouring of prayer for Luka and our family. Amazed. Then came the flood of letters from people we didn't know. It was absolutely beautiful and so encouraging.

It was God's people in fast action! The body of Christ stepping up and crying out for their brothers and sisters. It was human compassion, empathy, faith and care at its best.

I remember hearing some prayers via recorded messages, some prayers of real faith. I remember the sense that our story was bigger than I understood, and God wanted to use it to reach out and help others. I remember hearing the song about chains being broken and 'There's an Army rising up'. I remember within hours of hearing that song for the first time when it played on YouTube spontaneously, two people messaging me and saying Luka's story has brought our Army (The Salvation Army) to its knees like never before! An Army - rising up. I remember being beautifully touched by the fact that if God could use our Luka-Angel's story to help people be saved or grow in their faith it was worth it! As a person who never communicated personal information on Facebook, I was driven to put my story out there as I had been called to do for such a long time now. It was time to 'Speak Up', a word that had been given to me several times through people or God's voice in my mind.

There were over 30,000 people that we could count (according to hits on our church Facebook page) invisibly holding hands together and praying for our Luka-Angel to be made well. God heard, He moved! We were praying in his will.

I felt at one point very strongly that the enemy was trying so hard to rob our girl of life, but even in that, I knew God was stronger and had a different plan! I saw images of her telling her story to many people and God moving. I saw images of her dancing on a stage. I knew God had more for my Luka-Angel here on earth and I was so filled with hope and so grateful! Even in the worst of days I was filled to overflowing with hope. Some days when I could manage to have a sense of humour about it, I would think about each thing that went wrong as additions to Luka-Angel's great story she would tell one day!

My eyes were up. Luka was being held by God's hand. She was at peace and she was safe. We were being carried by angels into the room where she lay, and God's people had built a safe haven around us.

Chapter 43

Trust

'Trust in the Lord, with all your heart, and do not lean on your own understanding.' Proverbs 3:5-6 (ESV)

Recently a young friend of mine, who we have been taking to church as a family on and off for the last few years, came to me after I led worship at church and said, "Angela, I am having some problems with trusting in God." My friend is only fourteen years old, and is fostered. I know from my own experiences fostering, that trust can be a major issue for these vulnerable kids. So it came as no shock when she went on, "Angela, throughout my life I have had many people walk away from me, or desert me. People have let me down. So I am having trouble trusting God, and I am not sure what to do about it."

Her insight into her trust issues at her age, spoke to me of someone who had been taught well about some things she may encounter due to her life's circumstances, or someone who was very self-aware. I was delighted in her honesty and her sharing and of course could only meet such a comment naturally with understanding and grace. "That makes perfect sense," I said to her, knowing after years of following Jesus whole heartedly, I still encounter trust issues along the way. "It's okay." I told her. "You can come to God just as you are. You can talk to him and say 'I am not sure whether I can trust you yet'. He knows anyway, but don't let it stop you talking to him and seeking to get to know who he is."

I told her that on top of the fact that people she should have been able to trust had broken her trust, she couldn't even see God, and that's hard. I explained that's where faith comes in. It can be a journey to trusting God, just like it takes time to know who you can trust when you first encounter people.

This morning, as I re-read again the sixth chapter of Daniel, my heart engaged closely. I just love this story in the Bible. Daniel seeks each day to trust God and live an upright life. He seeks to display loyalty and trust to his King, even though he was captured and taken prisoner. Daniel saw his family, his home and many people he knew destroyed. His circumstances were dire but he chose to keep his eyes securely fixed on God. He chose to be loyal and faithful in the circumstances he found himself in. Daniel is then noticed and elevated to a high leadership position within this foreign Kingdom, so much so, that even the King deeply loves and cares for Daniel.

Daniel, even in the face of death, refuses to deny his faith in God, and continues to pray and meet with God despite the threats. Daniel's loyalty and faithfulness to the leader in charge of him (King Darius), is only trumped by his loyalty and faithfulness to the God who created him.

It tugs at my heart when I read of Darius not being able to sleep, or do anything all night after he is cruelly tricked by those jealous of Daniel who consequently is thrown into the lion's den to be eaten. Darius gets up first thing in the morning, and even though afraid and worried, rushes to the den to call out and see if Daniel's God has saved him. Daniel 6:23 (EXB) says, *'So they lifted him out and did not find any injury on him because Daniel had trusted in his God.'*

In a mind blowing twist, King Darius writes to everyone, of every language, declaring that from now on everyone in his own kingdom *"must fear and respect the God of Daniel. Daniel's God is the living God; he lives forever. His kingdom will never be destroyed and his rule will never end. God rescues and saves people and does mighty miracles in heaven and on earth. He is the one who saved Daniel from the power of the lions."* (Daniel 6:26-27)

Daniel's trust in God and his uprightness and saving power, changes the course of history and the law for an entire kingdom!

Somehow, although I have seen God do incredible miracles and save my little girl several times, I am finding it hard to trust him with my Jazz. Somehow, I struggle in my pain and my worry at times, endeavouring each time to give it over to God once and for all, but it keeps rearing its ugly head. Fear creeps in like a thief and begins to rob my bank of trust when I least expect it. Fear is followed fast by worry that sneaks up on fear's back, and is carried along until I identify them and put them back in their place!

Last night as my heart was overcome with sadness over what we have been through and what we still have to go through, all I could do was cry (and write). This journey is pain filled; most times it physically hurts my heart, as I feel the pain of my grief.

Today though, is a new day. I will count my blessings today! Today I choose to see the life and the light all around me. Today I choose to think about all the amazing things I have seen. Today I will consider that my God *'is a mighty God who rescues and saves people',* who rescued and saved my Luka-Angel, who heard our prayers. This God *'whose Kingdom will never be destroyed and whose rule will never end.'* (Daniel 6). He is the one who saved Luka from the power of death! She lives today and is a walking story to his saving grace, his power and his miracles. It was when the doctors could do nothing to make that new heart start, that God stepped in. It was when death appeared to be knocking on her door that my mighty God jumped in her way, picked her up and saved her, running her fast through the door of life like a prince on a stallion rescuing his princess from the grip of darkness.

Chapter 44

Living Life to the Best

(Jesus said) "I have come in order that you may have life – life in all its fullness." John 10:10 (GNT)

Recently I asked Jazz if he would like to ride a bike beside me as I went for a run along the foreshore and beach footpath. Riding for Jazz has always been very difficult. The only option for riding a bike is choosing a flat footpath, and I usually need to push him for a lot of the way. Jazz loves to ride! Sadly I saw him come to the realisation that riding was just too hard for him early last year. My Dad had been visiting and we went for a ride around our neighbourhood and to our local duck park. I said I was happy to run rather than ride as it would give me the freedom to push Jazz when he needed some help. I knew if there was any incline, I would be needed.

I hadn't realised just how hard riding had become for Jazz, as it had been some time since we had ridden bikes together. There came a point when it was just too hard for Luka-Angel. This particular day I was keenly aware of the energy it took to push my son who was now three quarters of my size.

Rainbows in the Storm

I spent most of my run as his engine (he has referred to me as his engine on many occasions). He has had this little joke for some time now, that when he stops peddling and his bike loses momentum, if I am not there to catch him, I 'fail' his test. The first time I recall him doing it was when he was riding his scooter. He had slowed right down as there was a slight incline too hard for him to get up, and he looked as though he was going to topple straight over. I quickly sped my running up and landed my hands in the middle of his back and started to push. "I was testing you Mum!" He said with a cheeky smile, "You always know when I need you! You are always there to catch me... but you only just made it that time!" My heart felt such joy that he was testing me, believing I would be there to catch him. Life for years had entailed me piggy backing both Luka-Angel and Jazz (in turns) whenever we went on family walks. They just got too big for me though, and that was when the scooters became our life saver. I found it really special to realise that Jazz's take was that I was always there to catch him. This has certainly put pressure on every ride since, and there has been one time when Jazz declared with great disappointment that I had failed that time.

As usual, I have side tracked. So back to where I was ... I asked Jazz recently if he wanted to come for a ride alongside me while I went for a run at the foreshore. To my joy and surprise he said "yes". This was the first time in ages Jazz was willing to go for a ride. The sun was going down and the two of us talked incessantly as we moved along the water's edge. It was so great to have him one on one (with four kids, this can be hard to find time for). It was an absolutely beautiful night and I could see Jazz was really enjoying himself. In these moments, when I push my son along on a bike whilst I jog, I relish in knowing I can assist him to enjoy life, and I am thankful for my legs and heart that work. At times, I feel aware that it may look strange and people may wonder why I am doing such a thing. Perhaps they judge my son as lazy, or even incompetent for his age. However, most of the time in these moments, I choose not to care what anyone around me is potentially thinking. The reality is that I can't know what they are thinking anyway. I guess the bigger he gets, the more aware I am of how strange it must look to others.

Jazz had so many questions that night. Sometimes I find it hard to get into Jazz's thoughts or feelings. He can be very reserved and guarded. This particular night as the moon lit our path I felt such openness, great conversation and joy from him.

Part of the way through the ride out of nowhere, Jazz said to me, "Mum, I am ready for a heart transplant now. Can you put me on the list?" This nearly floored me, and a mix of terror, sadness and relief filled my heart. Terror, because I am not ready, sadness that this is even a conversation to be had, relief that he is no longer afraid or unable to talk about such things. As many people jogged or walked past us chatting and laughing, I wondered if anyone could even comprehend the statement that had just hit my ears from my ten-year-old son. I withheld the tears that threatened to escape and said, "Okay Jazz, thank you for letting me know. That is a big conversation and one we would need to discuss with Dad. We need to wait for the right time to put you on the list, and we can talk about that."

"I am not scared anymore Mum," he assured me.

I wonder every day how I am going to go through this again. Every day there is a moment when I fear missing the boat for Jazz (a very real possibility), and then fear putting him on the list and having to go through this all over again. Some days it brings me completely undone. Some days it makes my heart race so fast I feel like I could pass out. Some days I just chuck it straight up to God and ask him to carry it for me, telling him I trust him, reminding him I will not stop asking for miraculous healing. I often consider the story Jesus told of the woman who persisted in prayer, and he said that this is how we should pray. We should not give up (Luke 18). I am never at peace with this. I know peace. I have incredible peace that passes understanding, but I am never at peace with the fact that my ten-year-old needs a heart transplant, or that my daughter had to have one (and now has the 'post' journey to contend with). It just seems so wrong. It seems so against God's plan for abundant life with no tears, pain or sadness.

As I shoved my involuntary processing aside, and got on with the ride with Jazz, we took in the sights and the sounds of the ocean under the ever so still, moonlit evening. We even saw dolphins surfing the waves.

Towards the end of our one hour ride Jazz said to me loudly, with firm enthusiasm, "Mum, I just want to live my life to the best that I can! You know?!!"

"Oh?" I enquired. "Do you mean after heart transplant and like what you said before? Are you thinking about what life would be like with a new heart that works properly?"

"No Mum. I mean now. I want to live my life to the best that I can, now. Every day!"

In that one moment, inspiration and awe filled me.

Here is a kid who can't run, who can't ride a bike on his own, unless it is completely flat or downhill, who misses out on competition sport and who can't run the field with his friends when they play soccer at lunch time. Here is a boy who gets tachycardic throughout every day, even just from walking up the set of eight stairs at home. A kid who has to see doctors every few months and has had to have many needles, tests and procedures, and is still able to say, "I just want to live my life the best that I can."

He told me it was the best night and he wanted to do that every night! My lower back whispered quietly to me that it wouldn't be possible to do that every night, but how I wish we could.

I have desired to live life to the full for so long now. Sometimes I get it right, other times I let negativity, resentment, un-forgiveness, fear, feelings, 'busyness', other people's expectations, frustrations, mundane things like housework and apathy get in the way. Jesus came to give us life in all its fullness; it was his desire for us.

These are the reasons we must keep taking holidays and adventures. The reasons why we must stop the housework some times (that just keeps renewing itself and magically multiplying), and enjoy the moments playing basketball or kicking a soccer ball with our kids. The reasons why we should stop when our little girl says, "Can you be a dog Mum?" or "Can you play dolls with me?" Life to the full surely is living in a constant state of forgiveness and grace towards others (how hard is that?), laughing loudly, stopping and looking your child in the eye, really listening to someone you love, smiling, doing a dare, stepping outside of your comfort zone, acting silly to make our kids laugh, riding bikes, going on nature walks, not allowing fear to stop us from doing something that seems insane. Life to the full is sometimes going away from our kids for a night to visit our aging parents. Life to the full is what I see my kids do every day.

When Luka couldn't dance yet, she stretched and she prepared, and she watched YouTube videos on ballet terminology and positioning. She prepared. She held hope fast. That hope was one of the things that pushed her through hard physiotherapy post heart transplant, major operations, dark days and loneliness. She lived life to the full in the moments, and remained filled with hope for her future.

Rainbows in the Storm

She lived life to the full even in hospital. Smiling, laughing, watching movies, making us laugh with silly faces, writing special cards and letters to people, showing gratitude to nurses and doctors, caring for others around her.

Surely life to the full starts with our relationships. Then spills over into moments throughout our day as well as the planned times for adventure, exploring and holidays. Surely life to the full means dispelling fear - throwing it in the bin every time it creeps up. Stepping up and pursuing a dream or doing something we have always dreamed of doing, or abandoning our insecurities and inhibitions, in order to be bolder and braver. The sentence from Jazz that night and the question from him, "Mum, what is something you have always wanted to do but never done," compelled me to finally sign up for a full marathon (this was something I had wanted to do for some time now, but fear of failure had always stopped me).

At times I think I could write a dictionary of Luka-Angel's terms, made up words and funny puns. My favourite right now is that when others say 'YOLO' (You Only Live Once), Luka-Angel says 'YOLT' (You Only Live Twice)! This 'YOLT' attitude that I have seen in her so many times is simply amazing! It sees her dancing in the rain, acting the fool to make someone laugh, jumping off high bridges into the water below, daring to adventure despite physical challenges!

I don't know about you, but when my ten-year-old says with joy and strength, "I want to live my life the best that I can. Every day," it compels me to want to do the same!!

Chapter 45

Luka-Angel's First Run

'For you make me glad by your deeds, Lord; I sing for joy at what your hands have done.' Psalm 92:4 (NIV)

When it is darkest, light can only shine its brightest. Not because of the light itself, but because of the dark.

In my deepest sorrow and pain, my deepest sadness, I have experienced some of my most joy-filled moments. Perhaps in normal circumstances, these moments may not have been more than just a passing moment in time.

No words can describe the plethora of emotions I felt at the Athletics Carnival on Friday (approximately seven months post-transplant). Ever since it was possible for Luka-Angel or Jazz to attend school Athletics Carnivals, I have had to prepare myself for days. It is the hardest thing to sit beside your child as they watch their friends get to participate in something they are just not able to do. For either of them, a simple running race could have meant life or death. So many times I wanted to just give in and tell them to go for it, but that would have been like telling your five-year-old child to cross a busy highway to get to Mr Whippy, and then hope they make it to the other side. It just wouldn't be worth the ice-cream.

Having said that though, I tried as much as I could to allow them to participate in whatever they could. It always took courage to approach teachers and ask them simple things like, "Can Luka please have a much shorter run up for the long jump?" Even though the teachers at the school were always so kind and accommodating, I always felt awkward, perhaps as though I was 'helicopter parenting'. All I could do was endeavour to get the balance of allowing them to participate in a safe way, yet take a risk and hope for the best.

Friday was the first Athletics Carnival where my daughter was actually able to run in the races! I was so excited days before I couldn't stop talking about it and smiling. The afternoon before the carnival around 4:30pm, it suddenly dawned on me that Luka-Angel had never actually run before. I walked her to the park a couple of doors away from home to do some practice runs. Her first run, she just didn't know what to do with her hands. As they flapped around by her side we had a giggle. I told her to make little fists and pump her arms up and down as she ran. To my surprise she went at quite a reasonable pace. Seeing Luka run for the first time across our local park made my soul leap for joy.

All the way to the carnival on the Friday I chatted, and gave tips. I told both my kids to look ahead when they raced, to never look sideways or behind. I told them to either pretend they were running to the best prize, like meeting their favorite hero, or to picture that a tiger was chasing them. I prattled on, hardly able to contain my excitement or nervous energy. By the time we were nearly there Luka-Angel looked very unhappy. "What's wrong?" I asked when we got out of the car. She didn't want to tell me. Suddenly it hit me in the face.

"Do you feel too much pressure from me?"

"Aaahh, ye-e-es!" she said rolling her eyes as if that was obvious.

"Sorry my Angel", I said, "I am just SO happy that I finally get to see you participate in a running race. There is no pressure whatsoever! I just am excited you can now run. I don't care if you come first or last, I just am happy you finally get to join in. Sorry." I said, realising that I had been putting some pressure on her, caught up in my own excitement.

As they called out for her age group I felt my hands and my voice begin to shake. I had been waiting thirteen years for this moment. Well, probably twelve years just to see my daughter run.

My Aunty Yvonne stood beside me as the girls lined up. Lucas waited down at the finish line. I remember my voice chatting nervously and carrying on to my aunty that I hope she doesn't trip over, and how cute it was the night before when she told me that she couldn't work out how people run in a straight line and stay in one lane. She wondered if she would be able to do that. I found myself rambling about not being able to see properly and I wish I had brought my glasses. We tried to fix our eyes on the one we thought was Luka, looking for the little yellow ribbons she had tied to her wrist in support of her team 'The Warriors'. I told Aunty Yvonne that Luka had told me strictly that I wasn't allowed to yell and cheer too loudly. Aunty Yvonne assured me not to worry because she could if she wanted to, as Luka hadn't told her the same.

'BANG!' The gun went off, interrupting my voice! I watched completely silent as Luka's arms pumped hard beside her. I could hardly believe my eyes when half way through the race it was clear she was coming third. I watched her arms pump so hard, and observing her long, slightly awkward strides, I wondered whether I should have told her to lift her knees a little more. Finally relaxing, I yelled spontaneously, "WOOOOHOOO!" I recognized it as the same kind of sound I have made on a roller coaster, or jumping off a small cliff into a fresh water creek. It wasn't the sound I had made before at a carnival. It was the sound of exhilaration, adrenalin, fun. It was the sound of PURE JOY! Alongside me I had been aware of Aunty Yvonne's unashamedly country twang yelling at the top of her lungs, "Go Luka!!! Go Luka!!!"

Tears filled my eyes and a big lump filled my throat! As the race finished, a Mum of one of Luka's friends called out, "Hey Angela, wasn't that amazing??!! How do you feel?!!" I yelled back, unconcerned of the tens of people I was yelling over the top of, "THAT WAS HER FIRST RUNNING RACE EVER!" Over the next few minutes, other mothers came up to me sharing in my joy, and even though their own daughters had run in the same race, somehow, they were celebrating my girl. They were celebrating the miracle they saw, as my daughter got to run in her first race ever. Perhaps they had seen my downcast face at other Athletics Carnivals. Some of them had caught me in years gone by, when the tears had accidentally spilled from underneath my sunglasses. Today they could see the change. The miracle that they had prayed for too, they could see with their very own eyes.

Lucas and I met at the finish line as he said with a broad smile, "She did so well! She came in third!" "Yes", I said, "she was fast! I can't believe she can actually run now!" I blinked back the tears and said to my cousin Triniti and Aunty Yvonne, "I can't let her see me cry. She told me not to get too excited."

I managed to convince Luka to get a photo with two of her friends as she walked off the track. Then, feeling the joy turn fast to tears of relief from years of pent up sadness, I turned to my husband who was about to drive off to a conference in Sydney and said, "I'll walk you out to the car." Leaving the stadium I was grateful I had made the excuse to take a moment, as I unfolded into loud sobs. I was torn between sobs of deep relief and laughing from my joy.

This was no ordinary joy. This was pure joy and it felt familiar. It felt like the joy I had experienced months before in Melbourne. The day we found out Luka-Angel's dormant heart muscle had miraculously kicked into action for the first time. This was a gratitude feeling that no one has yet invented a word for. This was us being gifted with hope on the most hopeless of days. Light in our darkness, hope in the direst of circumstances. Pure, untainted, uninhibited, unexplainable joy can only come after the deepest trauma and sadness. No other joy I have ever experienced can even be compared. The closest comparison I can think of is the worst labour pains followed by a perfectly healthy baby.

Luka was finally able to *run* and it felt as though she had won a gold medal at the Olympics!

Chapter 46

God's Little Gifts

'You have searched me, Lord, and you know me. You know when I sit and when I rise, you perceive my thoughts from afar.' Psalm 139:1-2 (NIV)

Luka-Angel is the most amazing and resilient person. She endures needles with ease, joy and sometimes even a smile on her face. She has had needles that hit a nerve and left her sore for weeks on end, attempts at bloods that have faltered and made her vein waterfall blood out (I did nearly faint in one like this whilst Luka sat in the big chair waiting for me to recover. Needless, no pun intended, to say I was pretty embarrassed). She has had needles that left her with deep dark bruises, some where they couldn't find the vein, and it took two unsuccessful attempts by one person unfolding in the next person's attempts.

I truly sit in awe of her as she interacts with doctors with such maturity and faces needles head on without flinching.

I often pray that God will guide us each step, each day.

Yesterday she needed another needle (she seems to have them every two to three weeks at the moment). We had a choice of so many pathologists around where we live. Interestingly, we chose one we had never been to before. We didn't even know if it would be open, but we headed there anyway.

As the young lady took Luka-Angel's blood, she interacted with Luka asking her questions about what she likes to do. While she filled up one container of blood, then another, and then another, it became apparent through the conversation this girl knew a thing or two about dancing.

I couldn't help but ask her, "Are you a dancer?"

"Yes," she replied with a big smile.

"I used to dance for the Australian Ballet". She had been chosen for a cast in a professional ballet for the Sydney Opera House at the age of just nine years old. Here she was taking Luka-Angel's blood.

"Dancing becomes a part of you. A part of who you are," she said to my already convinced daughter.

And we walked away shaking our heads at yet another special encounter.

God sends us so many little blessings. He wraps them up in pathologists, baristas, security guards, friends, art teachers, shopping assistants, neighbours, friends, family, actors and dancers off T.V shows. We only need to stop for a moment to realise these encounters are little gifts from God. Wrapped up just for us, to show us he is interested, and that he cares about every little detail of our lives.

We seem to receive these gifts constantly and sometimes we miss them! It never ceases to amaze me that my big God is all knowing and he is interested in us.

Chapter 47

Indescribable

'Thanks be to God for his indescribable gift.' 2 Corinthians 9:15 (NIV)

Last Thursday was Luka-Angel's 14th Birthday. I was both reflective and elated the day before as I shopped for some presents for her. Every time I bought something I felt like telling the shop assistant how special this birthday was for us, because Luka was here. We nearly lost her, in one moment we did lose her, and now it is her 14th birthday and she is well and she is here. This was a story I felt like declaring to everyone. Instead, it played out in my heart and my mind as I walked around, but I said nothing. As I purchased, I reflected. I didn't realise how much this was impacting me, until I got home and fell onto the lounge, arms full of bags in a torrential pouring out of tears. I am sure when Lucas encountered me he must have thought, *'I have always known she doesn't like shopping, but I didn't realise she hated it that much!!'* As always, I recovered before the kids got home from school.

Thursday morning around 7am I went into Luka-Angel's room and climbed on the bed and lay down beside her. I rubbed my nose against hers and said, "Happy Birthday my precious girl! You nearly didn't make this one Luka – but you are here, and I am so happy. Come on, it's time to get your presents!" Luka quietly smiled back at me and I thanked God so much that this was my morning, aware that it could have played out so differently.

That night around 7pm, Luka lifted her leg into the split position (as she does regularly) and we heard a big 'crack'. The pain clearly showed on her face as I said, "Was that your hip or your leg?"

"My leg," she said nearly crying and as usual putting on her brave face. Being out for dinner was clouded by the pain she was in.

The next morning Luka was due to go on a school excursion, an 8 kilometre obstacle course and run through the mud. I had started to feel very concerned that day - perhaps we had made a poor decision, perhaps her body wasn't ready for such a thing.

All night I worried and tossed and turned and wondered with the arrhythmia she was still experiencing whether an 8 kilometre run could be dangerous for her. I prayed and prayed God would make very clear the next morning whether she shouldn't go. I felt silly for having said yes to this excursion only seven months post-transplant. Although I felt like I had been so unwise, I prayed that God would make a way and if she shouldn't go that he would intervene.

I went in and woke her up at 6am and the first thing she said was, "Mum, my leg has been in so much pain all night I have hardly slept. I can't even roll over." I resigned myself to taking her to the doctor. It seemed the 8 kilometre run was not going to happen for her today. I wondered about God's protection, and wondered how many times he protects when we don't even realise it. He sees all, knows all, and I believe he knew that going on the long run was not the best thing for Luka-Angel's heart at this time.

Luka could only limp and her pain was great.

As the doctor examined her he said it appeared she may have torn a tendon in her mid-upper thigh.

I was so disappointed. Luka had been asked to dance on Sunday to the song 'Indescribable' as part of our worship time for our church's 25th birthday celebration. I knew it was going to be very powerful. All of a sudden it seemed as though her dance wouldn't be happening.

All the way to the ultra sound place I prayed and prayed that God would make very clear what was wrong with her leg, and that he would bring healing to it. Luka sat beside me in the car with great fear on her face and said, "What if I can't dance anymore? What if this injury means no more dancing for me? I have only just started!" I told her it was okay, and that if God had designed her to dance it would be in his time and all would be well. I told her not to worry about dancing on Sunday, but we would pray if it was meant to be, the injury and the pain would disappear.

"Mum, I have decided that if God has designed me to dance, nothing can stop that," she said. "Nothing can get in the way of his plans!"

During the ultra sound, to my surprise it seemed clear that nothing significant had been torn.

The pain continued through Saturday but seemed a little better than Friday.

Late Saturday night, Luka decided she would dance the next morning, and had her first opportunity to rehearse the dance. It was late at night as we had been out at a youth event, so she only had time for three practice runs. Through some pain she mapped out the dance, still unable to do the splits or cartwheels as planned.

The next morning to my surprise Luka said she was really excited! She was finally getting the opportunity to do what she was born to do – to dance and bring her gift to people! We talked through the fact that this dance to Chris Tomlin's song 'Indescribable' was very apt. This was a moment when people would be able to see God's indescribable power through his dancing miracle! The little girl whose heart he had healed!

I wondered how she would go. She still had a slightly sore leg, and had not had the opportunity to practice properly due to her leg injury on Thursday night.

In her white flowing dress she sailed gracefully across the stage as the lyrics played, *'From the highest of heights to the depths of the sea. Creation revealing your majesty…Indescribable, uncontainable you placed the stars in the sky and you know them by name. You are amazing God."* Many people were touched and impacted that morning, as they saw God's power revealed in a little girl who had never been able to dance; a girl whose heart God had held gently and safely, both before and after her transplant. I contemplated whether this heart had danced before. My little girl a young woman now, just turned 14, with all the energy in the world, dancing, doing the splits and cartwheeling across the stage.

In the car on the way home Luka said to me, "Mum, I felt closer to God as I danced today. I even felt him there with me, helping me!" Then she broke into great excitement saying, "I watched the dance back on video just before Mum, and I even did a trick I have never been able to do. I didn't even plan to do it. I didn't even realise I had done it until I watched it back! God really was helping me!"

It was clear to me this is one of the things she was born to do. Clear to me that God's healing power will continue to be seen through her life.

Every morning when she used to wake up, just getting dressed or brushing her teeth was hard, sport and dancing were out of the question. At this point, I can hardly comprehend where we have been and the roller coaster journey of the last eight months. But, I am also aware that there are still great challenges ahead.

When Luka-Angel wakes now she takes a handful of tablets, then again later in the day. Her immune system is suppressed, yet somehow she has thus far avoided too much sickness. The road is still long, but for now, we are living life to the full and my daughter can dance!

I have no doubt as I continue to allow myself to be carried in the hand of my Creator God, as I continue to keep perspective and keep my eyes on him, as we as a family continue to enjoy each other and life, we will continue to know peace and joy.

There is so much I could fear. Fear tries with all its might to creep in, especially when darkness falls, my defenses are down and the house goes quiet. But I will continue daily, to refuse fear and worry and accept peace and trust. When the storm clouds in the distant sky threaten to come overhead and burst, I will look for the rays of sunshine that remind me I still have so much to be thankful for. And when it rains, I will look for the rainbows. I know I still have so much to hope for. My Luka-Angel is filled with God's light, his strength and great courage and this is an act I want to follow!

> 'I prayed to the Lord, and he answered me.
> He freed me from all my fears.'
> Psalm 34:4 (NLT)

Chapter 48

Beautiful Things Out of the Darkness

> 'He has made everything beautiful in its time. He has also set eternity in the human heart; yet no one can fathom what God has done from beginning to end.'
> Ecclesiastes 3:11 (NIV)

Out of the hardest of circumstances and the darkest of days some beautiful things can emerge. Irritation and discomfort inside an oyster, creates a pearl; similarly with hard pressure and high temperatures a diamond is formed.

So much beauty has pushed itself to the surface through our toughest of times. I remember not long after my children's diagnosis, some of the darkest weeks of my life. But as a result of the hardship came some beautiful realisations that have formed some of our strongest family values and mandates.

1. Every day counts.

2. Appreciate each other.

3. Delight in the little things.

4. Stuff is not important, people are.

5. Making time for fun matters.

6. There is always something to be thankful for (even on the hardest days).

7. There is always someone else worse off, reach out to others in their own need.

8. Holidays and adventures are important.

9. Many things of this world we think matter, actually don't.

10. God is stronger than us, he can strengthen us and he knows better than we do.

This last one brings me to something Luka-Angel said about six months before her transplant. One day, after she came home from school, I went to her room to catch up on her day and she said to me, "Mum, sometimes I have felt that I have the hardest stuff to face, more than anyone else in my class (this was new to me as she never complained). But today Mum, I realised that there are people in my class who have things way worse than me. Like T – her parents are divorced. And M – she doesn't have a dad in her life. As I thought about them Mum I felt really sad for them, and I realised, what I have to face is easy. It's easy because I have a Mum and Dad who love me so much and who are together."

Sometimes, it's not a terrible thing to look out from our own pain, and realise there are other people around us in pain too. Perhaps in a sense without belittling our own, or even making any kind of comparison, we can remember to reach out, and be available to others who may need our support. Focusing on our own pain at the expense of being available to others in their pain is easy to do, but a very insular way to live. Investing in the lives of those around you is so important. I want to acknowledge that sometimes I find this hard to live out.

Out of the emergence of our darkness came these realisations that have eventuated in many amazing, adventurous family holidays. We are not people who get in patterns or habits. Perhaps it's the life of two Salvo Officers' kids who from one October to the next, didn't know if they would be staying where they lived or moving on. Somehow, we are not creatures of habit. Nearly every holiday destination is different. Often when we travel around we don't know where we are staying the next night or stopping for lunch, we kind of 'fly by the seat of our pants'. Sometimes things have been a disaster, and we've ended up sleeping in our car, or eating sao biscuits for dinner (not exaggerating). Other times though we have discovered the most extraordinary places or had the greatest of adventures.

One of my biggest delights is watching my children have fun together. I like to be there in the middle of it, so sometimes I have to refrain my notion to go and get in on it. I need to remember it's good for siblings to have their own adventures and fun, sometimes without an adult in their world. Kids know how to play with abandon and how to become real spies, or fairies. Adults can only 'pretend'.

In some of my darkest days in Melbourne when Luka was sleeping in ICU or when I had been cooped up in the ward and needed some fresh air, I found delight in the simplest things. A cup of coffee became like a reward from heaven. Feeling the sunshine on my back or looking at the formation of the clouds in the sky brought me out of the walls of the hospital, and into the awareness of something greater. Some days that hospital room felt so small, but other days it felt like my whole world.

It seemed that even though we were in the darkest of days, the brightest of lights still managed to seep through, shedding light and warmth on our darkness.

God's provision was so evident.

God provided other people for us through that time in the most unlikely of places. One such person was the ICU nurse who felt more like a sister. I remember a family member telling me as she came out from the room that the nurse, Steph, was a Christian. Not much later, as I played worship music to my precious sleeping daughter, I heard a voice join in, "Bless the Lord oh my soul, oh my soul, worship his holy name. Sing like never before, oh my soul, I'll worship your holy name." Although tempted to turn around, all I could do was listen to her sweet voice, ever so quietly singing along to the music I played softly in Luka-Angel's ear. I felt like I was in the room with a sister. Then the next song came on, "When darkness seems to hide his face, I rest on his unchanging grace. In every high and stormy gale, my anchor holds within the veil." I wept quietly, my head on Luka's bed, as close to her arm as I could get around the tubes as Nurse Steph's voice sung over us. This truly was a gift from God.

Then there was Cher and his wife Lorinda. In them I found the warmest, kind, chatty couple. They certainly were open people and up for a good conversation. The night I met them, it was around 10pm. I hadn't eaten any dinner, and I tore myself away from ICU to go to the parents' room to try and eat some of my mum and dad's left over Chinese dinner. My sister stayed behind to be with Luka. As I walked into the parent's room, my initial disappointment that three other people were already in the room was quite quickly dispelled. I went to the fridge, found the plastic bag with the left over Chinese and popped it in the microwave, aware I had no appetite but knowing because I could hardly walk, perhaps eating was an important thing to do. I sat on the lounge chair not so far from the three people at the table and said a polite hello.

As I pushed my food around the plastic container, barely able to swallow a thing, Lorinda leaned over with the warmest brown eyes and an accent I couldn't quite place and said, "Are you Angela?"

"Yes," I said somewhat surprised.

"Hello, I am Lorinda, this is my husband, Cher, and this is his mum. I feel like I know you," she revealed. "I have had some great conversations with your family and have heard about Luka. You have a beautiful family."

Seeing Cher's name badge, I questioned, "Do you work here Cher? Is it Shar or Cher sorry?"

Making a joke on his name being just like the 80's singer but you wouldn't catch him in a black 'g-string' leotard, he responded with a cheeky smile, "No, I don't work here. I've just come straight from work. I work at a different hospital." Together they went on to tell me of their baby H who had some major heart issues and was in ICU too. They said they'd seen our family pouring in to ICU and coming in and out of the parents' room and they had lots of great conversations with them. It appeared Cher's mum hardly spoke a word of English, but her interest showed me she understood a lot.

"How is your daughter?" Lorinda said in the most compassionate of tones and with a concerned face.

We talked so much that the ten minutes I planned to try and eat turned into forty-five minutes of great conversation and no more than two mouthfuls consumed. The beef and black bean was now dry, cold and chewy anyway and I assured myself that my body was probably very thankful for the two mouthfuls, having consumed very little else all day.

On noticing my lack of food intake, Lorinda leaned in and said, "You need to eat. Honestly, you need to look after yourself. You need your energy at a time like this."

Something in me felt loved, cared for and nurtured by this perfect stranger. It was touching to me, knowing her baby would require several heart operations over his life, and here she was reaching out to me.

I spoke to them of my faith, and assured them of my prayers for baby H, making a mental note to actually pray and not to forget.

"I am going to leave Jatz and cheese in the fridge for you every day," she said. "I keep getting given those little packets in the ward. I am breastfeeding and so they provide my meals, but I don't like cheese. I will leave Jatz and cheese in the fridge for you each day with your name written on it."

The next day, sure enough in the parent's room fridge were Jatz and cheese with 'Angela' scrawled across the label on top, and each day after that.

The following afternoon Lorinda walked in whilst I was in the parent's room. "Have you eaten today?" She said this, almost pre-emptively scolding me.

"Not really," I responded guiltily, "just the Jatz and cheese." She went on to tell me Cher was on his way up, and she would get him to buy something for me from the supermarket. Insistent, she asked me what I felt like.

Having explained to her I really don't have much of an appetite, she took the role of 'Mum' listing off several options.

"Perhaps yoghurt would be nice." I said with gratitude.

"Fine. There will be yoghurt in the fridge with your name on it next time you check."

Sure enough, hours later, I popped out of ICU feeling very hungry, and there in the communal fridge were four expensive yoghurts, with 'Angela' once again scrawled on the label.

I'm not sure if Cher and Lorinda comprehended what a blessing their care for me was over those days. They seemed to be in the room, each time my family had gone home. God had given me two strangers, who understood a little of what I was going through, to be my extra family.

Then there were some people we knew, who had already lost their son. Their second son has the same condition that stole their firstborn, and they are in and out of hospital regularly. While Luka was still 'sleeping' they rang a café at our hospital (even though they were in another state) and set up a tab for us. They did this at the same time their son was in another hospital. Then our church family and some friends continued to top the tab up for us. I found it strange that out of all the places to eat at the hospital, the café they chose had the name 'Sandrock'. Often when I went there I reflected on the foundation of my life, grateful that I had built my life on the rock for such a time as this. The winds and the rain beat hard on this house, but our lives were not built on the sand, so we could stand firm! This continually topped up tab meant there was always the possibility of buying breakfast after long nights in the ward, or not hesitating to shout our son a milkshake to lift his spirits, and buying coffee could be done without a thought for our budget. It was an incredible blessing and gift to us!

Other financial support from many of our friends, family, and even strangers, became an incredible blessing to assist us with extra flights to and from Melbourne and continues to make something like dance lessons for Luka possible! People's generosity and care, was mind blowing and uplifting!

Indeed, in this darkness, light shone brighter than we had ever seen!

Chapter 49

Cartwheels of Joy

'And those the Lord has rescued will return. They will enter Zion with singing; everlasting joy will crown their heads. Gladness and joy will overtake them, and sorrow and sighing will flee away!' Isaiah 35:10 (NIV)

It took me a while to notice Luka-Angel's new attire and daily routine post-transplant. It must have been a few months out, when I noticed she was wearing a dress that was shorter than her usual. She was beautiful and shining in her yellow dress and not ashamed of the large scar that peeked out the top of her dress revealing a part of her story. The self-adorned crown of gold flowers on her head was fitting! She truly was a brave warrior princess and I delighted in her beauty. We were on our way to visit my sister's church when I said to her, "Luka-Angel, that dress is a little short on you now. Perhaps now that you are getting taller you need to make sure your dresses aren't too short." I noticed how long her legs looked and cautioned her, "You'll have to be conscious of how you sit in church today, okay Luka?"

"Mum," she said laughing and instantly lifting her dress up to her waist with abandon. "It's okay – see I have bike pants on!"

"Oh," I said chuckling at her funny ways, "well that's a good idea."

"I wear them every day now Mum! You've always got to be prepared," she exclaimed with a big smile.

"Prepared for what?" I asked somewhat baffled.

As her hands hit the ground smoothly in front of me, she called out as she moved both gracefully and with strength, "You just never know when you'll want to cartwheel Mum!"

It didn't even take a second for me to realise that I had seen her cartwheel every day for the last few months since she achieved that goal in her recovery in physio! To this day, now ten months down the track, that still hasn't stopped, apart from the days she was sick in bed with immunity issues.

After all she had journeyed through, her joyful attitude and new lease on life amazed me. She was choosing to embrace the moment. I decided that this is an attitude I want to adopt. To be prepared every day, because you just never know when you might want to cartwheel!

I remembered the joy of cartwheeling in my teenage years and wondered at what point that had stopped. There is always something I can cartwheel about, even when times are hard.

Perhaps you remember cartwheeling too. Maybe it wouldn't hurt to take a moment to cartwheel in your day. Go on, I dare you!

Luka-Angel jumping for joy, four months post-transplant.

Epilogue

Gaining a Greater Perspective

> *'Can any of you by worrying add a single moment to your life?'* Matthew 6:27 (NIV)

Keeping perspective amidst health issues is vital to emotional survival.

It would be so easy for me to curl up in a ball of sadness and never leave my room again. When you see your children suffer the way that I do, you live with a broken heart. Living with a broken heart isn't easy, but it isn't the end either, there are still reasons to celebrate, laugh and know joy. I know there are other parents who have lost their children. I still have mine right here, and I don't take that for granted!

But I recall many times, when it has all felt too much and getting outside and getting a different perspective has been my absolute saving grace!

So often I have taken an opportunity to get a new perspective through my running. I love the open sky and I love the beach, so sometimes just taking a moment to take in the view of either the beach or the sky, has been a helpful reminder that the God who made them is even bigger than that, and life is more than our time on this earth.

It dawned on me as I drove south on the highway the other day, that if I were to only look in my rear vision mirror, or just look in my side mirrors or just look miles ahead of me on the road, or even only at the car in front of me, I would be in danger. I need to keep a broad perspective to stay safe. I need to look ahead, and also have glimpses behind and beside me constantly, to stay safe while I drive.

Similarly, it is vital I don't just stare into the future where many unknowns and fears lie dormant. It is vital I don't only look behind me, at happier days or at hard days, but glimpsing back every now and then and learning from them can be helpful to my perspective. I can't just look sideways and compare my journey to the journey of those around me. Comparison is a killer. However, glancing around me, looking out for others on my journey, and learning from the experiences of others is a helpful thing.

Having a broad perspective is vital for a safe drive. It is also vital for my mental health, my perseverance, my destination.

I could spend my moments so worried it would make me sick. Sometimes, that kind of worry tries so hard to strangle me. Usually at night, my sleep is often deprived and ransacked. Grabbing hold of these worrying thoughts and putting them in their place is imperative! For Mother's Day on Sunday (my first Mother's Day since Luka-Angel got her new heart), Luka wrapped up a picture for me. She had painted the backdrop sunshine yellow, and in gold writing it read, 'Worry achieves nothing. But trusting God changes everything.' The fact that she gave me a message that so often I have tried to embed in my spirit blew me away. Firstly, it was exactly what I needed at this time and I am often amazed at her gifted intuition and God-led spirit. Secondly, her words are completely right.

On this cold autumn day in May, as I sit on a bench seat overlooking the water, a beautiful, little, chubby bird sits beside my feet. I have never seen a bird like this up close before. He looks like the kind of bird who should be terrified of me. He isn't like a confident seagull ready to scrounge and see if I have any food, he looks vulnerable, yet strong, and very much like a little stuffed toy. He looks up at me and squeaks, letting me know he is there. I look down at him and say, "Hello little bird. You are very brave. Look at you, you are beautiful. Did you know God made you?" The bird squeaks again and then after a minute or so of the two of us gazing at each other, he flies off again as if his job was now done.

I have had moments just like this on a bench seat under the biggest tree in a park not so far from the hospital. This little bird had reminded me yet again, of what his other feathered friends often reminded me – Jesus own words, "Look at the birds of the air, they do not sow or reap and yet your Heavenly Father feeds them…. Who of you by worrying can add a single hour to your life?" (Luke 12:25)

As he flew off I felt thankful that I know these words; thankful that I have found them to be so true. The worry monster will regularly come and haunt me and try to ravage my soul. I will *not* let it! It has no place in my life. Like Luka-Angel's painting says 'Worry achieves nothing!' What good is worry? It is a waste of head space, a waste of thoughts and yet it is so easy to do.

Gaining a greater perspective is so important. Keeping my eyes up and outward-looking, not directly on my circumstances, is vital.

I am keenly aware that I have much to worry about. I have much to fear.

Just the other night Lucas was sitting in the office in our house when I heard a strange noise. It caught my attention and I called out, "Are you alright Lucas?" It was then he called for help.

As I ran to my husband's side and saw he was in the middle of the worst tachycardic moment I have witnessed him have outside of a hospital room, I called to Elijah, "GRAB THE DEFIBRILLATOR!" These are words I do not want to utter...ever!

As I stood by Lucas' side, waiting for Elijah to come, action and alert triumphed over panic and fear (this is not always the case).

Thankfully, Lucas recovered after a few minutes and there was no need for the defibrillator to be used.

I need to keep this action and alert on through any moments of fear or worry. I need to have a mind that is quick; quick to capture any thoughts that are useless and unhelpful. Don't get me wrong, living with illness means at times lots of unpredictable crying (I have never thought of myself as much of a 'crier' until I re-read this book)! Sometimes the feeling of utter despair and helplessness or sometimes a broken heart can tend to dictate your day if you're not careful. Living with serious illness in those your heart adores most, means sadness and grief. Even if deferred grief.

But there are things that help. Things like gaining a new perspective. Remembering life is more than this. Recalling that a better place awaits us, where there are no more tears or sadness, and where sickness does not exist. A place where life is as it was intended to be. One that is free, and whole and beautiful and where love reigns and hate is unheard of!

As I look up at the blue sky above me today, the clouds floating past and the trees that hold so much life, I remember that I am not alone. I remember that the One who created all of that, is far greater than I can even imagine, and that he is stronger than my pain. He has authority over sickness, and he is more powerful than my fear or worry. He can intervene. He has intervened. I have seen it with my own eyes. When the doctors could do no more for Luka-Angel, God stepped in. He held her close and breathed life, sweet life into her body. He breathed life into her new heart.

This is the perspective I want to keep, whatever lies ahead...

Some Tips on keeping perspective:

- Go outside, look up at the sky

    Take it in, remember how big God is. He is bigger than his creation, bigger than the sky. He is bigger than my problems. When I look at the sky I remember life is more than this. I literally lift my eyes away from the problems around me, and I see a bigger world. I remember that an eternity awaits and that this is merely a speck of time in the light of eternity.

- Turn worries into prayer

Every time I begin to worry, I start to pray. Sometimes I see myself physically picking up the problem, the worry, whatever I am concerned about, and placing it into my Creator God's hands. As I pray, I let go of my worry, and hand it over. 'Look at the birds of the air, they do not sow or reap and yet your heavenly Father feeds them. How much more valuable are you than they?' Luke 12:25

- Keep your eyes on Jesus

I remember to keep my eyes on Jesus who is my forerunner. He knelt in the garden of Gethsemane and pleaded with God to take this cup from him. He was overwhelmed with sorrow. He was able to say 'Not my will, but yours be done.' He recalled even amid his deepest darkest pain that God knew what was best and saw things from an eternal perspective.

Hebrews 12:2-3 '...fixing our eyes on Jesus, the pioneer and perfecter of faith. For the joy set before him he endured the cross, scorning its shame, and sat down at the right hand of the throne of God. Consider him who endured such opposition from sinners, so that you will not grow weary and lose heart.'

- Remain Thankful

There is always so much I can be thankful for. When I am thankful, it helps me keep perspective. I literally list off all of the things I am thankful for.

Philippians 4:6 'Do not worry about anything, but in everything with thanksgiving, present your requests to God and the peace of God which transcends all human understanding will guard your hearts and mind through Christ Jesus our Lord.'

Excerpts from a conversation with Luka-Angel twelve weeks post-transplant:

What is the most exciting thing about having a new heart?

DANCING

What has been the scariest thing in the last three months?

The nightmares in ICU

What has been some of the best things about the last three months?

- *Doing a cartwheel*
- *Moving to the little house in Melbourne when I was well enough and being a family again*
- *Receiving a special parcel of letters from my class*
- *When my friends and cousins visited me at the hospital*
- *Our family weekend holiday to Phillip Island*
- *Heart Camp (meeting other kids like me)*

What lessons has God taught you?

- *There is always someone else with a worse situation, be grateful for what you have.*
- *God is always with me, even when I am not aware. So I can always be brave and feel safe.*
- *God still does miracles*

YOU ARE MY SHELTER
By Angela Flemming Cairns

Verse 1

    Storms may come and storms may go
    Leave me lost with little hope
    And falling over
    Sometimes the storms I've had to face
    Have left me lost and in a daze
    And I am weary
    Pre-Chorus
    But I know that you are there
    And I see you still care

Chorus

    So I'm reaching out to you
    'Cause in you I find the truth
    I'll climb into your hand
    You will stretch out your wings
    Lift me up and bring your peace
    I'll climb into your hand
    You are my shelter
    You are my shelter from the storm
    You are my refuge
    You are my refuge in the storm

Verse 2

    Why's this life so full of pain
    I'm caught again in the pouring rain

My heart is broken
But you are God in whom I trust
My refuge, strength – you are enough
And you've already won.

(You can listen to You Are My Shelter – Angela Cairns on YouTube. Other songs available on YouTube by Lucas and Angela Cairns: Stronger – Pulse Band; Limitless – Pulse Band)

Luka-Angel's FIRST BLOG, posted 31st May 2016

'Look on the Colourful Side'

My name is Luka-Angel Lillian and this is my first blog EVER!

My greatest challenge is that I have a rare heart condition called Restrictive Cardiomyopathy. I also have Hypertrophic Cardiomyopathy. This restricts me from sport, fast movement, going up hills and stairs, even walking very far. The hardest part is that it restricts me from doing what I love the most....DANCING!!

All I have ever wanted to do is DANCE!

It is like eating to me...

I just love to do it! The more I can't do it, the more determined I am to do it!

Your challenges may seem harder or seem easier to face than mine — BUT — a challenge is a challenge! It is never easy to go through a challenge whatsoever!!

However, if you look at a challenge like a BAD STORM there are all different kinds of storms and they have different effects: cyclones, lightning, rain, hail, cold weather, loud thunder — but on the other side, lies a RAINBOW.

For me, that rainbow is a heart transplant. In June, I am going to go on a list of people who wait for a heart transplant. It sounds scary — and it is, however, my excitement far outweighs the nerves. For on the other side of that storm — there is a rainbow.

I wonder what rainbow is on the other side of your storm?

Luka-Angel (ten weeks post-transplant) on a special family trip to Phillip Island had just conquered walking up a hill unaided for the first time in her life!

I have many storms yet to face. Some days I feel frightened of what's next. Some days I still grieve. Some days I feel strong, brave and determined and I remember that God will carry me. Each day, no matter how I feel, I will choose to focus on hope and drink in the peace of God. Although I know there are storms ahead, I also know there are rainbows yet to be seen, both in this life, and in the next.

Ecclesiastes 3:4 (ESV)

'There is a time to weep,

and a time to laugh;

a time to mourn,

And a time to dance...'

Dear Reader,

God wants you to be able to live your life in freedom and peace, despite your circumstances. He wants you to know you are completely loved by him, just as you are. Always loved! This love never fails and it never gives up and it has no conditions!

You may want to pray this prayer to acknowledge and accept Jesus' saving power into your life personally...

Dear God,

I am sorry that I have not always made good choices. Sometimes I have made choices that have hurt others, hurt you and hurt me. This is not the way you wanted me to live. Your desire for me was to live free of pain, suffering, self-destruction and free from sickness. The consequences of choosing against you, is everything that does not come from you – loneliness, pain, sadness and death. I have heard the free gift you offer to me is eternal life.

Today God, I thank you for your son Jesus and that he was willing to take the punishment for the things I have done wrong, once and for all. Thank you that he came to save me and make a way for me to know you, my Creator, intimately. Help me to get to know you more. Speak to me - I want to recognise your voice. Help me to live the way you want me to live. Show me how to love others well, how to love myself well and how to love you fully. I don't always grasp or understand you or your ways.

Show me more of who you are God, I open up my heart and my life to you, help me to trust you. I want you to take up residence in my life as my leader, my guide, my peace bringer and my hope giver. I want you to fulfill your purposes in me. Please protect me and those I love with your presence.

I pray this prayer in the powerful name of your son, Jesus, Amen

Printed in the United States
By Bookmasters